THE NEW JEWISH TABLE

MODERN SEASONAL RECIPES FOR TRADITIONAL DISHES

TODD GRAY AND ELLEN KASSOFF GRAY

WITH DAVID HAGEDORN

Photographs by RENEE COMET

ST. MARTIN'S PRESS
NEW YORK

THE NEW JEWISH TABLE. Text copyright © 2013 by Todd Gray and Ellen Kassoff Gray.
Foreword copyright © 2013 by Joan Nathan. Photographs copyright © 2013 by Renee
Comet. All rights reserved. Printed in China. For information, address St. Martin's Press,
175 Fifth Avenue, New York, N.Y. 10010.

www.stmartins.com

Photographs on page xxii and additional photographs on pages 299–303
courtesy of Emily Clack.

Design by Stephanie Huntwork

ISBN 978-1-250-00445-1 (hardcover)
ISBN 978-1-4668-3253-4 (e-book)

First Edition: March 2013

10 9 8 7 6 5 4 3 2 1

In loving memory of those who started us
upon our epic culinary journey:
Lillian Malitsky,
Hilda Donahue (aka Muzzy),
Rose and Harry Henkin,
Herb Iris, John W. Gray, and Neil Wornum.

CONTENTS

WINTER

SPRING

HOLIDAY MENUS

ACKNOWLEDGMENTS

Thank you for your faith in this project. With much love and appreciation:

Renee Comet, David Hagedorn, Carole Spier, Katherine Latshaw, BJ Berti, and of course, Harrison Gray, Ed and Lisa Kassoff, and Bradley and Weezie Gray.

Our two floor cleaners, Zeus and August . . . faithful shepherds

FOREWORD

A SHORT WALK FROM THE WHITE HOUSE is a popular local restaurant, Equinox. A gathering place for Washington lawyers and deal makers, it also welcomes presidents and their wives who want to have a quiet meal alone in the real world.

Todd Gray is Equinox's chef and owner, along with his wife Ellen Kassoff Gray. Together, they have built a local and seasonal farm-to-table restaurant, and a life together. In addition to their now three restaurants, Todd and Ellen are the proud parents of son, Harrison. Ellen grew up in Washington, the daughter of a local Jewish family. Todd grew up Episcopalian, in Fredericksburg, Virginia, where he could count all the town's Jewish residents on one hand. The two have bonded over food and have made a success of sharing their culinary differences.

Today, more than ever before, millions of people marry outside of their faith. For some reason, perhaps because of our history and shrinking religious culture, doing so is a difficult decision to make for the Jewish partner in a couple; a decision that often has to be treated gingerly with parents. Smartly, Ellen realized one way for Todd to be accepted in her family would be a connection over Jewish food, especially with her father. "They bonded over Jewish deli," said Ellen. "I think chefs have more of an appreciation of the Jewish food culture than the non-Jewish spouse in most intermarried couples.

So when Todd and Ellen were engaged in 1994, her father decided to acquaint his future son-in-law with the Jewish culture he grew up with in a way they could both relate to: pastrami. They traveled from Washington to New York, where they ate not only pastrami, but corned beef, gefilte fish, and herring at Katz's, the Second Avenue Deli, and the Carnegie Deli.

On the couple's first Hanukkah together, Todd tried a recipe for sufganiyot, or jelly doughnuts, that Ellen had brought back from Israel. But the doughnuts turned out soggy and the dough didn't hold together. He has since revised the recipe, redeeming himself with the apple cider sufganiyot with blueberry sauce on Equinox's Hanukkah menu.

Now on Jewish holidays at their home, Todd brings epicurean interpretations to simple dishes, but also enjoys the culinary traditions that Ellen and her family have taught him. For Hanukkah, Todd, who usually cooks New American, slightly Virginian food, takes his father-in-law's twenty-four-hour braised brisket and cooks it sous vide (in a vacuum) for thirty-six hours. He makes a citrus-infused gravlax, as well as Ellen's Aunt Lil's matzo ball soup: "I dice the carrots, celery, and onions into a mirepoix," he told me, "rather than keeping them in big chunks."

I have known Todd and Ellen for years and have tasted their food in their restaurants and at their home. Todd is always one to volunteer his time and expertise for a good cause. When I was the honorary chair of the District of Columbia's Jewish Community Center's annual fundraiser, he made an absolutely delicious kosher dinner. He brought his characteristic goodwill and gentleness to the event, where we all tasted some of the most delicious kosher food ever.

The New Jewish Table: Modern Seasonal Recipes for Traditional Dishes is filled with the lore of Ellen's family's passion for Jewish food and Todd's youthful explorations of Pennsylvania Dutch cuisine and his chef's training. It is a delightful blending of recipes, tips, and tales, with the culinary traditions that nurtured both reinterpreted for everyone to cook in Todd's sure and professional hand.

—JOAN NATHAN

INTRODUCTION

FROM OUR TABLE TO YOURS

ELLEN: This book really represents the blending at our table in the truest sense, a culinary convergence, as our dear friend and mentor, Joan Nathan, refers to it. *The New Jewish Table* would not have come to be were it not for Joan, who penned an article in *The New York Times* in 2009 entitled, "At Hanukkah, Chefs Make Kitchen Conversions," highlighting culinary blending in marriages between Jews and non-Jews. Joan was the one who actually recognized that ours would be an interesting story to tell. Until she wrote that piece, we never realized how different, yet similar, our backgrounds were.

TODD: Above all, though, the emphasis of *The New Jewish Table* is on seasonality, with the hope that readers make every effort to source locally and support our nation's farmers, food artisans, and watermen.

To that end, we have divided the book into four seasons—Fall, Winter, Spring, and Summer—each with six chapters: Brunch, Starters, Lunch, Dinner, Sides, and Desserts. We suggest you browse the chapters, you may find a recipe in Brunch that sounds like lunch to you, or one in Lunch that might be just what you want for dinner. Sidebars linked to specific dishes throughout the book relay anecdotes, moving memories, or pertinent food methodology. Every recipe has been given a dairy, parve, or meat designation.

Additionally, we have included comprehensive menu suggestions for four Jewish holidays (Rosh Hashanah, Yom Kippur, Hanukkah, Passover) and an Appendix of culinary fundamentals—here you'll find recipes for many of our favorite dressings, sauces, condiments, and stocks; basic prep information for various ingredients; and explanations of frequently used cooking methods.

From our blended table to yours, happy cooking!

GROWING UP

ELLEN: In a nutshell, I grew up in a madcap traditional Jewish household with two working parents and three brothers, went to Bethesda Chevy Chase High School, got a degree in economics from the University of Maryland in 1986, and then moved to Israel to live on a kibbutz. I told my parents it was to get in touch with my farming side and my culture, but really I was just a hippie living it up commune style. After the kibbutz, I wound up working in the kitchen of a scuba boat on the Red Sea—making fritters.

TODD: I was born on Governors Island in Manhattan. My dad, Brad, was a flight surgeon in the army and was stationed there. We wound up in Fredericksburg, Virginia, via Charlottesville. My mother, Weezie (her real name is Louise, but everybody calls her Weezie), is from Lancaster and of Pennsylvania Dutch stock, but once she moved to Virginia, she embraced all things Southern, including the cooking traditions of the Chesapeake Bay.

My older brother, Brad, and I both went to an Episcopalian boarding school, then I went to the University of Richmond. I had been working in a restaurant as a busboy and was enthralled by the excitement and energy of it. The chefs there kept telling me to go to culinary school; the managers wanted me to go into hotel management. I interviewed at Cornell and looked at the Culinary Institute of America, finally deciding on the CIA.

ELLEN: What really attracted him to the business was the partying and the hanging out.

TODD: Well, I can't argue with that, but my parents weren't having any of that. I needed two years of practical cooking experience before the Culinary Institute of America would take me, so I moved back home. My parents helped get me a job at their favorite restaurant, La Petite Auberge, in the summer of 1985. The chef owner there, Christian Renault really put me through the paces by having me work every job in the front and back of the house. I learned the foundations of cooking, how to run a dining room, all about wine service, and the business side of things. That's what really inspired me to become a restaurant owner.

ELLEN: Fast forward—eighteen years later, Christian's son, came to do a *stage* (that's an internship) with Todd at Equinox after he finished cooking school. And now he's the chef of La Petite Auberge.

TODD: It all comes full circle.

PARALLEL LIVES, INTERSECTING

ELLEN: Our food backstories came full circle, too. The Jewish foods and traditions that I grew up with were very different from Todd's meat-and-potatoes upbringing, but as young adults, we were both drawn to Mediterranean foods. I got my first taste of this style of cooking when on the island of Crete while backpacking through Europe during my junior year. The olives, the cheeses, the figs, that dreamy yogurt, those lovely

tomato, cucumber, and olive salads dressed with that vibrant Greek olive oil, oregano, and mint—I had never had food as fresh as those things. And the flatbread pizzas and pastries filled with pistachios, pine nuts, and honey—I went crazy for it and still do. And then Israel, with the couscous, falafel, apricots, and pomegranates. This is the way I like to eat.

TODD: My appreciation for Mediterranean foods came from my French and Italian training. In the winter of 1992, I went to work at Galileo under Roberto Donna, this young, Italian chef who was all the rage in Washington. I thought I'd stay a year, but I was there for almost eight, first as a cook, then sous-chef, and finally executive chef. For me at Galileo, it was all about risotto, handmade pastas, olives, burrata, parmesan and ricotta cheeses, hazelnuts, figs, veal, cod, truffles, artichokes, all kinds of salami, olive oil, balsamic vinegar, artichokes, pesto, eggplant, tomatoes.

ELLEN: The year I lived in Israel was the time of the first Intifada and my parents insisted I come home. They were worried about my being in the middle of all the *mishegoss*. I learned a lot there at that time, especially about food. I got a job at the *Journal* newspaper writing ad copy and met the food columnist there, Ray Lane, who had me writing articles about foods in Israel. Then he sent me to Israel on a press junket with food journalists in 1988 to write about Israeli wine. That was my entrance into the food world.

In 1993, I came back to Washington. I moved to Mount Pleasant and started working as a sales rep for Sysco, one of the biggest food distributors in the country. That's how I met Todd—on a cold call to Galileo that year.

TODD: As life altering as the offer to work for Roberto Donna was, it didn't compare to 1993's seminal event—meeting Ellen.

I was smitten immediately. I asked her out on a date and she said, "I don't date customers." And I replied, "Don't worry—I won't buy anything from you."

Our first date was for brunch at a Dupont Circle restaurant called Childe Harolde. We discovered that college friends of mine from Bethesda were social friends of Ellen's. It turns out we had a lot of people in common, had gone to a lot of the same concerts over the years, so our lives had already intersected, we just didn't know it at the time.

ELLEN: Todd and I are convinced that while we were growing up, we were often doing the same exact thing at the same exact time—watching the same television show, going to the same concert or movies. We are soul mates. We were born six months apart in 1964 and just know that we've been in the same room at the same time on several occasions before we ever actually met. We led parallel lives, but with lots of intersections.

A MARRIAGE AND MISSION: OPENING EQUINOX

TODD: We may be soul mates, but it took Ellen a little while to realize it. At first, she blew me off. To get on her good side, and see a lot more of her, I suggested she work for a company where I could be a good customer, like D'Artagnan, and buy lots of foie gras and truffles from her. She became their Mid-Atlantic rep and I was one of her best customers, needless to say.

ELLEN: That's when we took our love for food and drink to a whole new level, where our journey together really began. Roberto was getting nominated for James Beard awards and we'd go to New York for the ceremonies, going to all the parties and hanging out with superstar chefs. This was my first taste of really heavy consumption—marathons of eating and drinking with those guys and trying to keep up. All that red wine!

It was at least ten years before I drank a glass of red wine after those years. I became a Sauvignon Blanc and Chablis lover on that night in New York.

TODD: Around this time, I met Ellen's Family. She brought them to Galileo, so I could make a good impression on them on my turf. That progressed to Ed and me making food trips to New York, where we started bonding over deli fare. You could say the relationship was cemented with lox and cream cheese.

Back in Washington, Ed and Lisa invited me

to their house around Hanukkah, quite an honor because Ed was going to make his famous latkes. I remember seeing the nonstick sauté pan with the plastic handle on the electric range and Ed flipping latkes in three times as much oil as I would have used. I mean, it was splattering all over the wall, the back of the range, the clock, the controls for the burners. And Ed asks me, "So Todd, am I doing it right?" and I said, "I think there might be a little too much oil in there." He thought about it for a second and said, "Only my future son-in-law could get away with telling me how to make latkes." And at that point, Ellen and I were engaged.

ELLEN: We were married in April 1995 at Tarara Winery in Leesburg, Virginia, and honeymooned in Northern California. We hiked by day and ate in three restaurants every night, hitting twenty restaurants in six days. When we came back to DC, Todd was promoted to Executive Chef at Galileo where he stayed for seven years.

TODD: Eventually, I asked Roberto's advice and he was completely supportive. He let me raise money while I worked for him and even helped me do it. In 1998, we signed the lease for Equinox and opened in May of 1999.

ELLEN: That honeymoon trip to California had changed us forever. It was so inspirational. We knew we wanted to open our own restaurant, an American restaurant. We were inspired by Alice Waters, Thomas Keller and Michael Chiarello. We wanted to serve straightforward, refined food that was fresh, bright, farm-driven, and all about local sourcing. That was Equinox's vision and mission statement from Day One. Our vendor list is ten times the length it was when we started; the restaurant has evolved and matured, but has always remained true to what we wanted it to be.

TODD: Part of Ellen's commitment to farmers has to do with the fact that she became a vegetarian in 1995. She called me one day and said, "No more meat for me."

ELLEN: It was a ninety-degree day in August and I was driving around town with fifty ducks in the back seat that I had to deliver to various chefs around town. Let's just say that seeing those ducks in the rearview mirror, plus the odor in the car, just clicked for me and I was done. And with what I came to learn about factory farming, I never looked back. These days, I'm pretty much a vegan.

BLENDING TABLES

ELLEN: Food-wise, things in our house growing up were active. Other than the usual ritual foods, the smoked fish and borscht my Grandpa Harry Henkin loved, the deli foods my father kept us in, kugels, Passover brisket, and the like, my mother bought into the convenience culture of the '50s: frozen and canned foods, big grocery stores, chicken sold by part in Styrofoam squares, casseroles made with condensed soup. My only knowledge about kosher kitchens came from my Aunt Lil in the Bronx (actually my great aunt) who was strict about observing the dietary laws.

TODD: As food people and parents, we just really saw the value in getting back to the roots of both our families, blending the Pennsylvania Dutch and Jewish influences with the American and Mediterranean ones.

ELLEN: As time went on, Todd got more comfortable with the Jewish holidays and what they meant. He started making macaroons for Passover and then decided to bring that inspiration to Equinox in the form of special Seder and Hanukkah menus. Aunt Lil's matzo ball soup, his version of it, was the first thing he put on the menu, using foie gras in the matzo balls. Then he did his version of brisket using French techniques and learned how to make kosher dishes, often working in Italian ingredients.

TODD: The next thing I knew, our friends and regulars heard that we were doing these menus and started coming in. It caught on as a successful menu format and became part of our repertoire. *The New Jewish Table* is a reflection of that blending.

Keeping Kosher: Being Mindful of Our Food

ELLEN: The laws that govern observant Jews when it comes to eating are called "kosher" or "kashrut," words that come from the Hebrew root *Kaf-Shin-Reish,* meaning fit, correct. From this one can infer that the very nature of kosher is to

do what is moral and virtuous. Keeping kosher is not so much about a Rabbi blessing the food as it is about preserving and respecting the spirit of the things that are consumed; this may explain why many people are drawn to kosher food today regardless of their religious beliefs.

Kosher laws prescribe that meat and dairy foods must not be eaten in the same meal but allow foods that are neither meat nor dairy, which are called "parve," to be eaten with either. Grains, vegetables, and fruit are all parve, as are eggs and fish (so it's permitted to serve smoked salmon and cream cheese together on a bagel). These rules of kosher are not very complicated to begin with but people who observe them require two sets of kitchen and dining accoutrements in order to keep the meat and dairy meals separate, and all the pots, pans, dishes, and utensils can make keeping kosher a bit more expensive.

For food to be kosher is relatively simple: There are about ten golden rules that must be followed, ranging from how an animal is slaughtered to which parts may be eaten. The rules governing slaughter methods are clear: An animal must be healthy and must not suffer in slaughter; therefore kosher slaughter is considered the most humane. The Torah states that the soul of an animal is contained in its blood; therefore blood must be drained from the animal's body for the meat to be considered kosher. The separation of meat and dairy symbolically follows the basic Torah principle that one should not eat an animal in its own milk. All kosher fish must have scales and fins, which explains why shellfish are not eaten. When something is harvested from your garden it is naturally kosher (unless of course it has bugs), meaning the laws of kashrut favor natural whole

foods. Keeping kosher is actually very poignant and soulful eating, and the theology is fascinating.

Being in the restaurant business, Todd and I find that principles like these arouse a natural interest and admiration. The core of keeping kosher goes right along with our own philosophies. The very essence of our restaurant reflects our reverence for the earth and all its natural resources; by showing respect for food and its production we try to do our part to preserve the planet and all its creatures.

TODD: This book is certainly not a strictly kosher cookbook, but we do identify each recipe as meat, dairy, parve, or in some cases, mixed. There are many recipes for which dairy ingredients add a flavor I prefer to that of oil or margarine, but where feasible, I have offered ingredient alternatives that transform dairy recipes to parve and mixed recipes to either meat or dairy.

ELLEN: Kosher for Passover has its own set of dietary rules (and Sephardic Jews have a separate set from the Ashkenazi), but the general rule is to avoid all foods that are leavened and to omit flour and shelled beans such as lentils or chickpeas. In the spring, many foods are labeled "Kosher for Passover," and with the increasing attention paid to marketing during this holiday there is no shortage of these items available in your grocery store. Todd and I, however, are advocates of home-cooked—no matter whether it's an entrée, a snack, or a side dish, it's always better coming from your own kitchen.

FALL

TODD: The autumnal equinox, when the day and night are in equilibrium, really underscores what we are all about. We named our restaurant Equinox because of my affinity for having everything in balance and in its right season.

To me, fall is culinarily the most productive time of year. It seems that one day I'm going crazy canning, jarring, and preserving all the end-of-summer gifts like tomatoes and corn, and then the next there's a chill in the air and my thoughts are turning to butternut squash, pumpkin, root vegetables, mushrooms, Brussels sprouts, cabbage, pears, and apples.

I know that fall is on for sure when I get my annual call from John Henry, in Middleburg, Virginia, telling me that the chestnuts are in. I usually get a hundred pounds the first week and another hundred the last week. At the restaurant, it's the dishwashers' greatest nightmare—splitting and peeling all of them—and I put them in everything, from soups to pastas and desserts.

ELLEN: Fall is all about the Jewish holidays to me. It begins with the two most important ones, Rosh Hashanah and Yom Kippur, and ends with Hanukkah, less significant perhaps, but still full of the traditions, symbols, and foods that we Jews hold so dear. Whether it's the apples and honey of Rosh Hashanah, the break-the-fast meal after Yom Kippur, or the latkes my father insists on making at Hanukkah, food always seems to be at the center of everything we do.

BRUNCH

YUKON GOLD AND SWEET
POTATO LATKES 3

RICOTTA CHEESE BLINTZES 6

CHOPPED LIVER WITH SWEET
MARSALA ONIONS 8

PICKLED HERRING IN CITRUS DILL
CRÈME FRAÎCHE 10

MACARONI SALAD WITH ROASTED
PEPPERS AND BABY CARROTS 11

FRITTATA OF WILD MUSHROOMS
AND MUENSTER CHEESE 12

KIPPERED SALMON SNACKS 15

YUKON GOLD AND SWEET POTATO LATKES

MAKES SIX 5-INCH LATKES

TODD: My first latke collaboration with Ellen's dad inspired me to create a dish at Equinox that became a signature there: Sweet potato latkes with horseradish cream and salmon caviar have been on the menu there since 2003. This is the recipe my sous-chefs and I developed. We prefer to use Yukon Gold potatoes because they are a little sweeter than russets, so they brown better, especially when combined with sweet potatoes as they are here.

ELLEN: Duplicate Todd's dish by mixing some crème fraîche with freshly grated horseradish and topping it with salmon roe, or opt for the toppings I grew up with: sour cream, applesauce, or cherries.

2 medium Yukon Gold potatoes

2 medium sweet potatoes

1 medium yellow onion

2 large eggs, lightly beaten

½ cup matzo meal

1 tablespoon minced fresh thyme leaves

1 tablespoon salt

½ teaspoon freshly ground black pepper

½ cup canola oil

FOR SERVING (OPTIONAL):

Crème fraîche, freshly grated horseradish, and salmon caviar

or

Sour cream and applesauce or fresh or frozen cherries

Mix the latkes. Grate the Yukon Gold and sweet potatoes on the large-mesh side of a box grater or in a food processor. With your hands, squeeze out any liquid and transfer the potatoes to a medium-size bowl. With the same grater, grate the onion into the bowl with the potatoes. Add the eggs, matzo meal, thyme, salt, and pepper. Using a wooden spoon or your hands, mix together until ingredients are well blended.

Cook the latkes. Preheat the oven to 250°F. Heat a 12-inch nonstick sauté pan over high heat; add ¼ cup of the oil and heat until it begins to smoke. Working in batches to cook three cakes at a time, shape the potato mixture into 5-inch round cakes about ½-inch thick, adding each to the pan as you do so. Lower the heat to medium and cook the cakes without moving them until brown on one side—about 4 minutes; turn them over and cook until the other side is brown—about 4 minutes more. Remove the cakes from the pan and transfer to a paper towel–lined plate to drain. Meanwhile, heat the remaining ¼ cup oil in the pan and shape and cook the remaining potato mixture. When the first batch of latkes has drained, transfer them to a serving plate and keep warm in the oven. Serve with the topping of your choice.

The Ritual of Latkes

ELLEN: It makes sense that Yukon Gold and Sweet Potato Latkes are the lead recipe in our book because they are the first dish that Todd and my father made together. Making the latkes for Hanukkah was a ritual that my father insisted on undertaking by himself every December, so I was shocked when he asked for Todd's help, especially since he was already skeptical about my marrying a non-Jew. That Todd was a chef greatly helped him work through that, though.

TODD: Watching Ellen's father make those latkes, I remember thinking, "That's so much oil!" So I said, as delicately as possible, "You know, Ed, you could probably get by using a lot less oil. You don't really have to submerge them." He looked at me like I was crazy, but now he makes them the way I do.

ELLEN: Todd also taught my dad that potatoes didn't have to be gray. No Jewish man understands anything about oxidation until a chef like Todd comes along and teaches it to him.

TODD: I learned from him, too. He inspired me to develop a dish using them at Equinox. We were getting these terrific heirloom sweet potatoes from Tuscarora, a cooperative in Pennsylvania, and my then sous-chefs, Tony Chittum and Brendan Cox, and I had a serious conversation about how to make latkes with them. Then we had to decide if they were actually latkes or more like a pommes rösti? The egg, matzo meal, and shredded potatoes make them more of a latke, so we went with that. Out of that latke base came a great signature dish that has been on the menu since 2003: sweet potato latkes with horseradish cream and salmon caviar.

ELLEN: Joan Nathan turned us on to making them with zucchini, too (a recipe is on page 239). She has a recipe for it in her cookbook, *The Jewish Holiday Kitchen*. We love making them in the summer when we have way more zucchini than we know what to do with.

RICOTTA CHEESE BLINTZES

MAKES 10 TO 12 BLINTZES

TODD: For this blintz recipe, I incorporate a bit of orange zest to provide a delicate citrus accent to the filling. For serving, I add a few fresh orange segments as a garnish, but you may wish to experiment with adding different jams or fruit to the cheese filling (see Falling for Blintzes, page 7). While I think blintzes should be assembled and cooked when you plan to serve them, you can still do much of the prep ahead of time by making the batter and the filling the day before or even making the crêpes a couple of weeks ahead and freezing them, wrapped well in plastic wrap and aluminum foil.

CRÊPES:

1 cup whole milk

2 large eggs

1 cup all-purpose flour

1 tablespoon granulated sugar

½ teaspoon salt

4 tablespoons unsalted butter (½ stick), melted

Cold unsalted butter for greasing sauté pan

FILLING:

1½ cups ricotta cheese

½ cup cream cheese (4 ounces)

1 large egg yolk

1 teaspoon freshly grated orange zest

2 tablespoons honey

¼ teaspoon salt

Confectioners' sugar and fresh orange segments for serving

Prepare the batter. Whisk together the milk and eggs in a small bowl; then whisk in the flour, sugar, and salt until well combined. Pour the batter through a mesh strainer into another small bowl. Stir in the melted butter. Cover the bowl and refrigerate for at least 1 hour.

Prepare the filling. Using a wooden spoon, mix the ricotta cheese, cream cheese, and egg yolk together in a medium-size bowl until well combined. Add the orange zest, honey and salt and stir until combined. Cover and refrigerate until you are ready to fill the crepes.

Cook the crêpes. Line a 10-inch plate with paper towels. Heat an 8-inch nonstick crêpe pan or skillet over medium heat. Rub the pan with cold butter and immediately add ¼ cup crêpe batter. Cook until the crêpe is slightly caramelized on the bottom—about 2 minutes. Using a pancake turner, turn the crêpe over and cook the second side until slightly caramelized—about 2 minutes more. Transfer the crêpe to the paper towel-lined plate. Repeat this process until all the batter has been used; place additional paper towels between the cooked crêpes.

Fill the crêpes. Spoon a dollop of filling onto each crêpe, covering about a third of the area nearest to you but leaving an empty margin at the sides. Fold the margin at each side up and over the filling; then roll up the crêpe—like a cylindrical envelope. Turn "flap down" until ready to cook.

Cook the blintzes. Heat the oven to 350°F. Butter a baking dish large enough to hold the blintzes loosely in one layer. Heat a 10-inch nonstick sauté pan over medium-low heat; melt 1 tablespoon butter in it, coating evenly. Working in batches and adding another 1 tablespoon butter for each batch, brown the blintzes until golden, turning gently with a spatula—about 2 minutes on each side. Arrange the blintzes flap-side down in the prepared baking dish. Bake until the filling is set—5 to 8 minutes. Using a slotted spatula, transfer the blintzes to a serving plate or individual plates. Sprinkle with confectioners' sugar; serve immediately, with orange segments as an additional garnish.

Falling for Blintzes

TODD: It's funny the historical claim people make to a dish like blintzes. I think every culture has some form of rolled up, filled pancake—egg rolls, crêpes, summer rolls, even burritos come to mind. I admit my expectations were high for blintzes because I had heard how amazing they were from Ellen so many times. Well, once I tasted them, I just didn't get it. They were these pasty squares of flabby dough out of a box, frozen and reheated. Half the time, the filling was still cold in the center.

ELLEN: Well, we certainly were not making them from scratch in our house, growing up. For years I thought the only way they came was frozen in a package. We considered it exotic when my grandmother fried them in butter and got them all golden brown and crispy rather than just heating them up in the oven like my mother did. To mix things up, we'd have the cottage cheese-filled ones one week and fruit-filled ones the next.

TODD: Let me tell you, it certainly makes a world of difference when you make them from scratch and it couldn't be much easier to do. And changing up the fillings is simple: Just start out with the cheese filling as a base and top it with a spoonful of preserves or marmalade before folding up the crêpes. Strawberry, peach, raspberry, blueberry, and apricot preserves would all be excellent, or an orange marmalade—but be sure to use artisan products or homemade if you can. To really own the dish, use preserves from a fruit that is in season, then garnish with slices of the fresh form of that fruit.

CHOPPED LIVER WITH SWEET MARSALA ONIONS

MAKES ABOUT 3 CUPS

ELLEN: Chopped liver is straight out of the Bronx for me. I can still picture my great-aunt, Lillian Malitsky, hand-chopping the eggs on the counter of her apartment there, and adding them to the blender with the sautéed livers, golden caramelized onions, and some leftover chicken stock.

TODD: How many times did I purée country-style chicken livers, onions, Marsala wine, and garlic in a blender, put it on a little piece of toast with black pepper and a little piece of sage, and serve it as an *amuse-bouche* at Galileo, only to discover from Ellen that I was making chopped liver all along?

3 tablespoons olive oil

½ pound chicken livers, cleaned (see Chicken Liver Prep, page 9)

2 garlic cloves, sliced

2 teaspoons salt

½ teaspoon freshly ground black pepper

2 medium yellow onions, thinly sliced

3 tablespoons canola oil

3 fresh sage leaves

3 oz Marsala wine

3 hard-boiled eggs, peeled and finely chopped

Toasted bread slices or crudités for serving

Cook the chicken livers. Heat the olive oil in a large sauté pan over medium-high heat. Add the chicken livers. Sauté for 3 minutes, stirring frequently; stir in the garlic, 1 teaspoon of the salt, and ¼ teaspoon of the pepper; turn the heat to low and cook, stirring gently, until the livers are fully cooked but still a touch pink in the center—4 to 6 minutes more. Using a slotted spoon, transfer the livers to a bowl and set aside. Discard the cooking juices from the pan.

Caramelize the onions. Heat the canola oil in the pan that you used to cook the livers over medium heat, add the onions, and stir in the remaining 1 teaspoon salt and remaining ¼ teaspoon pepper. Cook for 15 minutes, stirring frequently so the onions cook evenly. When the onions begin to turn an amber color, add the sage leaves and stir in the wine. Continue to cook until the onions are a soft caramel color—10 to 15 minutes more. Drain the onions in a colander and discard the sage leaves.

Make the chopped liver. Place the chicken livers and onions in the container of a small food processor that is fitted with a metal blade. Pulse the processor until the livers and onions form a mixture with the consistency of a coarse paste. Transfer the chopped liver to a small bowl and fold in the chopped egg with a rubber spatula; adjust the seasoning as necessary. Cover, and refrigerate for at least 1 hour. Serve chilled, with slices of toasted bread or crudités.

CHICKEN LIVER PREP.

One thing to keep in mind when dealing with chicken livers: You must take the time to clean them well to prevent any unpleasant bitterness creeping into your cooked dish. Cut the lobes of the liver apart. Using the tip of a sharp paring knife, remove the sinew that runs into the meat and trim off any yellow spots or unevenly colored areas. Rinse the livers under cold running water and pat them dry thoroughly with paper towels before sautéing. (You can store them in the refrigerator for 2 days or freeze for up to 1 month.) Watch out for splattering—the livers contain water, so they are likely to pop during cooking, and the hot fat can really burn you if you're not careful.

BAGELS AND ME

When I opened Restaurant Nora, one of my partners was famous for making bagels. He invited several of us to his place, where he demonstrated his from-scratch techniques, and we were treated to a Jewish breakfast of his bagels with lox, cream cheese, capers, and onions. This was my first introduction to Jewish cuisine, although I have fond later memories of chopped liver pâte made with chicken fat, hard-boiled eggs, lots of onions, spices, and herbs. I'm sure I ate a lot of Jewish food growing up in Vienna, Austria, since many of my father's friends were Jewish businessmen. When they had to flee the country in the 1940s, my father still maintained relationships with them, even running a movie house and an amusement park until they returned at the end of the war. I was just never made aware of Jewish cuisine until I came to this country and had my experience with bagels. I had no idea what a bagel even was!

—NORA POUILLON, author and chef owner
of Restaurant Nora, the first certified organic
restaurant in the country

PICKLED HERRING IN CITRUS DILL CRÈME FRAÎCHE

SERVES 6 AS A BUFFET OFFERING

TODD: I didn't really know from herring until I met Ellen and her family. But on many an occasion, and especially at Sunday brunch, pickled or creamed herring would find its way onto the table right out of a jar. When I first tasted it, I found it oily, fishy, and tart from vinegar. So I decided to soften it up and give it a little bit of an upgrade by mixing it with some crème fraîche, citrus zest, and dill. I like to garnish this dish with skinless segments of orange, lemon, and lime—you may wish to do the same.

1 ½ cups crème fraîche or sour cream

1 teaspoon freshly grated orange zest

¼ teaspoon freshly grated lemon zest

¼ teaspoon freshly grated lime zest

1 tablespoon chopped fresh dill leaves

1 tablespoon chopped, rinsed, and drained capers

3 scallions, thinly sliced crosswise, including some of the green part

1 tablespoon freshly squeezed orange juice

1 jar pickled herring (approximately 6 ounces), lightly rinsed and drained well

Mixed salad greens (washed and spun dry) and toasted sliced rye bread or crostini for serving

Place the crème fraîche in a medium-size bowl. Stir in the citrus zests, dill, capers, scallions, and orange juice, mixing until blended. Add the herring fillets, stirring to coat evenly. Cover and refrigerate for at least 6 hours. Serve on a bed of salad greens, accompanied with toasted rye bread slices or crostini.

LEARNING TRUE DELI

Growing up in Richmond in the 'fiftys and 'sixtys, life was somewhat limited in the food department. People mainly ate at home. However, joy was to be found at the New York Deli with its new-to-us foods: My favorite was the "Sailor Sandwich"—grilled knockwurst with Swiss cheese on rye and an authentic kosher pickle, or so we were told. And Russian Salad—defrosted carrots and peas and onions in a mayonnaise dressing. Everything was served by large and stern black waitresses.

Thank the Lord, Johnny Apple came along and took me by the hand around Manhattan, to the Carnegie, Stage, and Katz's delicatessens. I learned fast and had a ball. But even now, I sometimes slip, and order a chicken liver on rye, with mayo and lettuce. How's that for Southern fusion?

—BETSEY PINCKNEY APPLE,
widow of journalist R. W. Apple, Jr.

MACARONI SALAD WITH ROASTED PEPPERS AND BABY CARROTS

SERVES 8

ELLEN: When Todd and I began formulating menus for Muse, the café we operate at Washington's Corcoran Gallery of Art, we wanted to include a lot of cold salads. Who doesn't love macaroni salad? During my childhood it made a regular appearance on the Kassoff family Sunday brunch table—right out of the deli containers it came in.

TODD: What I grew up on came from the grocery store and it was always some weird yellow color, mayonnaise-y, and sweet. Improving on that doesn't really take that much—for me, some roasted red peppers, heirloom carrots, and scallions do the trick.

½ pound dry elbow macaroni

2 tablespoons olive oil

1 bunch baby carrots (about 4 ounces), preferably from your local farmers' market

½ roasted red bell peppers, finely chopped (recipe in Chef's Appendix)

1 bunch scallions, thinly sliced crosswise, including some of the green part

1 cup mayonnaise

1 tablespoon honey

1 teaspoon salt

¼ teaspoon freshly ground black pepper

Cook the macaroni. Bring a large pot of salted water to a boil over high heat. Stir in the macaroni and cook according to the package directions until al dente (done but still firm to the bite). Drain the macaroni in a colander, rinse under cold running water, and drain again. Transfer the macaroni to a large bowl; toss with 1 tablespoon of the oil to keep it from sticking together.

Prepare the carrots. Bring a medium-size pot of lightly salted water to a boil. Add the carrots; lower the heat so the water simmers and cook, uncovered, until the carrots are crisp-tender—test one. It should be a bit firm when you bite through it. Drain the carrots in a colander and rinse under cold running water; transfer to paper towels to dry completely. Cut the carrots on a slight diagonal into ¼-inch thick slices.

Make the salad. Add the carrots, roasted pepper, scallions, mayonnaise, remaining 1 tablespoon oil, honey, salt, and pepper to the bowl with the macaroni. Mix with a wooden spoon until well combined. Cover and refrigerate until ready to serve.

FRITTATA OF WILD MUSHROOMS AND MUENSTER CHEESE

MAKES ONE 11-INCH FRITTATA (ABOUT 12 SERVINGS)

ELLEN: After Harrison was born, we would put him in the stroller and walk to the Dupont Circle Farmers' Market on Sunday with our German shepherd, Samson, in tow. We'd get mushrooms from the mushroom lady and eggs from the egg guy, then go home and make frittatas. The mushrooms you add don't have to be wild—you could just use button mushrooms or crimini—but Todd and I really love shiitake and oyster mushrooms because they have more depth.

TODD: Ellen loves Muenster cheese, but I had never even heard of it until I met her. Any melty cheese works well; I'm partial to fontina, probably from my Italian restaurant background.

12 jumbo eggs

1 cup whole milk

1 tablespoon olive oil

2 garlic cloves, minced

¾ pound mixed wild mushrooms (any varieties you wish)

2 cups coarsely chopped fresh, washed, and spun-dry baby spinach (about ½ pound)

1 tablespoon salt

½ teaspoon freshly ground black pepper

2 tablespoons finely chopped fresh parsley

1 tablespoon unsalted butter

1 cup grated Muenster cheese (about 4 ounces)

Sour cream or Rémoulade (recipe in Chef's Appendix) for serving

Prep the frittata. Preheat the oven to 350°F. Whisk together the eggs and milk in large bowl, mixing well; set aside. Heat the oil in an 11-inch ovenproof nonstick sauté pan over medium heat. Add the garlic and mushrooms, sauté until soft—about 3 minutes. Add the spinach and cook, stirring, for 1 minute. Stir in the salt, pepper, and parsley; cook until the vegetables are cooked—about 2 minutes more. Transfer the vegetables to a medium bowl and set aside.

Cook the frittata. In the sauté pan used to cook the vegetables, melt the butter over medium heat, coating evenly. Stir the egg mixture again and then pour into the pan; gently fold in the cooked vegetables and about half of the cheese. Cook, without stirring, for 3 minutes (leave the heat at medium so the bottom of the frittata does not brown—it will also cook in the oven for a while and you don't want the bottom to get too caramelized). Transfer the pan to the oven and bake until the frittata is set—about 12 to 15 minutes; sprinkle the remaining cheese over the top of the frittata when about 5 minutes of baking time remains. Remove the frittata from the oven and allow to rest for 5 minutes. Cut into wedges and serve warm, with a dollop of sour cream or Rémoulade.

A WORD ABOUT EGGS

Farm-fresh organic eggs are going to give you a better frittata than those you generally find in a grocery store. The chickens are being fed better, they lead a better life, and their eggs' whites are less watery and their yolks more flavorful. All of these factors translate to the plate in my experience.

KIPPERED SALMON SNACKS

SERVES 6 AS A BUFFET OFFERING

ELLEN: I grew up with canned "Kipper Snacks," which are smoked, cooked, skinless, boneless herring fillets. We ate them right out of the can, piled up on Ritz crackers and topped with a dollop of sour cream.

TODD: My dish is a little more refined than that, but is still meant to be a very quick, easy-to-make snack that you can pile up on toast, crackers, slices of French bread, or even cucumber rounds. I mix flaked, store-bought hot-smoked salmon (see Of Kipper Snacks and Cured Salmon, page 16) with sour cream and brighten the fish up with lemon juice and chives. It makes a great addition to a brunch table.

1 cup sour cream

1 tablespoon freshly squeezed lemon juice

2 tablespoons minced fresh chives

¼ teaspoon salt

⅛ teaspoon freshly ground black pepper

½ pound hot-smoked (kippered) salmon

Lemon wedges, cucumber rounds, and toast or crackers for serving

Make the sauce. Mix the sour cream and lemon juice in a small bowl; stir in the chives, salt, and pepper. Taste the sauce and adjust the seasoning if you wish. Cover and refrigerate (for up to 3 days) until ready to serve.

Flake the salmon. Peel the salmon away from its skin, being sure to leave any dark flesh (the blood line) with the skin. Flake the salmon into bite-size pieces (you can use your fingers). Transfer the sauce to a small serving dish; place on a serving platter large enough to hold the salmon. Arrange the salmon around the sauce and garnish the platter with lemon wedges. Pass plates of cucumber rounds, toast, or crackers at the table.

Of Kipper Snacks and Cured Salmon

TODD: Ellen's family loves any kind of fish that comes in a can or jar, in oil-stained white paper packages from a deli, or in vacuum-sealed portions from a grocery store refrigerator case. It took me a while to figure out what everything was and keep them all straight.

ELLEN: My parents were at our house one Sunday and Todd was all excited: Charlie the Fisherman had brought some fish to the back door of Equinox the day before. "You're going to love this hot-smoked salmon I got yesterday!" he told us. My father and I took one look at it and said, "You can call it whatever you want, but that's kippered salmon."

TODD: That's when I realized that kippered just means hot-smoked. So the canned kipper snacks that Ellen and her father love so much are just hot-smoked skinless, boneless herring fillets.

ELLEN: Well, Dad didn't know from hot-smoked and cold-smoked until Todd came along and I'm not convinced that he does yet.

TODD: They are two different processes. They both start out with salt-curing the fish—that helps preserve the fish by extracting water from it, thereby reducing the environment in which bacteria can grow. In cold smoking, the cured fish is smoked far enough away from the source of the smoke, usually burning wood chips, that its flesh doesn't cook. In hot smoking, the cured fish is close enough to the smoke source that the fish winds up getting fully cooked. The flesh of cold-smoked fish, because it is only cured, still has the moist, firm texture of raw fish. Hot-smoked fish is flaky, as cooked fish is. To get some of the terms straight:

- Kippers or kipper snacks are cured, hot-smoked fish (usually salmon or herring) fully cooked to 145 degrees internal temperature.

- Hot-smoked salmon is smoked and fully cooked. Also known as kippered salmon.

- Lox is salmon that has been cured, usually in a brine of water, salt, sugar, and oil, but not smoked.

- Smoked salmon is what you usually find in a deli. It has been cured and cold-smoked. Nova Scotia, Scottish, and Norwegian smoked salmon are all forms of cured, cold-smoked salmon.

- Gravlax is cured, but not smoked, salmon. It is usually cured with sugar, salt, dill, and seasonings, then wrapped and weighted down to extract moisture from it.

STARTERS

CURRIED BUTTERNUT SQUASH SOUP
WITH GRILLED SOURDOUGH BREAD 19

PANKO-CRUSTED FISH CAKES 23

WEEZIE'S INDIAN SUMMER GAZPACHO
WITH PESTO CROUTONS 24

SWEET AND SOUR EGGPLANT ON CRISPY
GARLIC TOAST 27

MINI PASTRAMI REUBENS WITH SPICY
RUSSIAN DRESSING 28

CURRIED BUTTERNUT SQUASH SOUP WITH GRILLED SOURDOUGH BREAD

MAKES ABOUT 8 CUPS

TODD: *Zuppa di zucca*, pumpkin soup, is a fall soup I started making at Galileo years ago. It was one of the most popular dishes on the menu, partly due, no doubt, to its appealing color—that vivid orange we all associate with the fall. When my mother first tasted that soup, she gave me a glance over her glasses and said, "Have you ever tried putting a little curry in this?" She grew up in the heart of the Pennsylvania Dutch country, but she became a very Southern Virginia-inspired cook when she married my father, Brad, and settled in Fredericksburg in the late '60s. It's not unusual to find references to curry in old Virginia cookbooks. Mary Rudolph gives a recipe for "A Dish of Curry After the East Indian Manner" in *The Virginia Housewife*, published in 1828. Mom always loved to put curry in things when I was growing up—soups, chicken dishes, even salad dressings—so it's no surprise that I heeded her advice for this recipe.

½ cup canola oil

2 butternut squash (1 small, 1 medium—enough to yield 5 cups chopped)

1 medium yellow onion, chopped

4 garlic cloves, sliced

2 tablespoons curry powder

4 cups vegetable stock, preferably homemade (recipe in Chef's Appendix)

3 cups heavy cream

1 tablespoon salt

¼ teaspoon freshly ground black pepper

2 small Granny Smith apples, peeled, cored, and diced

1 tablespoon unsalted butter

¼ cup toasted pumpkin seeds (see Chef's Appendix)

6 slices Grilled Sourdough Bread (recipe follows)

Prep the squash. Peel the squash. Cut them in half and scoop out the seeds. From one of them, neatly dice enough of the flesh to equal 1 cup and set it aside for the garnish. Coarsely chop the rest—you should have about 4 cups.

Cook the soup. Heat the oil in a medium-size heavy saucepan over medium heat. Add the 4 cups chopped squash, onions, and garlic and cook for 5 minutes, stirring frequently. Stir in the curry powder and then add the vegetable stock; bring the stock to a boil, then lower the heat and simmer gently, stirring occasionally, until the squash can be easily pierced by a fork—20 minutes. Stir in the cream, salt, and pepper; cook for 15 minutes more.

Blanch the squash garnish. Meanwhile, bring a medium pot of water to boiling over high heat. Add the reserved 1 cup diced squash and boil for 1 minute. Drain in a colander and then blot dry on paper towels.

(recipe continues)

Purée the soup. Working in batches, transfer the soup to the container of a blender or food processor fitted with a metal blade, and process until the mixture is smooth. Pour each batch through a fine mesh strainer into a clean saucepan; cover and keep warm over low heat.

Sauté the garnish and serve the soup. Melt the butter in an 8-inch nonstick sauté pan over medium heat, coating evenly. Stir in the apples and blanched squash; cook, stirring occasionally, until soft—about 5 minutes. Ladle the soup into individual bowls, spoon on some of the sautéed garnish, sprinkle with pumpkin seeds, and pass the grilled bread at the table.

GRILLED SOURDOUGH BREAD

You can double, triple, or even quadruple this recipe, depending on the size of your guest list. Start with good quality sourdough bread in boule or loaf form (if using a baguette, use twice as many slices).

Preheat the oven to 325°F. Arrange 6 slices of sourdough bread on a baking sheet. Evenly drizzle 2 tablespoons olive oil over them. Sprinkle with salt and freshly ground black pepper. Turn the slices over and repeat the drizzling and seasoning. Place the baking sheet in the oven and bake until the slices are toasted and golden on both sides—3 to 4 minutes per side. (You may alternatively toast the slices in a panini press, in which case you won't need the baking sheet.)

The Story on Broth, Stock, and Quick Stock

TODD: Although the words *stock* and *broth* seem to be used interchangeably, they are, in fact, different. Stock is made with bones and broth is made with meat or with meat and bones. The essential ingredient in a stock is bones; they contain collagen, which gives stock a gelatinous quality and becomes syrupy when reduced. Stock is meant to be used as an ingredient to make something else, say a soup or a sauce (or a broth for that matter),

whereas a broth could be served as the end product because, by virtue of being made with meat, it is richer. Though it is commonplace to use vegetables in stocks and broths, they are not essential to the process. We do that now because it bumps up the flavor of both.

ELLEN: Whatever it's called, whenever I make a roast chicken, I take the carcass afterwards and simmer it in salted water for 45 minutes—no vegetables.

TODD: Actually, that's called a quick stock.

ELLEN: I strain it, cool it, and freeze it in ice cube trays. That way I can pop out however many I need to make a quick cup of soup, just adding some rice or noodles or vegetables. It's a great way of utilizing the whole bird.

PANKO-CRUSTED FISH CAKES

MAKES FOUR 3-INCH DIAMETER FISH CAKES (4 STARTER OR 2 ENTRÉE SERVINGS)

TODD: Think of these as kosher crab cakes. You could offer them with no sauce at all, or with just some sour cream or with tartar sauce (chopped pickles, capers, and mayonnaise). Or add some chopped capers to Spicy Russian Dressing (page 287), which turns it into rémoulade sauce. I like the rémoulade because the tartness of the capers and their texture add some extra oomph to the sweetness and texture of the cakes. You can also make these as mini-cakes to pass around as cocktail party hors d'oeuvres.

1½ pounds assorted white fish, such as halibut and rockfish

2 sprigs fresh thyme

2 garlic cloves

2 bay leaves

1½ cups ¼-inch cubes of bread (brioche or white sandwich bread are good here)

3 scallions, finely chopped, including some of the green

3 tablespoons mayonnaise

1 teaspoon whole grain mustard

½ teaspoon freshly grated lemon zest

¼ teaspoon Old Bay Seasoning

1 teaspoon salt

¼ teaspoon freshly ground black pepper

2 cups panko bread crumbs

¼ cup canola oil

Sour cream or rémoulade (recipe in Chef's Appendix) for serving

MAKE IT PARVE: *Serve these cakes with one of the mayonnaise dressings in the Chef's Appendix instead of with sour cream or rémoulade.*

Poach the fish. Cut the fish into 2-inch cubes. Wash it under cool running water, drain on paper towels, and pat dry with a dry paper towel. Bring 3 quarts of water to boiling in a large pot over high heat; add the fish, thyme, garlic, and bay leaves. Lower the heat to medium-low and simmer gently, uncovered, for 5 minutes. Drain the fish in a colander and discard the garlic and herbs; set the fish aside to cool.

Mix the cakes. Flake the fish into a large bowl (use your fingers). Add the bread cubes, scallions, mayonnaise, mustard, lemon zest, Old Bay Seasoning, salt, and pepper; mix well with a wooden spoon or rubber spatula. Cover and refrigerate for at least 1 hour.

Cook the cakes. Put the bread crumbs in a shallow dish. Shape the fish mixture into 4 cakes, each about 3 inches in diameter and 1 inch thick, and roll each in the crumbs, pressing with your hands to adhere. Heat the oil in a large sauté pan over medium heat. Add the cakes to the pan, lower the heat to medium-low, and cook until the cakes are golden-brown on each side—about 2 minutes per side (to help them caramelize evenly, do not move them while they cook). Transfer the cakes to a paper towel-lined plate to drain. Serve with a dollop of sour cream or rémoulade.

WEEZIE'S INDIAN SUMMER GAZPACHO WITH PESTO CROUTONS

MAKES 12 CUPS SOUP

ELLEN: Indian summer has such a pleasant ring to it. It immediately conjures up a farm market with a cornucopia of produce, which straddles the seasons of summer and fall. Every Labor Day weekend, we go down to Todd's parents' place in Irvington. It's on the Chesapeake Bay in Virginia's Northern Neck. We arrive in the early afternoon for a late lunch, and Weezie, Todd's mother, always has her famous gazpacho ready for us.

TODD: Her given name is Louise, but everyone calls her by her childhood nickname—not even my father calls her Louise. Mom's gazpacho is something she's always been known for. Her secrets: Use V-8 for extra flavor, leave the soup fairly chunky, and give it plenty of time in the refrigerator for all the flavors to meld. I added the pesto croutons because we have so much basil in our backyard every year that I have to come up with ways to use it, never wanting to waste a good harvest.

GAZPACHO:

2 large ripe tomatoes, preferably an heirloom variety, cored and quartered

1 medium english cucumber, peeled, seeded, and chopped

1 medium Vidalia onion, quartered

1 small green bell pepper, cored, seeded, and chopped

6 cups V-8 Juice (four 12-ounce bottles)

¼ cup olive oil

⅓ cup red wine vinegar

½ teaspoon Tabasco Sauce

1 tablespoon Worchestershire Sauce

1½ teaspoons salt

¼ teaspoon freshly ground black pepper

Make the gazpacho. Working in batches if necessary, place the tomatoes, cucumbers, onions, and green peppers in the container of a blender or food processor fitted with a metal blade. Process just until the vegetables begin to liquefy. Add the juice, oil, vinegar, Tabasco Sauce, Worchestershire Sauce, salt, and pepper; process until the mixture is a coarse puree. Transfer to a food storage container, cover, and refrigerate for at least 6 hours before serving.

BASIL PESTO:

4 cups packed fresh basil leaves

1½ cups olive oil

½ cup toasted pine nuts (see Chef's Appendix)

3 garlic cloves

½ cup grated Parmesan cheese (2 ounces)

½ teaspoon salt

⅛ teaspoon freshly ground black pepper

CROUTONS:

1 small baguette, cut into 1-inch cubes

3 tablespoons olive oil

¼ teaspoon red pepper flakes

¼ teaspoon salt

Pinch freshly ground black pepper

Make the pesto. Bring a large pot of water to a boil. Stir in the basil and cook for 15–20 seconds then immediately drain in a colander. Rinse under cool running water and then, with your hands, completely squeeze out the water and transfer the basil to a cutting board or wooden bowl. Coarsely chop the basil with a kitchen knife or demi-lune. Place the basil, ¾ cup of the oil, the garlic, and pine nuts in the container of a blender or food processor; process briefly to form a coarse purée. With the blender running, add the remaining ¾ cup oil and continue to process until the mixture forms a fine paste. Transfer to a small bowl and stir in the cheese, salt, and pepper; taste the pesto and adjust the seasoning if you wish.

Make the croutons. Preheat the oven to 350°F. Toss the bread cubes with the oil, red pepper flakes, salt, and pepper on a baking sheet (Ellen likes to spray the oil over the bread); spread evenly. Bake the croutons for 10 minutes, then stir. Continue to bake until toasted and crunchy—about 10 minutes more. Remove from the oven and cool on the baking sheet on a wire rack. Transfer the croutons to a large bowl and toss with ¾ cup of the pesto. (Cover and refrigerate or freeze any leftover pesto.) When ready to serve, ladle the gazpacho into individual bowls and top with croutons, or pass the croutons at the table.

SWEET AND SOUR EGGPLANT ON CRISPY GARLIC TOAST

MAKES 4 CUPS EGGPLANT COMPOTE (ABOUT 6 APPETIZER SERVINGS)

ELLEN: Chinese foods and Jews seem to go together like Christmas and a Christmas tree, so sweet and sour anything was always welcome in our house.

TODD: Sweet and sour eggplant—it's like a ratatouille. It's even better the day after it is made, when the flavors have had a chance to meld. When we go on road trips, Ellen makes a big batch a couple of days before and loads it into Tupperware so we can snack on it without having to stop. You can eat it cold, but it's best served at room temperature or even a little warm, by the spoonful on garlic toast.

3 ripe tomatoes

¼ cup olive oil

2 medium eggplants, peeled and cubed (about 4 cups)

1 medium yellow onion, cut into small dice

2 tablespoons minced garlic

¼ cup sugar

1 teaspoon ground cumin

½ cup Champagne vinegar

½ cup cider vinegar

2 cups vegetable stock, preferably homemade (recipe in Chef's Appendix) or water

1½ teaspoons chopped fresh oregano

1½ teaspoons salt

⅛ teaspoon freshly ground black pepper

Garlic Toast (recipe follows)

Prep the tomatoes. Bring a medium-size pot of water to boiling over high heat. Drop the tomatoes into the water and cook for 1 minute. With a slotted spoon, transfer the tomatoes to a bowl of ice water to stop the cooking. Use a paring knife to peel the tomatoes; then core each one and squeeze out the seeds. Chop the tomatoes.

Make the eggplant mixture. Heat the oil in a large sauté pan over medium heat; stir in the eggplant and onions, cook for 5 minutes. Stir in the tomatoes and garlic, cook for 5 minutes more. Stir in the sugar and cumin and cook for 2 minutes; add both vinegars. Continue to cook, uncovered, until the liquid is reduced by three-quarters—about 5 minutes. Add the stock, oregano, salt, and pepper. Cover the pan, lower the heat to low, and cook for 30 minutes more. Taste the mixture and add more salt or pepper if you wish. Set aside to cool slightly. Serve in a bowl, garnished with Garlic Toast, or pass the toast separately.

GARLIC TOAST

Preheat the oven to 350°F. Mince 2 garlic cloves. Whisk together ¼ cup olive oil, the garlic, ⅛ teaspoon salt, and a dash of freshly ground black pepper in a small bowl. Cut a small baguette into ⅓-inch thick slices and arrange on a baking sheet. Brush the tops of the slices with the oil mixture. Turn baguette over and brush the other side with the olive oil mixture. Bake the slices until the tops are golden brown and crunchy—for 10 to 12 minutes.

MINI PASTRAMI REUBENS WITH SPICY RUSSIAN DRESSING

MAKES 8 SMALL SANDWICHES

TODD: Whenever I went to New York with the great Italian chef Roberto Donna, he'd always say, "Oh, we have to go to Carnegie Deli and get Reuben sandwiches." Everybody loves Reubens—the gooeyness of the cheese, the dressing oozing out, the buttery crunchiness of the rye bread, the tang of the sauerkraut, the fatty richness of the meat. I prefer them with pastrami instead of corned beef (but feel free to use either, or turkey for that matter) because of the spice the peppery crust adds. Many a time when the Kassoffs wind up at our house on Sundays, Reubens hit the pan and get cut up into bite-sized pieces for noshing. Using party rye is neater and more suitable for serving at cocktail parties.

16 slices party-style marbled rye bread

Spicy Russian Dressing (recipe follows)

1 cup sauerkraut, drained (from either a jar or package)

½ pound sliced pastrami

16 slices Swiss cheese

Dill pickles for serving (recipe page 275)

Arrange 8 slices of bread on a work surface. Spread each with a teaspoon or two of the Russian dressing. Then layer the sauerkraut, pastrami, and cheese on them, distributing evenly; top each with another slice of bread. Working in batches if necessary, cook the sandwiches in a panini press until the cheese is melting and bread is well toasted. (If you don't have a panini press, heat a little olive oil in a sauté pan over medium heat and cook the sandwiches in it until the bread is toasted and caramelized—place a skillet on top of the sandwiches to press them if you like.) Serve family style, passing the remaining Russian dressing and some dill pickles at the table.

SPICY RUSSIAN DRESSING
MAKES ABOUT 1½ CUPS

With a fork, blend 1 cup mayonnaise with ¼ cup ketchup, 1 tablespoon sour cream, ¼ teaspoon Tabasco Sauce, ¼ teaspoon salt, and ⅛ teaspoon freshly ground black pepper in a small bowl; stir in four finely chopped cornichon pickles and 2 tablespoons finely chopped scallions (include a little of the green part). Cover and refrigerate until ready to use.

LUNCH

PUMPKIN RISOTTO WITH MASCARPONE
CHEESE 31

ELLEN'S FALAFEL WITH PICKLED
VEGETABLES AND MINTED LEMON
YOGURT 33

GRILLED SARDINE SANDWICH WITH
ZESTY MAYONNAISE 36

PULLED CHICKEN SALAD WITH
CRANBERRIES AND TOASTED PECANS 38

BAKED SALMON WITH POTATOES AND
GREEN OLIVES 41

PUMPKIN RISOTTO WITH MASCARPONE CHEESE

SERVES 4

TODD: This recipe is a little unusual for a risotto (see Making Risotto, page 32) in that a purée is added to it. The purée adds texture and concentrated squash flavor and intensifies the risotto's color big time. The dish isn't driven by any sense of Jewishness, really. It's just something that typifies what I would cook: It's Italian, seasonally driven, creamy, soothing—perfect for lunch on a cool, fall day.

1 small butternut squash, peeled, seeded, and coarsely chopped (about 2 cups)

3 cups vegetable stock, more as needed, preferably homemade (recipe in Chef's Appendix)

½ cup water

1 teaspoon honey

¼ teaspoon curry powder

1 tablespoon salt

1 small pumpkin or kabocha squash

1 medium celery root, scrubbed clean

2 tablespoons olive oil

1 medium yellow onion, minced

3 cups Arborio rice

1½ cups dry white wine (such as Chablis)

6 to 7 cups hot chicken stock or vegetable stock, preferably homemade (recipes in Chef's Appendix)

¼ cup Mascarpone cheese (about 8 ounces)

3 tablespoons unsalted butter (½ stick)

½ cup grated Parmesan cheese, plus more for serving (Parmigiano Reggiano is best)

Puree the butternut squash. Place the butternut squash in a 4-quart saucepan with the 3 cups vegetable stock, the water, honey, curry powder, and ¼ teaspoon salt. Bring to simmering over high heat; lower the heat to medium and simmer until the squash can be easily pierced with a fork—about 5 minutes. Transfer the mixture to the container of a food processor or blender and process until pureed, adding more vegetable stock or water if needed to create a smooth mixture.

Blanch the pumpkin and celery root. Peel the pumpkin, cut in half, and discard the seeds. Cut enough of the flesh into small dice to yield 1 cup, reserve the remainder for another use. Peel the celery root and cut into small dice; if there is more than 1 cup, reserve the excess. Bring a large pot of water to boiling, add the diced vegetables, and cook until tender but still firm to the bite—3 to 4 minutes. Drain in a colander and rinse under cold water to stop the cooking.

Make the risotto. Heat the oil in a medium-size saucepan over medium heat. Add the onions and cook, stirring occasionally, for 2 minutes. Stir in the rice and cook for 2 minutes, stirring occasionally (this technique is called toasting). To deglaze the pan, stir in the wine and continue cooking, stirring once or twice, until the wine has been completely absorbed by the rice or has evaporated—about 3 minutes. Lower the heat to medium-low. Add the stock in three 2-cup additions, adding the butternut squash purée with the second

(recipe continues)

addition; after each addition allow the rice to absorb the liquid (do not stir) and then free the rice from the sides of the pan with a wooden spoon before adding more stock. Remove pan from the heat and stir in the Mascarpone cheese, butter, Parmesan, 1½ tablespoons salt, ¼ teaspoon pepper and diced vegetables. If the risotto is thicker than you wish, stir in a little more stock. Serve, passing additional Parmesan cheese at the table.

Making Risotto

ELLEN: What is really terrific about risotto is that it's so diverse. Whether you make it with squash in the fall or asparagus in the summer, it's a dish that can be eaten in every season.

TODD: In my years working at Galileo, chef Roberto Donna instilled in me that risotto is something to be taken very seriously. To Italians, it is much more than just a bowl of rice.

Contrary to what many American chefs dictate, risotto does not need to be stirred constantly. Short and sweet, this is how you make it: Start out by properly toasting the rice and use a good wooden spoon so the rice doesn't get ground when you do stir it. Add the stock in batches. Stir it in, then leave the rice be, allowing it to absorb the stock while softly simmering. Repeat the process until the rice is done.

Risotto needs to seem creamy, even though no cream has been added. The rice's slowly released starch gives it that quality. The grains should be al dente, with just the slightest bite left to them, not crunchy in any way nor completely soft. As to the final texture, a Venetian chef once told me, "When you move the risotto, it should have waves like the sea." That's well put.

ELLEN'S FALAFEL WITH PICKLED VEGETABLES AND MINTED LEMON YOGURT

SERVES 4

ELLEN: My love affair with falafel began in Israel in 1987 when I discovered it for the first time at a shop in Tel Aviv. The counterman would spit out impatiently, "Chopped salad? Chopped salad?" I thought that meant salad, meaning the shredded lettuce and tomatoes kind of salad, but came to realize it was actually a mix of diced pickled vegetables. A few years later, Todd and I were in a falafel shop in New York and the counterman hissed at me, "Chopped salad? Chopped salad?" and I knew immediately he was an Israeli. It took me right back.

TODD: The acidic nature of the pickled vegetables really complements the nuttiness of the fried chickpeas in the falafel. The vegetables improve in flavor after they've marinated for at least 24 hours and taste best at room temperature, so plan ahead (see Pickled Foods Belong in Your Repertoire, page 164).

PICKLED VEGETABLES:

3 cups water

1 cup apple cider vinegar

½ cup sugar

1 star anise

12 black peppercorns

1 teaspoon coriander seeds

1 teaspoon fennel seeds

2 bay leaves

2 sprigs fresh thyme, broken into short pieces

2 garlic cloves, crushed

2 cups finely shredded green cabbage (about ½ pound)

1 cup matchstick-cut carrots (see julienne in Chef's Appendix)

1 red onion, thinly sliced

1 jalapeño pepper, sliced ¼-inch thick (optional)

Pickle the vegetables. Combine the water, vinegar, sugar, peppercorns, coriander, fennel, bay leaves, thyme, and garlic in a medium saucepan. Bring to boiling over high heat; immediately remove from the heat and set aside to cool at room temperature. Combine the cabbage, carrots, and onions in a large, heatproof bowl, add the jalapeño if using, and toss the vegetables to mix well. Pour the pickling liquid through a mesh strainer into another saucepan; discard the spices. Bring the liquid back to boiling and then pour it over the cabbage mixture; stir gently to mix. Cover the bowl and refrigerate until the vegetables are pickled—for at least 24 hours and up to 3 days.

Make the falafel. Preheat the oven to 300°F. Mix the falafel according to the package directions. Roll the falafel mixture into walnut-size balls, flattening each slightly in the palm of your hand. Pour 3 inches of oil into a heavy saucepan. Heat the oil to 325°F over medium heat (measure on a candy thermometer). Working in batches as appropriate for the pan you are using, fry the falafel in the hot

(recipe continues)

FALAFEL:

One 10-ounce package good quality falafel mix

Canola oil for frying

Salt

Freshly ground black pepper

4 pita breads, cut in half

Minted Lemon Yogurt (recipe follows)

Vidalia onion marmalade for garnish (optional)

MAKE IT PARVE. *Take my suggestion for a hummus dressing (see Topping Off Falafel, below) instead of using the Minted Lemon Yogurt.*

oil, turning once, until golden brown and cooked through—3 to 4 minutes per side. While the falafel cook, arrange the pitas on a baking sheet and put in the oven to warm. Using a slotted spoon, transfer the falafel to a paper towel–lined plate and sprinkle with a little salt and pepper. To serve, spoon some Minted Lemon Yogurt into the bottom of each pita half, then spoon in some of the vegetables, dividing equally, and add 3 falafel. Dot some onion marmalade over the top if you wish.

MINTED LEMON YOGURT
MAKES 1 CUP

Place 1 cup plain or vanilla low-fat yogurt in a small bowl (Ellen favors vanilla). Add to it 3 finely chopped fresh mint leaves, ½ teaspoon freshly grated lemon zest, ½ teaspoon freshly squeezed lemon juice, ¼ teaspoon honey (if you're using plain yogurt), and a sprinkling each of salt and black pepper. Whisk together until combined; cover and refrigerate until ready to serve.

Don't Nix the Mix

TODD: We experimented with making falafel mix from scratch, but found that the batter did not hold well for more than four to six hours and the texture was not consistent from one hour to the next. Then we discovered terrific prepared mixes on the market. The mix can be made the day before and still hold up well. The other consideration was this: The mix version is what everyone expects when they order falafel, so no need to reinvent the wheel here.

ELLEN: We had the same experience with matzo balls. My Aunt Lil always used a mix and you couldn't get matzo balls lighter than the ones she made. Todd experimented with making the balls from actual matzo, but we found the texture was never as good. Certain convenience foods have their place in every pantry.

Topping Off Falafel

TODD: I like to bring a complex mix of tastes in this sandwich, adding jalapeño peppers to the pickled vegetables for a spicy accent, and finishing the whole with a sprinkling of Vidalia onion marmalade—a condiment I purchased. Minted yogurt makes a refreshing dressing, but you could also just take some hummus and/or tahini and puree it with some fresh garlic and a little water and salt.

GRILLED SARDINE SANDWICH WITH ZESTY MAYONNAISE

MAKES 4 SANDWICHES

TODD: Sardines are small, oily fish from the herring family. Ellen was always crazy about canned sardines and can debone them with surgical precision in about five seconds, a skill she learned from her grandfather, Harry, when she was a little girl (see Sardines, Fresh and Canned, page 256).

ELLEN: After Todd and I were married, I discovered the fresh variety, which takes the sardine sandwich experience to a totally different level. They are a cinch to prepare on a George Foreman–type grill. Todd puts chives in his mayonnaise, but I like to sneak in some thinly sliced red onions, too.

16 fresh sardine fillets, pin bones removed (see Chef's Appendix

1 tablespoon olive oil

Salt

Freshly ground black pepper

8 slices rye bread

Zesty Mayonnaise (recipe follows)

Arugula or soft, sweet lettuce leaves

Grill the sardines. Preheat a George Foreman grill according to the manufacturer's directions (you can preheat your oven to Broil if you don't have this handy machine). Drizzle the sardine fillets with the oil; sprinkle with salt and pepper. Arrange the fillets in the George Foreman grill or on a broiler pan. Cook for 4 minutes; transfer to a paper towel-lined plate to drain.

Assemble the sandwiches. Toast the bread. Arrange all 8 slices on a work surface; spread each with some Zesty Mayonnaise. Top each of 4 slices with arugula and 4 sardines; lay more arugula over the sardines and top with another slice of toast. Cut each sandwich into halves or quarters and serve.

ZESTY MAYONNAISE

MAKES ABOUT ⅔ CUP

With a fork, blend ½ cup mayonnaise with ¼ teaspoon freshly squeezed lemon juice, ¼ teaspoon freshly grated lemon zest, a dash of Tabasco Sauce, ¼ teaspoon salt, and a pinch of freshly ground black pepper in a small bowl; stir in 2 tablespoons minced fresh chives. Cover and refrigerate until ready to use.

PULLED CHICKEN SALAD WITH CRANBERRIES AND TOASTED PECANS

SERVES 4

TODD: This dish, a favorite of three White House administrations, has been a signature item at Equinox since we opened in 1999 and remains the most popular lunch dish there. The secret to making great chicken salad is to poach the bird whole (using, of course, the best quality farm-raised animal you can afford), then pull the dark and white meat from the bird by hand and shred it into bite-sized pieces. The coarser texture creates more surface areas for the dressing to cling to.

ELLEN: Growing up, chicken salad was a way to deal with leftovers from a roast chicken dinner. Or something you got at a deli. Todd's version updates the Waldorf salad a little bit, with the inclusion of dried cranberries, cashews, and celery.

TODD: The bonus here is the poaching liquid. Reduce that broth and freeze it for another use, such as sauce or soup making.

½ cup dried cranberries

1 whole poached chicken, about 3 pounds (recipe follows)

1 cup mayonnaise

1 tablespoon olive oil

1 tablespoon freshly squeezed lemon juice

2 teaspoons salt

¼ teaspoon freshly ground black pepper

1 cup minced red onion (about 2 medium onions)

1 cup minced celery

½ cup chopped toasted cashews (see Chef's Appendix)

2 tablespoons chopped fresh parsley

Soak the cranberries. Put the cranberries in a small bowl. Cover with boiling water and set aside to soak while you do the next step.

Shred the chicken. Pull or cut the chicken from the bones and pull the meat into bite-size pieces, shredding with your hands. Place the meat in a large bowl.

Make the salad. Drain the cranberries in a strainer. With a fork, mix the mayonnaise, olive oil, lemon juice, salt, and pepper in a small bowl. Add the onions, celery, cranberries, cashews, and mayonnaise mixture to the bowl with the chicken; mix thoroughly with a wooden spoon. Mix in the parsley. Cover and refrigerate for at least 1 hour before serving.

POACHED CHICKEN

Prep the ingredients. Trim any excess fat from the chicken. Rinse the chicken under cold water and place it in a large pot. Coarsely chop 1 carrot, 2 stalks celery, and 1 large yellow or white onion and crush 3 garlic cloves. Add these to the pot along with 3 sprigs fresh thyme, 2 bay leaves, 1 teaspoon salt, and ½ teaspoon freshly ground black pepper. Add water to cover.

Poach the chicken. Cover the pot with the chicken and bring to boiling over high heat, lower the heat to low, and simmer until the chicken is done (the leg joints will be loose when moved)—about 1 hour. Remove the pot from the heat; transfer the chicken to a colander to drain. Pour the broth through a strainer into a food storage container or bowl; reserve for another use. Discard the vegetables and herbs.

BAKED SALMON WITH POTATOES AND GREEN OLIVES

SERVES 6

TODD: When you want to offer something for lunch that is more substantial and formal than a sandwich or salad but still light, a nice piece of salmon baked in a bath of wine, butter, and shallots is a good way to go. In this dish, the potatoes and green olives add a Provençale profile while making the meal complete. As the fish bakes, juices from the salmon combine with the cooking liquid. The potatoes absorb some of this liquid and the rest gets reduced and thickened into a concentrated sauce after the salmon is baked. It's easy to prepare and comes together fast. Use any good quality cracked green olives in brine, but I prefer Cerignola, those meaty, bright green olives from Foggia in Southern Italy.

2 medium Yukon Gold potatoes

4 medium shallots, sliced (about 1 cup)

2 tablespoons unsalted butter

6 boneless, skinless salmon fillets (about 5 ounces each)

1½ cups pitted, sliced green olives (cracked green or Spanish olives both are good)

1 cup dry white wine (such as Chablis)

1 cup vegetable stock or chicken stock, preferably homemade (recipes in Chef's Appendix)

1 tablespoon salt

⅛ teaspoon freshly ground black pepper

2 scallions, sliced crosswise, including part of the green (¼ cup)

¼ cup very thinly sliced fresh basil leaves

¼ cup seeded and diced fresh tomatoes

Cook the potatoes. Peel the potatoes and cut into ½-inch dice. Place in a 2-quart saucepan; add water to cover. Cover the pan and bring to boiling over high heat; cook for 4 minutes. Drain in a colander.

Cook the salmon. Preheat the oven to 375°F. Rub the butter over the sides and bottom of a flameproof baking dish large enough to hold the salmon fillets in one layer. Sprinkle the shallots over the bottom of the dish. Arrange the salmon on top; add the potatoes and olives. Pour in the wine and broth; sprinkle the salt and pepper over all. Heat the dish over high heat until the liquid is not quite boiling and then place in the oven. Bake until salmon is cooked through—8 to 12 minutes.

Finish the sauce. Transfer the salmon to a serving platter and keep warm. Place the baking dish with the sauce on the stove top again and bring to simmering over medium heat, stirring constantly; stir in the tomatoes and heat through. Stir in the scallions and basil and then immediately pour the sauce over the salmon and serve.

MAKE IT PARVE. *Use margarine or canola oil instead of the butter and be sure to choose vegetable stock, not chicken stock.*

DINNER

SALT-BAKED RED SNAPPER 43

BEEF STEW WITH GLAZED FALL
VEGETABLES 46

HONEY-GLAZED CHICKEN THIGHS WITH
BULGUR PILAF 48

BAKED VEAL ROAST 50

MEDITERRANEAN-STYLE FISH STEW 53

SALT-BAKED RED SNAPPER

SERVES 4

TODD: This is the ultimate cool technique, using salt and egg whites to form an igloo around a fish and create a steam chamber. It makes a stunning presentation that never fails to mesmerize guests when you break the crust open and reveal a beautiful whole fish in all its glory with lemon and herb-scented steam rising from it. Make sure the fish is completely free of scales.

1 whole red snapper or sea bass (about 3 pounds), cleaned

4 sprigs fresh thyme

2 sprigs fresh rosemary

2 garlic cloves, crushed

1½ pounds kosher salt (1 large box)

3 egg whites, lightly whisked together

Grated zest of 1 lemon

1 teaspoon coarsely ground black pepper

2 tablespoons olive oil

Lemon wedges and good olive oil for serving

Prep the fish. Preheat the oven to 350°F. Wash the fish well in cold water and dry with paper towels. Stuff the cavity of fish with the thyme, rosemary, and garlic. Place the salt in a large bowl and add the egg whites, lemon zest, and pepper; mix well with your hands to incorporate everything. Spread one-third of the salt mixture over the bottom of a baking dish large enough to hold the fish. Lay the fish on top and drizzle with the oil. Pack the remaining salt mixture around and on top of the fish, leaving the head uncovered.

Bake the fish. Place the baking dish in the oven and cook until the eyes of the fish are pearly white—30 to 40 minutes. Remove from the oven and set aside to rest for 5 minutes. Then—at the table or in the kitchen as you prefer—crack open the salt crust with a wooden spoon; gently lift out the fish and transfer it to a large platter. Slice into serving portions and serve family style, passing a plate of lemon wedges and a decanter of good olive oil at the table.

BEEF STEW WITH GLAZED FALL VEGETABLES

SERVES 6 TO 8

TODD: Many cultures have some form of stewed beef dish in which the lesser cuts of the steer are slow cooked to coax tenderness out of them. There are few methods of cooking that surpass braising for concentrating flavor, but using proper technique is key: It's what separates an average rendition from a great one (see On Braising, page 119).

ELLEN: Jewish households were big on the stewed meats—they were affordable and could withstand long cooking times unmonitored during the Sabbath. In the '50s, you'd just buy packages of random beef chunks labeled "stew meat," sear them (maybe) in a Dutch oven, throw canned mushroom soup or dehydrated onion soup mix in there, add some chunks of carrots, potatoes, and celery (maybe), and cook it all into submission. In Todd's version, all the great fall root vegetables (turnip, rutabaga, celery root, and sweet potato) get glazed separately and added to the stew at the end. That way they are beautiful and cooked perfectly.

TODD: The stew stands on its own as a meal, but we love it with Saffron Rice (page 201, but leave the peas out) or over buttered noodles.

3 pounds beef stew meat (preferably shoulder cut), cut into 2-inch cubes

1 teaspoon salt

½ teaspoon freshly ground black pepper

2 cups all-purpose flour

¼ cup canola oil, more if needed

1 carrot, coarsely chopped

1 medium yellow onion, sliced

2 celery ribs, sliced crosswise

6 whole garlic cloves

1 tablespoon tomato paste

1 bottle Cabernet Sauvignon wine (750 milliliters)

Brown the meat. Preheat the oven to 350°F. Toss the beef with the salt and pepper in a large bowl. Put the flour in a second large bowl. Heat the ¼ cup oil in a flameproof casserole over medium-high heat. Working in batches, add the beef to the flour and toss to coat; then transfer to the heated casserole, shaking off the excess flour as you do so. Sauté until the beef is golden brown, turning to brown both sides—about 5 minutes per side. Remove from the pan and set aside.

Braise the stew. Lower the heat to medium and in the same pan, adding a little more oil if needed, sauté the carrots, onions, celery, and garlic until lightly caramelized—10 minutes. Stir in the tomato paste and cook for 5 minutes more. Add the wine, and cook until the liquid has reduced by half—about 10 minutes. Add the stock, herb bouquet, and seared meat. Raise the heat to medium-high and bring the liquid to simmering. Cover the pan and transfer to the oven. Cook until the meat is tender—about 1 hour.

**2 quarts veal stock,
preferably homemade (see
About Veal Stock, and recipe
in Chef's Appendix)**

**1 herb bouquet (see Chef's
Appendix)**

**Saffron Rice with Peas
(omit the peas) for serving
(optional, page 201)**

GLAZED VEGETABLES:

1 medium turnip

1 medium rutabaga

1 medium celery root

1 medium sweet potato

⅓ cup canola oil

1 teaspoon salt

**¼ teaspoon freshly ground
black pepper**

**2 cups chicken stock,
preferably homemade (recipe
in Chef's Appendix)**

1 tablespoon unsalted butter

MAKE IT MEAT. *Use margarine
or olive oil instead of butter to finish
the glazed vegetables.*

Make the glazed vegetables. Meanwhile, peel the turnip, rutabaga, celery root, and sweet potato and cut each into ½-inch dice; you should have about 4 cups total. Heat the oil in a large sauté pan over medium heat. Add the vegetables and sauté for 3 minutes. Stir in the salt and pepper, then the chicken stock; bring to simmering and then lower the heat to low and cook, uncovered, until the vegetables are tender, approximately 15 minutes. Stir in the butter until melted and the vegetables become glazed; drain vegetables in a colander.

Complete the stew. With a slotted spoon, transfer the meat from the casserole to another casserole or a large bowl; pick out and discard the braised vegetables and herb bouquet. Strain the braising liquid into the casserole with the meat. Stir in the glazed vegetables. Taste the stew and add more salt or pepper if you wish. Serve with Saffron Rice if desired.

ABOUT VEAL STOCK

Veal stock can be very challenging to make at home for the simple reason it takes 24 hours of simmering in order to gain full strength and flavor. Reduced veal stock—called demi-glace or *fond du veau*—is made by boiling veal stock until it is substantially evaporated and thickened into a syrup consistency. It is a foundation in the classical kitchen and fortunately is available readymade at good grocers and online. Demi-glace may be diluted with water to make veal stock for use in a recipe such as the Beef Stew with Glazed Fall Vegetables (use 2 to 3 parts water to 1 part demi-glace); without it, it is very difficult to make a good brown sauce. It's well worth the effort to make your own veal stock and demi-glace, and should you wish to make them from scratch my recipes are in the Chef's Appendix. On the other hand, if you are pressed for time, by all means buy one of the prepared versions, such as Demi-Glace Gold brand—this is a fine and practical option.

HONEY-GLAZED CHICKEN THIGHS WITH BULGUR PILAF

SERVES 6

TODD: This dish was a staff favorite at Equinox. We'd save up the thighs and drumsticks from whole chickens (the breast meat was used for entrées) until we had enough for a "family" meal, then bake and glaze them and serve them with rice or couscous. Here I'm using bulgur wheat as a nod to Ellen's Mediterranean cravings. Pilaf usually means rice, but I apply that term to any grain dish cooked in stock and enhanced with sautéed onions and garlic. "Pilafized bulgur wheat" would be a more accurate way to put it, but it doesn't sound as nice.

12 chicken thighs

2 teaspoons salt

¼ teaspoon freshly ground black pepper

2 cups all-purpose flour

¼ cup canola oil

½ cup honey

⅓ cup balsamic vinegar

¼ cup soy sauce

1 tablespoon freshly squeezed lemon juice

Brown the chicken. Sprinkle the chicken thighs with the salt and pepper. Put the flour in a large shallow bowl. Heat the oil in a large sauté pan over medium-high heat. Working in batches, dip the thighs in the flour, turning to coat and shaking off the excess, and then place in the sauté pan. Turn the heat to medium and cook the thighs, stirring occasionally and turning once, until they are golden brown on both sides—3 to 4 minutes per side. Transfer the thighs to a paper towel-lined plate to drain.

Make the basting sauce. Preheat the oven to 350°F. Whisk together the honey, balsamic vinegar, soy sauce, and lemon juice in a small bowl. Arrange the chicken thighs in a baking dish large enough to hold them in one layer (use two dishes if you wish). Brush the thighs with the sauce; turn them over and brush the other side with the sauce.

Bake the chicken. Place the baking dish in the oven and cook for 10 minutes; remove from the oven and baste the tops of the thighs with sauce again. In this manner, bake the chicken until done, basting every 10 minutes—for a total baking time of 30 to 40 minutes. Remove from oven and brush once more with basting sauce.

BULGUR PILAF:

2 tablespoons olive oil

1 medium yellow onion, finely minced

1 garlic clove, finely minced

2 cups bulgur wheat

4 cups hot chicken or vegetable stock, preferably homemade (recipes in Chef's Appendix)

3 scallions, finely sliced crosswise, including some of the green

1 tablespoon chopped fresh parsley

2 tablespoons freshly squeezed lemon juice

2 teaspoons salt

¼ teaspoon freshly ground black pepper

Make the bulgur. Meanwhile, heat the oil in a medium sauté pan over medium heat. Add the onions and garlic; cook, stirring, until translucent and shiny—about 5 minutes. Stir in the bulgur and add the hot stock; cook for 5 minutes. Remove the pan from the heat, cover, and set aside to let the bulgur absorb the liquid for 15 minutes. Then drain any excess liquid through a sieve and return the bulgur to the pan. Fluff with a fork and add the scallions, parsley, lemon juice, salt, and pepper, fluffing again to mix. Taste the pilaf and add more salt or pepper if you wish.

To serve, make a bed of the bulgur pilaf on a platter and arrange the chicken thighs on top.

BAKED VEAL ROAST

SERVES 6

TODD: This is really an upscale version of pot roast. Veal is a bit lighter than beef, but still hearty and flavorful, so it's a good choice for a fall dinner. Fennel, cumin, and coriander add some complexity to the meat, which, by virtue of being younger than beef, has a subtler flavor. The shoulder is a good piece of meat to use because it has interior fat that melts during the cooking process, imparting tenderness and preventing the meat from drying out. You may have to put in a special request with the butcher to get this cut, but it's worth doing.

3 pounds boneless veal shoulder roast or veal top round

2 tablespoons olive oil

1 tablespoon Aromatic Spice Blend (see Chef's Appendix)

Salt

Freshly ground black pepper

2 carrots, coarsely chopped

2 celery stalks, chopped

1 medium yellow onion, diced

3 garlic cloves, crushed

6 button mushrooms, chopped

1 cup dry white wine (such as Chablis or Sauvingon Blanc)

2 springs fresh rosemary

2 springs fresh sage

2 cups Roasted Chicken Jus (recipe in Chef's Appendix)

Prep the roast. Preheat the oven to 450°F. Wash the roast under cold water; pat dry with paper towels. Trim off any unwanted fat. Rub the roast all over with the olive oil, and sprinkle with the Aromatic Spice Mix and some salt and pepper, patting into the surface to adhere.

Mix a mirepoix. Mix the carrots, celery, onions, garlic, and mushrooms in the bottom of a roasting pan large enough to hold the veal. Add the wine to the pan and spread the vegetables evenly. Lay the rosemary and sage on top.

Roast the veal. Place the veal on the vegetables in the pan and place in the oven. After 5 minutes, lower the oven temperature to 350°F. Cook for 20 minutes more; remove the pan from the oven and baste the roast with the pan juices. Rotate the pan 180 degrees and return to the oven; cook, basting occasionally, until the internal temperature of the roast reads 135°F to 140°F on a meat thermometer—about 30 minutes more. Remove the pan from the oven; transfer the roast to a platter, cover with foil, and keep warm.

Make the sauce. Discard the rosemary and sage springs from the roasting pan. Transfer the vegetables and cooking juices to a small pot, and add the chicken jus. Heat to simmering over medium heat and cook for 15 minutes, skimming off any grease. Pour the sauce through a fine mesh strainer into a serving vessel, using a wooden spoon to press the vegetables through the mesh; keep warm.

To serve, cut the veal into ½-inch thick slices. Arrange the slices in a fan on each diner's plate and drizzle with sauce.

MEDITERRANEAN-STYLE FISH STEW

SERVES 6 AS AN ENTRÉE

TODD: Pretty much every culture, especially around the Mediterranean, has a version of fish or seafood stew: cioppino, kakavia, bouillabaisse. I especially love the latter, with its layered flavors of fennel, pernod, tomatoes, and saffron melding with white wine and juices from ultra-fresh fish.

ELLEN: I met Todd when he was working at Galileo and I was a sales rep for a big food company. In the summer of 1993, the chef, Roberto Donna, sent Todd to Italy for a month to *stage* (intern) at the hometown restaurant in Torino where Roberto got his start. I came over after he was done and we went to Nice. We were young and didn't have much money to spend, but one night we decided to splurge on a restaurant meal instead of just eating baguettes and ratatouille like we had been doing.

TODD: It turned out to be the greatest bouillabaisse I ever had—an inspiration that stayed with me throughout my career.

SOUP BASE:

3 tablespoons olive oil

1 small fennel bulb, thinly sliced

1 small yellow onion, finely sliced

2 garlic cloves, finely chopped

1½ pounds assorted fish trimmings (such as bass, halibut, or sole—see what your fish monger has available; it is usually quite cheap)

1 medium celery rib, thinly sliced

1 small carrot, thinly sliced

2 tablespoons tomato paste

2 cups dry white wine (such as Chablis)

2 cups V-8 Juice

Make the soup. Heat the oil in a 4-quart stockpot over medium heat. Stir in the fennel, onions, and garlic with a wooden spoon. Sauté for 3 minutes. Add the fish trimmings, celery, and carrots and lower the heat to medium-low; cook until the vegetables and fish are shiny and aromatic—for 3 minutes more. Add the tomato paste and stir into the vegetables; cook for 2 minutes to reduce some of the acidity. Add the wine and continue to cook until the liquid is reduced by half—about 4 minutes. Add the juice, stock, bay leaf, thyme, salt, and pepper. Raise the heat to medium-high and bring the liquid to simmering; cover the pot with a tight lid, lower the heat to low, and let the soup simmer for 30 minutes.

Purée the soup. Remove any coarse or bony fish trimmings and the thyme and bay leaf from the soup. Working in batches if necessary, transfer the soup to the container of a blender or food processor fitted with a metal blade and process to a smooth purée. (If using a blender, cover the lid with a kitchen towel to prevent it from popping off.) Pour the soup through a medium-mesh strainer (such

(recipe continues)

4 cups fish stock, vegetable stock, or chicken stock, preferably homemade (recipes in Chef's Appendix)

1 bay leaf

2 springs fresh thyme

1½ tablespoons salt

½ teaspoon freshly ground black pepper

STEW:

1 cup diced rockfish (about ¼ pound)

1 cup diced halibut (about ¼ pound)

1 cup diced cod (about ¼ pound)

½ cup diced ripe tomatoes (use canned if local tomatoes are not in season)

1 cup mixed finely diced carrots, fennel, and scallions

¼ cup Pernod (anise liqueur)

Saffron Mayonnaise (recipe follows)

Fresh fennel fronds for garnish (optional)

Garlic Toast (page 27) for serving

as a pasta basket) into a clean stockpot, using a wooden spoon to force any remaining vegetable pieces through the mesh; keep warm over low heat.

Complete the stew. Add all the diced fish, the tomatoes, diced vegetables, and Pernod to the soup. Raise the heat to medium-low and bring the mixture to a soft simmer. Lower the heat to low and cook the soup, stirring occasionally, until the vegetables are tender and the fish is fully cooked—about 10 minutes. Ladle the stew into individual bowls, top with a small dollop of Saffron Mayonnaise, and serve; pass the Garlic Toast at the table.

SAFFRON MAYONNAISE

MAKES ABOUT 1⅓ CUPS

Stir together 1 cup white wine (such as Chablis) and 1 finely minced large shallot in a small saucepan. Bring to boiling over medium heat; gently boil until the liquid is reduced to 1½ tablespoons (that's 4½ teaspoons). Stir in ½ teaspoon saffron threads and cook just until they are soft; pour the mixture into a small bowl and set aside until cool. Then stir in 1¼ cups mayonnaise, 1 teaspoon freshly squeezed lemon juice, and a pinch each of salt and freshly ground black pepper, mixing well. Cover the bowl and refrigerate until ready to use (or up to 1 month).

FISH MATTERS

Be mindful of the fish that you use for the stew—you want white fish basically. In Europe they use rascasse, red snapper, or red mullet. You don't need to use premium center cuts of fish. I wouldn't use trim exactly, because you want fish pieces to be firm and sturdy enough to withstand the simmering process and not disintegrate (but you do want the trimmings to enhance the flavor of the soup base). A delicate fish like flounder or trout will not do. I would stay away from oily fish, like bluefish or mackerel, because their flavor is too strong for such a nuanced dish.

SIDES

RED CABBAGE COLESLAW 57

ROAST POTATOES WITH ROSEMARY 58

BAKED SPAGHETTI SQUASH
WITH TOMATO FONDUE 60

BRUSSELS SPROUT PETAL SAUTÉ 63

CIDER-GLAZED ROOT VEGETABLES 65

RED CABBAGE COLESLAW

MAKES ABOUT 4 CUPS

TODD: This has been a signature side dish at Market Salamander, the gourmet market I helped open in Middleburg, Virginia, in 2005, since the day they opened. I use red cabbage for the slaw because it just looks more interesting than green—it's brighter. It's a good idea to think ahead about making this; the slaw improves when the flavors have a chance to meld, at least overnight.

1 small head red cabbage, finely shredded (about 3 cups)

1 carrot, grated

1 small red onion, halved lengthwise and finely sliced

2 scallions, thinly sliced crosswise, including part of the green (¼ cup)

1 teaspoon toasted fennel seeds (see Chef's Appendix), crushed with a mortar and pestle

1 teaspoon toasted mustard seeds (see Chef's Appendix), crushed

¼ teaspoon toasted coriander seeds (see Chef's Appendix), crushed

1 teaspoon salt

⅛ teaspoon freshly ground black pepper

1 cup mayonnaise

¼ cup apple cider vinegar

2 tablespoons sour cream

MAKE IT PARVE. *Use an additional 2 tablespoons mayonnaise instead of adding the sour cream.*

Place the cabbage, carrots, onions, and scallions in a large bowl. Add the fennel, mustard, and coriander seeds and the salt and pepper. Stir these ingredients to mix well. Whisk together the mayonnaise, vinegar, and sour cream in a small bowl; add to the cabbage mixture and mix well. Taste the coleslaw and add more salt or pepper if you wish. Cover and refrigerate for at least 6 hours.

ROAST POTATOES WITH ROSEMARY

SERVES 4 TO 6

TODD: We like to use red bliss potatoes because they are less starchy than russets or Idahos, and therefore caramelize well, so they lend themselves perfectly to roasting (see Roasting Potatoes, below). You can substitute with low-starch potatoes, like Yukon Golds or fingerlings. Cloves of garlic cooked in their skins add an interesting element to the dish (if you peel them, they would burn). If you press down on the sides of them with the side of your forks, the flesh should pop out easily. Eating a bit of roasted garlic with each bite of potato is just a delight.

1 pound Red Bliss new potatoes

½ cup canola oil

12 whole garlic cloves, in their skins

1 tablespoon unsalted butter

½ teaspoon salt

Pinch of freshly ground black pepper

2 large sprigs fresh rosemary, broken into 3-inch pieces

MAKE IT PARVE. *Substitute margarine or olive oil for the butter.*

Blanch the potatoes. Preheat the oven to 325°F. Bring a large pot of salted water to boiling over high heat. Meanwhile, cut the potatoes into quarters. Drop the potatoes into the boiling water and cook for 3 to 4 minutes. Drain in a colander and set aside to dry (pat dry with a kitchen towel if they don't air-dry quickly—they need to be dry in order to brown evenly).

Roast the potatoes. Heat the oil in a 14-inch ovenproof sauté pan over medium heat. Add the potatoes and cook without stirring until caramelized (slightly golden)—about 4 minutes. Stir in the garlic cloves. Transfer the pan to the oven and roast until the potatoes are cooked through and browned evenly—8 to 10 minutes.

Season the potatoes. Remove the pan with the potatoes from the oven and add the butter and rosemary; stir until the butter is melted and well incorporated. Add the salt and pepper; taste the potatoes and add more salt or pepper if you wish. Drain on paper towels, transfer to a serving bowl, and serve.

Roasting Potatoes

ELLEN: Knowing how to roast potatoes perfectly, so they are brown and crisp on the outside and fluffy on the inside, is a telltale sign of a good cook. Even though I grew up eating them (in a family with three boys, you eat a lot of things that are filling, and inexpensive), I was never very good at making them. Todd's were amazing, though, so it was one of the first things I wanted him to teach me how to make.

TODD: There's really not that much to it. You have to start out with a low-starch potato. When I use red bliss potatoes, I don't bother to peel them because the skins are thin and look so nice. I quarter them, blanch them in boiling water for several minutes, dry them, sauté them in hot oil to caramelize them on all sides, oven roast them, and then finish them with some butter and rosemary.

ELLEN: It is such an easy concept, and yet after 2 decades of marriage I still can't roast potatoes the way Todd does. I am better at it than I used to be, just out of sheer practice. But to this day when I call Harrison to dinner and tell him that we're having roasted potatoes with dinner, he asks if Todd made them. If I say yes, he's downstairs in two seconds flat. If not, I definitely have to call him a few more times.

BAKED SPAGHETTI SQUASH WITH TOMATO FONDUE

SERVES 4

TODD: Tomato fondue is basically just tomatoes stewed slowly with aromatics. It's not a bad idea to make a big batch, because you can put it on just about anything: sandwiches, fish, chicken, or with vegetables for a quick ratatouille.

ELLEN: If we ever had spaghetti squash growing up it was because my mother thought it looked interesting, brought it home, and then didn't know what to do with it. At that point it would sit in the fruit drawer of the refrigerator and rot.

TODD: When I saw spaghetti squash for the first time at the Culinary Institute of America, I found it fascinating to rake it and have those noodle-like strands that looked like spaghetti come out of it. It not only looks like pasta, you can treat it similarly—it works so well here with the stewed tomatoes, fresh thyme, and a final sprinkle of Parmesan cheese. It's rustic, tasty, seasonal, inexpensive, and very easy to prepare. It's not haute, but it's still elegant.

2 medium spaghetti squash (about 3 pounds total), split lengthwise, seeds removed

3 tablespoons olive oil

Salt

Freshly ground black pepper

2 tablespoons minced garlic

1½ cups chopped scallions (1 to 2 bunches)

1 teaspoon chopped fresh thyme leaves

Grated Parmesan cheese for serving (optional)

TOMATO FONDUE:

2 medium ripe tomatoes

1 yellow onion, finely minced

2 small garlic cloves, finely minced

⅓ cup V-8 Juice

Bake the squash. Preheat the oven to 325°F. Line a baking sheet with parchment paper. Rub 1 tablespoon of the oil over the cut surfaces of the squash and then sprinkle with salt and pepper; place cut side down on the prepared baking sheet. Bake the squash until the skin is blistered and the flesh is softened—30 to 40 minutes. Transfer the baking sheet to a wire rack and set aside until the squash is cool enough to handle.

Prep the tomatoes for the fondue. Meanwhile, bring a medium-size pot of water to boiling over high heat. Drop the tomatoes into the water and cook for 1 minute. With a slotted spoon, transfer the tomatoes to a bowl of ice water to stop the cooking. Use a paring knife to peel the tomatoes; core each one and squeeze out the seeds. Chop the tomatoes.

Make the fondue. Place the tomatoes, onions, and garlic in a medium saucepan. Stir in the juice, water, oil, sugar, salt, and pepper. Cook over low heat, stirring occasionally, until the tomatoes begin to form a soft pulp—for 20 minutes.

2 tablespoons water

1½ tablespoons olive oil

1 teaspoon sugar

½ teaspoon salt

⅛ teaspoon freshly ground black pepper

Season the squash. With a table fork, "rake" the flesh out of the squash skin into a large bowl. In a saucepan large enough to hold the squash, heat the remaining 2 tablespoons oil with the garlic over medium-low heat. Cook, stirring occasionally, until the garlic is aromatic—about 2 minutes. Add the squash to the pan and stir until coated with the oil and garlic. Stir in the scallions and ½ cup of the Tomato Fondue. Cook the squash mixture until heated through—6 to 8 minutes. Taste the squash and add more fondue, salt, or pepper if you wish (reserve the remaining fondue for another use). Serve immediately.

BRUSSELS SPROUT PETAL SAUTÉ

SERVES 6

ELLEN: In my childhood, Brussels sprouts were one of those items that came in a can or a bag. They were not looked upon with any great affection in our house, but once I had them fresh like Todd does them, it was a whole other story.

TODD: Quite honestly, I was never a fan of those halved or quartered Brussels sprouts that would stink up the kitchen when my mother made them. This technique, by which you peel apart the leaves of the sprouts as you would a small cabbage, will take you a bit of time to prep, but I promise you it's worth the labor. Petals take on a completely different mouth feel and a much more delicate flavor—gone is the bitter aftertaste and gaseous quality that Brussels sprouts often manifest.

36 Brussels sprouts (2 pints)

¼ cup unsalted butter

¼ cup olive oil

4 large shallots, sliced lengthwise

2 garlic cloves, minced

MAKE IT PARVE. *Use margarine instead of butter.*

Separate the petals. Cut off the bottom of each Brussels sprout with a paring knife and pull each leaf free from bottom to top, rubbing between your thumb and forefinger to separate; discard any that are blemished.

Blanch the petals. Bring a large pot of salted water to boiling over high heat. Add the sprout leaves and cook for 2 minutes. Drain the leaves in a colander and rinse under cold water to stop the cooking.

Make the sauté. Melt the butter with the olive oil in a large sauté pan over medium-low heat, stirring to combine. Add the shallots and garlic; cook for 2 minutes. Add sprout leaves and cook, stirring frequently, until tender and well cooked—about 5 minutes. Stir in the salt and pepper; taste the leaves and add more salt or pepper if you wish. Transfer the sauté to a serving bowl; serve hot.

CIDER-GLAZED ROOT VEGETABLES

SERVES 4

TODD: It used to be that the only root vegetables people were familiar with were carrots and potatoes. Turnips maybe.

ELLEN: And sweet potatoes, except we only really ate the ones out of a can when I was growing up—they'd get cooked to death in tzimmes.

TODD: Now folks are used to seeing parsnips, turnips, celery root, rutabagas. These vegetables are so delicious that it's best not to fuss with them much. Cooking them in stock and then glazing them with some vinegar and honey brings out their earthy flavor and adds extra depth and pizzazz—a professional touch.

ELLEN: I always associate honey with Rosh Hashanah, so these glazed vegetables always turn up on our holiday table.

1 large carrot

1 medium turnip

1 medium rutabaga

1 medium celery root

2 tablespoons unsalted butter

1 tablespoon olive oil

1 tablespoon honey

¼ cup apple cider vinegar

½ teaspoon salt

⅛ teaspoon freshly ground black pepper

2 cups vegetable stock or chicken stock, preferably homemade (recipes in Chef's Appendix)

2 sprigs fresh thyme plus the leaves from a third sprig

MAKE IT PARVE. *Substitute margarine or olive oil for the butter and be sure to choose vegetable stock, not chicken stock.*

Prep the vegetables. Peel the carrot, turnip, rutabaga, and celery root and cut each into ½-inch dice; you should have about 1 cup of each or 4 cups altogether (reserve any excess for another use).

Cook the vegetables. Heat the butter and oil in a large sauté pan over medium heat. Add the diced vegetables and sauté until the vegetables begin to caramelize (turn slightly golden)—about 5 minutes. Stir in the honey and cook for 1 minute. Add the vinegar and continue to cook, stirring, until it has evaporated—3 to 4 minutes. Stir in the salt and pepper. Add the stock and whole thyme sprigs. Raise the heat to high and bring the stock to simmering; lower the heat to medium-low, cover the pan, and simmer the vegetables until they are tender and turn slightly shiny—for 5 to 7 minutes more. Drain the vegetables in a colander and discard the thyme sprigs; transfer the vegetables to a serving dish and toss with the thyme leaves. Serve immediately.

DESSERTS

ALMOND BISCOTTI 67

APPLE STRUDEL 68

SWEET POTATO PIE WITH CANDIED GINGER 71

ETROG CAKE 75

MARBLE CAKE 77

ALMOND BISCOTTI

MAKES ABOUT 40 BISCOTTI

TODD: Biscotti are a good and simple alternative to a big, formal dessert. We often serve them at Equinox in a miniature version as an after-dinner cookie to dip in a little coffee or dessert wine, like vin santo. The trick is to not bake them so long the second time—that keeps them from getting too hard. Feel free to switch pistachios or hazelnuts for the almonds and adjust your flavoring accordingly, using vanilla instead of almond liqueur, for instance.

ELLEN: In the 80's the Stella d'Oro annisette toasts I grew up with morphed into biscotti!

2¼ cups all-purpose flour

1½ teaspoons baking powder

½ teaspoon salt

½ cup unsalted butter (1 stick), softened

1 cup granulated sugar

2 large eggs

2 tablespoons Amaretto (almond liqueur)

2 teaspoons freshly grated lemon zest

1 heaping cup lightly toasted whole almonds (with their skins; see Chef's Appendix)

1 large egg, lightly beaten, and turbinado sugar for brushing and sprinkling

Mix the dough. Preheat the oven to 350°F. Line a baking sheet with parchment paper (the paper will adhere better if you lightly spray the pan with nonstick cooking spray before laying the paper on it). Whisk together the flour, baking powder, and salt in a medium bowl. Using an electric mixer on medium-low speed, cream the butter with the granulated sugar in a large bowl. Add the eggs and beat until smooth—2 to 3 minutes, stopping occasionally to scrape down the sides of the bowl with a rubber spatula. Beat in the Amaretto and lemon zest until smooth. Gradually add the flour mixture, beating until just barely combined. Stir in the nuts with the spatula, mixing just until incorporated.

Shape and bake the dough. Turn out the dough onto a lightly floured work surface and divide it in half. Shape each half into 10-inch-long logs about 3 inches in diameter. Transfer the logs to the prepared baking sheet, placing them at least 2 inches apart and 2 inches from the edge of the sheet. Brush the tops of the logs with the beaten egg; sprinkle liberally with turbinado sugar. Bake the logs until lightly golden on top and firm to the touch—for about 20 minutes. Cool the logs on the baking sheet on a wire rack for at least 10 minutes; keep the oven on.

Slice and bake the biscotti. Transfer the logs to a cutting board and cut them straight across into even slices, about ½-inch thick. Arrange the slices, cut side up, on the baking sheet and return to the oven to bake until lightly golden and toasted—about 5 minutes. Transfer the biscotti to wire racks to cool completely. Store in an airtight container at room temperature.

APPLE STRUDEL

MAKES ONE 4×14-INCH STRUDEL, ABOUT 8 SERVINGS

TODD: Fall and apples go hand in hand (see Apple Memories, page 143). To Ellen and me, baking seasonal apples in pastry is an irresistible way to celebrate the pair, and you can't get much better than strudel (unless, of course, you're making Pennsylvania Dutch Apple Dumplings, page 142). When making strudel, bear in mind the key to working with phyllo is to get yourself set up properly before you start the process (see Phyllo Tips, page 70). Strudel is at its best baked to order and eaten warm, but you can cook it earlier in the day and then reheat if you must—just don't refrigerate it once it's been baked. If you wish, serve with lightly sweetened whipped cream or vanilla ice cream.

½ **cup golden or dark raisins**
½ **cup rum, or as needed**

6 **cups peeled, cored, and diced baking apples, such as Honeycrisp or Granny Smith (about 2 ½ pounds)**

2 **tablespoons unsalted butter, melted**

2 **tablespoons freshly squeezed lemon juice**

½ **cup light brown sugar**

1½ **teaspoons ground cinnamon**

¼ **teaspoon salt**

½ **cup granulated sugar**

6 **sheets phyllo dough (14×18 inches), more if needed**

Melted unsalted butter for brushing (about 4 tablespoons)

Vanilla ice cream and lightly sweetened whipped cream for serving (optional)

MAKE IT PARVE. *Use melted margarine instead of butter in the filling and also for brushing the phyllo sheets. Did you know phyllo is made with oil, not butter?*

Prepare the filling. Place the raisins in a small bowl. Add rum to cover and set aside to soak for 1 hour. Meanwhile, set a large colander over a large bowl. Place the apples in the colander and add the butter, lemon juice, brown sugar, 1 teaspoon of the cinnamon, and the salt; toss to mix. Set aside to macerate (infuse the apples with the seasonings) for about 1 hour, letting the juices accumulate in the bowl.

Complete the filling. Lift the colander from the bowl. Pour the accumulated juices from the bowl into a small saucepan. Transfer the apples from the colander to the bowl. Bring the juices to simmering over medium heat; simmer until reduced by half—about 5 minutes. Pour the juices over the apples and toss to mix well. Drain the raisins in a mesh strainer and then stir them into the apples.

Make a cinnamon-sugar sprinkling mix. Whisk together the remaining ½ teaspoon cinnamon and the granulated sugar in a small bowl. Set aside.

Layer the pastry. Preheat the oven to 375°F. Line a baking sheet with parchment paper (the paper will adhere better if you lightly spray the pan with nonstick cooking spray before laying the paper on it). One at a time, unfold five phyllo dough sheets and stack them on top of each other near the edge of a large work surface. Lay a slightly dampened (not wet) cloth over the top to keep them from drying out

(recipe continues)

PHYLLO TIPS

Make sure you check the expiration date of the phyllo package so you don't wind up with old sheets that stick together. I like to start off with twice as much phyllo as I need. That way if any sheets are dry or stuck together, I can just throw them away.

Take the phyllo out of the freezer so that it is thawed but still cool when you work with it (allow about 30 minutes for this). The next tip is to have your butter melted and a pastry brush ready before you open the phyllo package. You'll stack the phyllo sheets and peel off one at a time to work with—it's crucial to keep the stack covered with a damp, but not wet, cloth while you are working with the sheet you have just peeled off. Work as quickly as you can.

The process can be a little messy and time consuming, so it's okay to assemble the strudel 3 to 4 hours before baking (not longer, because the apples will start to weep and break down the phyllo, making it soggy). To do this, assemble the layers; brush the top with melted butter, cover it with plastic wrap, and refrigerate it for 2 to 3 hours. Let the strudel come to room temperature for an hour before baking.

while you work. Unfold the sixth sheet and lay it flat in your work area, with a long edge facing you. Very carefully brush the sheet with some melted butter, then sprinkle it liberally with the cinnamon-sugar mix. Lift the damp cloth; separate the top dough sheet from the stack and lay it directly on top of the sugar-sprinkled sheet (put the damp cloth back on the stack). Brush with butter and sprinkle with cinnamon-sugar as before. In this manner continue layering, buttering, and sugaring the dough sheets until you have a six-layer rectangle. Don't be alarmed by minor breakage of the dough, this is almost inevitable; try to orient the sheets so that unbroken areas support broken ones.

Fill the strudel. Working quickly, spread the apple filling over the phyllo, leaving a 3-inch margin bare along the edge closet to you and a 2-inch margin bare along the three other edges. Fold up the 3-inch margin of dough over the filling; then fold up the 2-inch margins at both ends; roll the filled area away from you all the way to the opposite edge to completely seal in the filling. With your hands, carefully lift the strudel and place it seam down on the prepared baking sheet.

Bake the strudel. Brush the top of the strudel with melted butter and sprinkle with more of the cinnamon-sugar. With a sharp knife, pierce the dough in a few places along the top to allow steam to escape during baking. Bake the strudel until the pastry is golden and the filling is bubbly—35 to 45 minutes. Cool on the baking sheet on a wire rack for 20 to 30 minutes; serve while warm.

SWEET POTATO PIE WITH CANDIED GINGER

MAKES ONE 9-INCH PIE

ELLEN: Growing up, both of my parents worked, so Annie, our housekeeper (these days she'd be called a nanny) would often cook for me and my siblings. On special occasions, she'd make sweet potato pie. I can practically taste it just thinking about it.

TODD: Back in the day, ground ginger in a jar was all you could get in a store, but crystallized ginger is now easy to find. It has a concentrated ginger flavor and a little bite to it, so adding it to the crust really takes this pie up a notch.

CRUST:

1¼ cups unsalted butter (2½ sticks), softened

1½ cups confectioners' sugar

1 teaspoon salt

2 large eggs

2 tablespoons crystallized ginger

4 cups all-purpose flour

FILLING:

2 medium sweet potatoes (about ⅔ pound)

½ cup vegetable stock, preferably homemade (recipe in Chef's Appendix), or water

½ cup granulated sugar

¼ cup light brown sugar

1 teaspoon ground ginger

¾ teaspoon ground cinnamon

½ teaspoon salt

1½ cups half-and-half

3 large eggs

Mix the crust. Using an electric mixer on medium-low speed, cream the butter with the confectioners' sugar and salt in a large bowl until light and fluffy—3 to 5 minutes. Add the eggs one at a time, beating until smooth and scraping down the sides of the bowl with a rubber spatula after each addition. Place the ginger on a cutting board and dust it with a little of the flour, then finely chop it. Gradually add the remainder of the flour and the chopped ginger to the butter mixture, beating until incorporated. Turn out the dough onto a lightly floured board and flatten into a disc. Wrap the dough in plastic food wrap and refrigerate until—at least 2 hours or overnight.

Bake the sweet potatoes. Meanwhile, preheat the oven to 325°F. Place the sweet potatoes on a baking sheet and bake until tender—about 45 minutes. Transfer the baking sheet to a wire rack and set aside until the potatoes are cool enough to handle.

Bake the crust. Roll out the dough on a lightly floured board, forming a round less than ⅛-inch thick. Transfer it to a 9-inch pie pan or tart ring and trim the edges to fit the pan. Refrigerate until firm—about 1 hour. Preheat the oven to 350°F. Line the dough in the pan with parchment paper, then fill it with pie weights or dried beans to keep the bottom of the crust from rising during baking. Bake the crust until the edges are golden—for 15 to 20 minutes. Remove the crust from the oven and lift out the pie weights and parchment

(recipe continues)

**Vanilla or ginger ice cream
for serving (optional)**

paper; return the crust to the oven and bake until the inside is light golden—for 10 minutes more. Remove from the oven and let cool on a wire rack. Lower the oven temperature to 275°F.

Make the filling. Peel the sweet potatoes, cut into large chunks, and place in the container of a food processor fitted with a blade. Add the stock and process until a smooth puree forms. Add the granulated and brown sugars; process until blended. Blend in the ginger, cinnamon, and salt. Add the half-and-half and then the eggs one at a time, processing until smooth after each addition. Pour the filling into the baked pie shell and bake until the filling is set and a toothpick inserted in the center comes out clean—45 to 60 minutes. Transfer the pie to a wire rack to cool completely.

To serve, remove the outer ring if you used a tart pan and transfer the pie to a plate. Cut the pie into wedges and serve, topping each piece with ice cream if desired.

ETROG CAKE

MAKES ONE 4×8-INCH LOAF OR 8-INCH ROUND CAKE

ELLEN: Etrog is a lemon-like citrus fruit readily available in Israel (see About Etrog, page 76), but as far as I can tell only one farmer grows it in the United States, so it is not always easy to find. Ask your specialty food store if they carry it or how to order it or check online. Around Sukkot (four days after Yom Kippur), you can order etrog and lulav "kits" from certain local synagogues or Jewish organizations.

TODD: Lemons are perfectly reasonable substitutes for this pound cake–like dessert.

2 etrogs (or 2 lemons)

1 tablespoon freshly squeezed etrog juice or lemon juice

1 tablespoon freshly squeezed lime juice

2¾ cups all-purpose flour

1 tablespoon baking powder

½ teaspoon salt

4 tablespoons unsalted butter (½ stick), softened

1¾ cups sugar

3 large eggs

1¼ cups freshly squeezed orange juice (3 to 4 juice oranges)

3 tablespoons Grand Marnier (orange-flavored liqueur)

Orange and blood orange segments for garnish (optional)

MAKE IT PARVE. *Use margarine instead of butter.*

Make a citrus seasoning mixture. Grate the zest of the etrogs with a rasp or citrus zester, being careful to get all the zest off of the citrus without cutting into the pith below the skin. Whisk together the lemon juice and lime juice in a small bowl; whisk in the etrog zest. Set aside 1 tablespoon of this mixture to use later for the glaze.

Mix the batter. Preheat the oven to 350°F. Spray a 4×8-inch loaf pan with nonstick cooking spray and line the bottom with parchment paper or rub the pan with butter and dust it with flour, shaking out the excess. Sift together the flour, baking powder, and salt. Using an electric mixer on medium speed, cream the butter with the 1¼ cups of the sugar in a medium bowl until light and fluffy. Add the eggs one at a time, beating until smooth and scraping down the sides of the bowl with a rubber spatula after each addition. Beat in the non-reserved portion of the citrus mixture. Add a third of the flour mixture, beating just to combine; add ½ cup orange juice, followed by another third of the flour mixture, another ½ cup orange juice, and finally the last of the flour, mixing only until just combined after each addition.

Bake the cake. Pour the batter into the prepared pan and bake until a toothpick inserted in the center comes out clean—45 to 55 minutes. Cool the cake in the pan on a wire rack for about 20 minutes, then turn out onto the rack to cool completely.

Make the glaze. Meanwhile, stir together the remaining ½ cup sugar, remaining ¼ cup orange juice, and the reserved tablespoon of the citrus mixture in a small saucepan. Heat over medium heat, stirring frequently, just until the sugar is completely dissolved. Remove the pan from the heat. Stir in the Grand Marnier. Let the glaze cool. To serve, slice the cake and place on dessert plates; drizzle the glaze decoratively over each portion—we like to use a ladle to do this. Garnish each plate with a few orange segments if you wish.

SUMMERTIME LEMON CAKE

Fresh raspberries are a perfect complement to the fresh, sweet-tart flavor of the Etrog Cake. So when raspberries are in season (and etrog is not), we make this cake with lemons and serve it garnished with wonderfully ripe, juicy berries. Irresistible!

About Etrog

ELLEN: One of the harvest rituals at Sukkot involves waving a palm frond (lulav) wrapped with myrtle (hadass) and willow twigs (aravah) and an etrog, a citrus fruit that grows abundantly in Israel. (It's also known as citron.) Sukkot is an eight-day holiday that takes place at harvest time, four days after Yom Kippur. The word sukkot refers to huts that Jews built in the fields during the harvest to maximize their time working there. Sukkot were also erected as temporary shelters during the forty years the Jews wandered in the desert. The holiday therefore is a time to celebrate the earth's bounty and to remember the hardships of the exodus.

TODD: I had never heard of etrog, let alone seen one, until Ellen told me about it. They look like lemons on steroids, only craggier. Although they are enormous, they are mostly pith; the citrus part inside is very small. Etrogs can be hard to find, so substitute lemons if you need to.

MARBLE CAKE

MAKES ONE 4×8-INCH LOAF

ELLEN: It wasn't too difficult to badger my father into buying one of these cakes on our weekly forays to the deli. To see these paper-lined cakes in the deli growing up was totally enticing. I'm sure displaying them prominently was meant to provoke impulse buying and it worked in the Kassoff family. At home, we'd top the slices with sour cream—there's just something about chocolate and sour cream together that is irresistible to me.

TODD: Marble cake has a lot of eye appeal, which we restaurant types always appreciate. It's also a fun thing to make with kids, letting them swirl the batters together and then see the final product. Use the best quality dark chocolate you can afford (see On Chocolate for Baking, page 208).

1½ cups all-purpose flour

½ teaspoon baking powder

¼ teaspoon baking soda

½ teaspoon salt

10 tablespoons unsalted butter (1 stick plus 2 tablespoons), softened

10 tablespoons cream cheese (5 ounces), softened

1½ cups sugar

3 large eggs

1½ teaspoons vanilla extract

4 ounces dark chocolate, melted and cooled slightly

Mix the batter. Preheat the oven to 350°F. Spray a 4×8-inch loaf pan with nonstick cooking spray and line the bottom with parchment paper, or rub the pan with butter and dust it with flour, shaking out the excess. Sift together the flour, baking powder, baking soda, and salt. Using an electric mixer on medium speed, cream the butter and cream cheese together with the sugar in a medium bowl until light and fluffy—about 3 minutes. Add the eggs one at a time, beating until smooth and scraping down the sides of the bowl with a rubber spatula after each addition. Beat in the vanilla. Gradually add the flour mixture, beating just until combined.

Marble the cake. Pour half of the batter into a small bowl. Fold in the chocolate, gently mixing just until the batter is chocolate colored. Spoon the white and chocolate batters into the pan in an alternating pattern and then pass the handle of a wooden spoon through them to loosely swirl together.

Bake the cake. Bake the cake until a toothpick inserted in the center comes out clean—45 to 60 minutes. Cool the cake in the pan on a wire rack for about 20 minutes, then turn out onto the rack to cool completely.

WINTER

TODD: To pay tribute to the changing of the seasons, we inaugurated the Winter Solstice wine dinner at Equinox in 2000. The idea was to showcase winter's bounty and firmly establish our cuisine's identity. So we sat down with our management team and our sous-chefs and discussed logistics. As you should when planning any dinner party, be it at home or in a restaurant, we listed foods and cooking styles of the season: roasted and braised meats, game, and game hens; thicker gravies and sauces; root vegetables, such as heirloom sweet potatoes, beets, turnips, and rutabagas; heartier side dishes, like braised cabbage and our famous truffled macaroni and cheese. Once we created the dishes, we paired them with suitable wines.

ELLEN: Of course I pushed for my own favorites to be worked into the menu, like borscht, knishes, tzimmes, and pickled beets. And lemon-ricotta fritters and pineapple upside-down cake for dessert.

TODD: The pickled beets for sure, because winter is all about breaking out all the great summer vegetables we lovingly preserved at the height of their freshness in the summer and fall.

ELLEN: People went crazy for those dinners. It started out as twelve people at a corner table in the dining room, then it evolved into a theatrical event that took up the entire restaurant. Todd would plate by candlelight in the dining room as Spanish guitarists strummed in the background.

TODD: It was just a way to boost people's spirits as winter set in. Cold air makes us crave comfort and yearn for rib-sticking foods. We don't want beef stew or braised lamb shanks in the summer, but come December and January, we embrace them, along with Sunday corned beef hash brunches and nights curled up by a fire as a big pot of matzo ball soup simmers on the stove.

BRUNCH

VEGETABLE KISHKA WITH SAGE
AND PAPRIKA 81

POTATO PIEROGI WITH FONTINA
CHEESE 82

BAKED GEFILTE FISH 85

CORNED BEEF HASH AND EGGS 88

BEET-CURED SALMON GRAVLAX 93

VEGETABLE KISHKA WITH SAGE AND PAPRIKA

SERVES 8

ELLEN: In the Old Country (that is, Eastern Europe), kishka, or stuffed derma, was a kind of sausage made with meal or flour and stuffed into a casing of beef intestine. The dish was also a favorite of Ashkenazi Jews, so it's not surprising that it found its way to the United States with the wave in immigration in the 19th and 20th centuries. I remember it from the deli as some enormous tube of bready, meaty stuffing slathered with brown gravy. As a vegetarian, that's not exactly on my radar these days, so Todd developed a vegetarian, actually vegan, version of the dish for me.

TODD: Gone are the casings and stodgy gravy. With some Lime Sour Cream or Zesty Mayonnaise, this makes a great addition to a winter brunch table.

4 celery ribs, chopped

2 medium carrots, chopped

1 large yellow onion, quartered

½ cup vegetable stock, preferably homemade (recipe in Chef's Appendix)

¼ cup olive oil

⅓ cup margarine (5 tablespoons plus 1 teaspoon)

6 roasted garlic cloves (see page 173)

5 large sage leaves, finely chopped

1 tablespoon smoked paprika

1 tablespoon salt

¼ teaspoon freshly ground black pepper

3⅓ cups matzo meal

Lime Sour Cream or Zesty Mayonnaise for serving (optional, recipes in Chef's Appendix)

Mix the kishka. Preheat the oven to 325°F. Combine the celery, carrots, and onion in a food processor fitted with a metal blade. Process until pureed; with the machine running, add the stock, oil, margarine, garlic, sage, paprika, salt, and pepper through the tube. Transfer the purée to a medium bowl and gradually add the matzo meal, stirring with a wooden spoon until well combined.

Shape the kishka. Tear five 8×12-inch pieces from a roll of aluminum foil and lay them on a work surface. Spoon the kishka mixture onto each piece, dividing equally and shaping into logs 2½ to 3 inches in diameter. Roll up the foil around the mixture, like a sausage, being sure the ends of the foil are tightly sealed.

Bake the kishka. Place the foil rolls on a baking sheet. Bake for 20 minutes; turn the rolls over on the baking sheet and then bake for 25 minutes more. Transfer the baking sheet to a wire rack and let the kishka cool slightly. Then unwrap, slice into medallions, and serve. Serve with Lime Sour Cream on the side if you wish.

POTATO PIEROGI WITH FONTINA CHEESE

MAKES 24 PIEROGI (4 SERVINGS)

ELLEN: Of course, my experience with pierogi growing up was with the frozen variety. Mom would boil them up, lightly pan-fry them in butter, then serve them with sour cream for dinner every now and then. With three brothers, that meant a portion size was at least ten each. To me, they are more suitable for brunch, especially on a winter day.

TODD: With my background in Italian cooking, using a traditional potato gnocchi dough as the base for these stuffed, ravioli-like dumplings was a natural. To make the dough more pliable and easier to roll, I stiffen it with extra flour. Fontina cheese works well for the stuffing because of its nutty flavor and oozy quality when melted. You can substitute any good melting cheese, such as Gruyère, Brie, or Taleggio.

1½ pounds russet (Idaho) potatoes (3 medium potatoes), with the skin on

1 quart kosher salt

1⅔ cups all-purpose flour

2 large egg yolks

Table salt

Freshly ground black pepper

½ pound Fontina cheese, cut into 1×3-inch strips, approximately ¼-inch thick

2 tablespoons olive oil

⅓ cup grated Parmesan cheese, preferably Parmigianno Reggiano

½ cup egg wash (see Chef's Appendix)

2 teaspoons unsalted butter (optional)

Sour cream for serving

Cook the potatoes. Preheat the oven to 325°F. Pour and spread a ¼-inch deep layer of kosher salt into a rimmed baking sheet. Place the potatoes on top and bake until tender (the skin should be buckled and blistered)—about 45 minutes. Remove from oven and cool the potatoes on the salt-lined pan.

Make the dough. Peel the potatoes and put through a food mill placed over a medium stainless steel bowl (you can push them through the grating disk on a food processor if you don't have a food mill). Add the egg yolks, flour, ¾ tablespoon table salt, and ⅛ teaspoon pepper; mix with your hands until blended to a firm dough. Turn out onto a lightly floured surface and knead for 2 to 3 minutes. Cover the dough with a dry kitchen towel and let rest for 5 to 10 minutes.

Form the pierogi. Cut the dough into quarters. Work with one quarter at a time and leave the remainder under the towel. Roll out the dough to ¼-inch thickness on a lightly floured work surface, forming a round 12 to 14 inches in diameter. Using a 4-inch round cutter, cut the dough into rounds. Brush each round with egg wash and place a piece of fontina cheese on top, near the edge. Sprinkle Parmesan on top and then fold up the empty portion of the dough round over the fontina, aligning the edges. Press the edges of each round together with the tines of a fork.

Poach the pierogi. Bring a large pot of salted water to simmering over high heat; simmer the pierogi for 2 minutes. Use a slotted spoon to transfer the pierogi to a large bowl; add the oil and toss to coat. Set aside to cool slightly or cover and refrigerate until ready to serve.

Sauté the pierogi. Heat a nonstick pan over medium heat. Drain the pierogi in a colander and then blot on paper towels to remove the oil. If you wish, add the butter to the pan—it will enhance the caramelizing of the pierogi. Add the pierogi to the pan; sauté, turning once, until golden-brown on both sides—about 4 minutes total. Sprinkle with table salt and pepper. Drain the pierogi on paper towels, and then transfer to a serving bowl. Serve, passing a small bowl of sour cream at the table.

PIEROGI AT THE READY

As a timesaver, you can prepare the pierogi through the poaching process (up to a day ahead) and refrigerate them until ready to finish and serve the dish. Or you can freeze uncooked pierogi and poach them frozen, doubling their cooking time, before proceeding as directed.

BAKED GEFILTE FISH

MAKES 18 FISH PATTIES (6 SERVINGS)

TODD: To me, gefilte fish out of a jar is an abomination, but my version, basically an interpretation of the French *quenelles be brochet*, is cheftastic. Choosing between the two is a no-brainer, in my opinion (see Gefilte Fish: Jarred or Fresh? page 87). I prefer to use rockfish, otherwise known as sea bass, for gefilte fish because it is indigenous to the Chesapeake region. I blend it with pike and flounder, but you could use any combination of the three. Any white, non-oily fish will do for that matter. I've even made them with salmon; the light pink color makes a nice change of pace. It's best to poach the fish balls a day ahead of time so they can rest in their cooking liquid for several hours. They can be eaten cold, but Ellen and I like to serve them warm—they make a great, non-meat brunch entrée.

1½ **pounds rockfish fillet**

½ **pound pike fillet**

½ **pound flounder fillet**

8 **cups fish stock, preferably homemade (recipe in Chef's Appendix)**

¾ **cup matzo meal**

4 **large eggs, lightly beaten**

2 **tablespoons sugar**

1 **tablespoon chopped fresh thyme leaves**

2 **tablespoons chopped fresh parsley**

1 **teaspoon freshly grated lemon zest**

2½ **teaspoons salt**

⅛ **teaspoon freshly ground black pepper**

Boiled Carrots with Prepared Horseradish (recipe follows) for serving

NOTE: *Vegetable stock or water can be used instead of fish stock.*

Prep the fish. Working in batches if necessary, place the rockfish, pike, and flounder fillets in the container of a food processor fitted with a metal blade and process until pureed. Transfer the fish to a large bowl. Bring the fish stock to simmering in a large saucepan over medium-high heat.

Mix the fish. Add the matzo meal, eggs, sugar, thyme, parsley, lemon zest, salt, and pepper to the bowl with the fish. Mix together with a wooden spoon until well combined. Shape the fish mixture into oval patties about 2 by 4 inches. Carefully lower the patties into the simmering fish stock, return to simmering, lower the heat to medium-low and simmer gently for 20 minutes. Using a slotted spoon, transfer the patties to a paper towel-lined tray. Strain the stock through a fine mesh strainer into the dish with the patties. Let the stock cool (it will gel) and then refrigerate overnight or at least 8 hours.

Bake the fish. Preheat the oven to 350°F. Using a slotted spoon, remove the fish patties from the gelatin and transfer to a lightly oiled baking sheet. Bake the patties until lightly caramelized on edges—about 20 minutes. Serve topped with a dollop of the gelatinous stock and some Boiled Carrots with Prepared Horseradish on the side.

(recipe continues)

BOILED CARROTS WITH PREPARED HORSERADISH

This is especially pretty made with a mix of orange and purple carrots, and even nicer if you flute the carrots lengthwise with a channel knife before slicing them—this results in slices with pretty scalloped edges. A channel knife is handy for cutting decorative strips of citrus zest, too; you can pick one up in nearly any gourmet shop.

Cut 3 medium carrots into ¼-inch thick rounds. Place in a small saucepan. Add water to cover, ½ teaspoon salt, and a grind or two of black pepper. Bring to boiling over high heat; boil until the carrots are tender—about 10 minutes. Drain in a colander and serve warm, with prepared horseradish on the side.

Gefilte Fish: Jarred or Fresh?

ELLEN: The advent of commercial kosher kitchens greatly increased the number of convenience foods available to Jewish households. Among the items that became widely available on grocery store shelves all over America was jarred gefilte fish, those cooked balls of ground fish lovingly referred to as "hot dogs of the sea."

Aunt Lil made gefilte fish from scratch, undergoing the laborious and messy process of passing fish through a meat grinder before forming the balls, cooking them slowly in a carefully prepared stock, baking them, and serving them with carrots and horseradish.

My mother embraced the jarred version completely, even keeping it on hand as a fridge snack, something that could be eaten cold right out of the jar after school.

Nestled on a lettuce leaf and garnished with little piles of white or red horseradish, gefilte fish made regular appearances on our family's table at holiday meals, where attendees invariably divided into two groups: the "I love gefilte fish!" contingent and the "How can you eat that disgusting stuff?" group.

TODD: I definitely fell into the latter camp.

Once I realized that gefilte fish is really just an interpretation of *quenelles de brochet* (poached ovals of pike mousse), the job was easy. I made a fish purée of rockfish, pike, and flounder, bound it with eggs and matzo meal, and formed the mixture into patties. Poaching them in fish stock imparts flavor.

You can serve gefilte fish cold but I like taking the extra step of baking them—it gives them some color and brings out the subtle flavor of the fish.

CORNED BEEF HASH AND EGGS

SERVES 6 TO 8

ELLEN: The most memorable canned item in our family pantry growing up was Libby's Corned Beef Hash. I can still picture the label, with the snapshot of a sunny-side-up fried egg on a plate with the hash and its little dices of potato—that represented culinary heaven to me. The more I tried to get my eggs to look that perfect, the more likely I was to break the yolks. One winter afternoon, our son came home from Hebrew school looking for a hearty Sunday fix. We had some leftover corned beef and Todd, with his affinity for all things fresh, whipped up this hash.

TODD: I'm not making the corned beef from scratch. It comes from the deli, already sliced. But the eggs have to be farm fresh; those factory-produced eggs with their dull, lifeless yolks and watery whites don't taste like anything.

¼ cup olive oil

1 tablespoon unsalted butter

3 cups shredded green cabbage

1½ cups finely diced yellow onions (2 to 3 medium onions)

1½ cups finely diced Yukon Gold potatoes (1 to 2 medium potatoes)

1 cup finely diced red bell peppers (1 large pepper)

2 garlic cloves, minced

2 pounds cooked corned beef, cut into ¼-inch thick slices

1 teaspoon minced fresh thyme leaves

12 scallions, finely sliced crosswise, including part of the green (1¼ cups)

Fried eggs for serving (see To Cook Eggs, page 90)

MAKE IT MEAT. *Use margarine instead of butter.*

Sauté the hash. Heat the oil and butter in a 12-inch nonstick sauté pan or cast-iron skillet over medium heat. Add the cabbage, onions, potatoes, peppers, and garlic and sauté for 5 minutes. Lower the heat to low and cook, stirring occasionally, until the cabbage is tender—5 to 7 minutes more. Add the corned beef and thyme and mix well; heat through, stirring to slightly break up the corned beef—6 to 8 minutes more.

Caramelize the hash. Place a heavy heatproof lid directly on top of the hash and press down to form a compressed cake. Continue to cook, until the hash browns—about 5 minutes. Then lift the lid, stir, and repress; cook until the hash browns again. Meanwhile, if you wish, fry the eggs in butter in a second skillet. Serve the hash from the pan (or turn out onto a platter), sprinkled with the scallions and topped with the eggs.

(recipe continues)

To Cook Eggs

TODD: With regard to various egg preparations for breakfast, the three most common are scrambled, fried, and poached.

To scramble eggs: In a small bowl, season 2 large, farm fresh eggs with salt and freshly ground black pepper, then lightly whisk them with a touch of water. (It helps lighten the scramble—this is my wife's secret.) Over medium heat in a nonstick omelet pan, heat 1 teaspoon of unsalted butter until it is foamy hot. Add the eggs, reduce the heat to medium-low, and allow the eggs to set for 20 to 30 seconds, untouched. Then, using a rubber spatula or wooden spoon, stir the eggs to break up the curds and continue to stir gently until they reach the desired doneness. I like my eggs a little damp; others like them cooked through or dry.

To fry eggs, two at a time: To ensure that you won't break the yolks or get any bits of shell in your eggs, crack them into a small bowl or ramekin first.

For sunny-side-up: Over medium heat in a nonstick omelet pan, heat 1 teaspoon of unsalted butter until it is foamy hot. Pour the eggs into the pan, reduce the heat to medium-low, and let the eggs cook until the whites are set, about 3 minutes, using the end of a rubber spatula to make sure the eggs are completely loosened from the bottom of the pan. Season with salt and pepper.

For over-easy: Repeat the technique for sunny-side-up eggs. At the 3-minute mark, flip the eggs over by lifting the pan several inches above the burner, tilting the far edge of the pan slightly downward and jerking the handle toward you. Return the pan to the heat and cook for:

15 seconds for over-easy

30 seconds for over-medium

75 seconds for over-hard or 1 minute plus 15 seconds

To poach eggs, two at a time: It's best to poach no more than 2 eggs at a time in a 3-quart saucepan. Have ready a plate lined with paper towels. Crack the eggs, 1 each, into small ramekins. In a medium saucepan over medium-high heat, bring 8 cups of water, 1 teaspoon of salt, and 1 tablespoon of white vinegar (it helps set the whites) to just under simmering (small bubbles on the outside of the pan). Reduce the heat to medium.

Holding the ramekin close to the water's surface, gently release 1 egg, then the other, into the water, leaving plenty of space between the 2 eggs. Allow the eggs to set untouched for 30 seconds, then use the edge of a rubber spatula to make sure neither egg is sticking to the bottom of the pan. Use the spatula to bring the white up, over, and all around each yolk. Let the eggs cook for another 2½ minutes (for soft-poached) and 30 seconds beyond that for medium-poached. Using a slotted spoon, remove the eggs from the water and drain them on the paper towel-lined plate before serving. Season with salt and pepper.

You can make poached eggs ahead of time by plunging soft-poached eggs in ice water and then refrigerating them in cold water. Reheat them in gently simmering water for 30 seconds.

BEET-CURED SALMON GRAVLAX

MAKES 2 POUNDS (AT LEAST 8 THINLY SLICED SERVINGS)

TODD: Gravlax is cured, but not smoked, salmon. It is usually cured with sugar, salt, dill, and seasonings, then wrapped and weighted down to extract moisture from it (see Of Kipper Snacks and Cured Salmon, page 16). I use grated beets instead of chopped dill in the cure for this gravlax—they infuse an earthy flavor and a vibrant, bright red color. Wrapped airtight and refrigerated, the salmon will keep for a week.

¼ cup Cointreau (clear orange-flavored liqueur)

One 2-pound salmon fillet, with the skin on

2 cups kosher salt

2 cups sugar

2 small beets, peeled and grated (about 1¾ cups)

1 tablespoon toasted fennel seeds, crushed with a mortar and pestle

1 tablespoon chopped fresh tarragon leaves

1 teaspoon freshly grated orange zest

1 teaspoon freshly ground black pepper

Cheesecloth, for wrapping, one piece about 3-feet long

Toasted bagels and cream cheese, for serving (optional)

Season the salmon. Rub the Cointreau over the salmon flesh. Combine the salt, sugar, beets, fennel seeds, tarragon, orange zest, and pepper in a medium bowl. Unfold the cheesecloth and lay it in a shallow pan large enough to hold the salmon, centering it so the edges are free to wrap over the fish. Spoon half the salt mixture into the pan, smoothing over the cheesecloth. Place the fish skin side down on top. Spoon the remaining salt mixture evenly over the fish, covering as much as possible.

Cure the salmon. Fold the cheesecloth edges up and over the fish. Place a heavy plate on top of wrapped fish and refrigerate for 24 hours.

Slice and serve. Remove the pan from the refrigerator. Unwrap the fish, brush aside the salt mixture, and lift the fish from the pan. Wash the fish under cold water to remove the remaining salt. Dry well with paper towels. Slice very thin, lift from the skin, and serve with toasted bagels and cream cheese.

STARTERS

NOT EXACTLY AUNT LIL'S MATZO BALL
SOUP 95

SWEET POTATO SOUP 98

BEET AND RED CABBAGE BORSCHT 99

CROSTINI WITH SMOKED TROUT
AND SOUR CREAM 100

CHICKPEA SALAD WITH FETA CHEESE
AND MINT 103

NOT EXACTLY AUNT LIL'S MATZO BALL SOUP

SERVES 6

TODD: Aunt Lil's matzo ball soup got quite a build-up in the Kassoff family long before I ever tasted it (see Aunt Lil's Chicken Soup, page 96), and it certainly lived up to the hype. It was rustic, homey, and satisfying, but needed some refining around the edges to bring it into the world of fine dining. Aunt Lil, for instance, didn't add noodles to her soup and cooked her matzo balls directly in the broth. At Equinox, we make the matzo balls separately to keep the broth pristine, then add noodles and a garnish of scallions and finely diced vegetables to give the dish a polished look.

ELLEN: Yes, your version is very pretty, and the broth is definitely bolder, but there's still nothing like Aunt Lil's as far as I'm concerned. What can I say? Blood is thicker than soup.

MATZO BALLS:

3 large eggs

2 tablespoons unsalted butter, melted

¼ cup club soda

1 cup matzo meal

½ cup chopped Caramelized Onions (recipe follows)

1 teaspoon salt

⅛ teaspoon freshly ground black pepper

SOUP:

One 3-pound whole chicken

1 large yellow onion, quartered

2 celery ribs, chopped

2 small carrots, chopped

1 medium turnip, chopped

6 garlic cloves, crushed

1 bunch parsley, washed and blotted dry

2 bay leaves

4 sprigs fresh thyme

Mix the matzo balls. Whisk together the eggs and melted butter in a large bowl. Whisk in the club soda and then whisk in the matzo meal, Caramelized Onions, salt, and pepper. As the mixture thickens, tap off excess batter from the whisk and switch to a wooden spoon or rubber spatula to finish mixing into a dough. Cover the bowl and refrigerate for 1 hour.

Make the soup. Meanwhile, remove the gizzard and liver from the chicken and reserve for another use. Wash the chicken under cold water and cut into eight pieces. Place the chicken in a stockpot large enough to comfortably hold it; add the onion, celery, carrots, turnips, garlic, parsley, bay leaves, thyme, peppercorns, and salt. Pour in water to cover the chicken. Bring to a simmer over high heat, lower the heat to medium-low, and simmer the soup for 1½ hours.

Cook the matzo balls. About an hour before serving the soup, bring a large pot of lightly salted water to boiling. Spoon two or three ladles of soup into the pot of water for added flavor. Shape the matzo dough into balls about 1½ inches in diameter, rolling them between your palms (moisten your hands with a touch of water first). Add the matzo balls to the boiling water, cover the pot, and simmer until cooked, about 30 to 40 minutes. Use a slotted spoon to transfer the matzo balls to a paper towel–lined plate to drain; keep warm.

(recipe continues)

12 black peppercorns

2 tablespoons salt

GARNISH:

2 cups finely diced carrots

2 cups finely diced celery

1 cup finely diced turnips

3 cups fresh egg noodles or
packaged dry noodles

½ cup thinly sliced scallions,
including some of the green

MAKE IT MEAT. *Substitute
margarine for the butter.*

Finish the soup. Transfer the chicken to a cutting board and allow
to cool. Pour the broth through a sieve into a bowl and discard the
vegetables; pour the broth back into the pot and keep warm. Pull
or cut the chicken from the bones and pull the meat into bite-size
pieces, shredding with your hands; set aside.

Garnish the soup. Preheat the oven to 250°F. Add the diced carrots,
celery, and turnips to the pot with the broth and simmer 10 minutes.
Place six large soup bowls in the oven to warm. Add the noodles and
chicken meat to the pot and simmer until the noodles are tender—
about 7 minutes more. Remove the bowls from the oven and spoon
3 matzo balls into each, add a generous spoonful of vegetables,
noodles, and meat, and then ladle in broth to fill the bowls. Sprinkle
the sliced scallions over the top of each bowl, dividing equally.

CARAMELIZED ONIONS
MAKES ABOUT 2 CUPS

Thinly slice enough yellow onions to equal 3 cups (2 medium onions).
Heat ¼ cup canola oil in a medium sauté pan over medium heat. Stir
in the onions and ¼ teaspoon salt and cook for 4 minutes. Lower the
heat to low and continue to cook the onions, stirring often, until they
turn amber in color—20 to 30 minutes. Drain in a colander and store
in the refrigerator until ready to use, for up to 4 days.

Aunt Lil's Chicken Soup

TODD: I remember the first time Ellen made her Aunt Lil's matzo
ball soup. It was in the nineties on a day I was out from work
with a nasty cold. She called the soup Jewish penicillin and made
it the way her Aunt Lil taught her to when she was a child, or at
least that's what she told me back then.

Maybe it was just that I was sick and liked the attention I was
getting, but to me that was one of the greatest chicken broths
I had ever had, full of poached chicken, chunky vegetables,
and fluffy matzo balls, which I had never eaten before in my
life. I started to make my own version of it, using matzo ball mix
and jacking it up with some chopped parsley and sage. On

the Passover menu at Equinox, I serve it with wide pappardelle noodles and a garnish of finely diced vegetables, just to add a touch of elegance to the dish.

ELLEN: Aunt Lil (Lillian Malitsky) was actually my great aunt because she was my father's mother's sister. She kept kosher in her little Bronx apartment, where I would sit on a stool in the kitchen and watch her make soup during family visits. Chicken soup and matzo ball soup were her signature dishes. What made them so special were the depth of the flavor and the silkiness of the stock. Maybe I'm just romanticizing the memory, but there was always some indefinable something extra in Aunt Lil's soup.

SWEET POTATO SOUP

MAKES ABOUT 6 CUPS (4 SERVINGS)

TODD: People often think that we chefs always use fancy, expensive ingredients, but the reality is that we are always conscious of the affordability of ingredients. A restaurant's success, after all, hinges upon the abiltity to maintain a low food cost. Sweet potatoes are abundant, inexpensive, loaded with "good" carbs, and fairly well beg to be made into a winter soup—but they need help. Using the finest vegetables available, rich stock (see The Story on Broth, Stock, and Quick Stock, page 20), on-point seasonings and the correct garnishes is crucial (see About Soup Making, page 244).

1/3 **cup canola oil**

3 **medium sweet potatoes, peeled and chopped**

1 **small yellow onion, chopped**

2 **celery ribs, chopped**

1 **carrot, chopped**

2 **garlic cloves, crushed**

1 **teaspoon ground cumin**

1/4 **teaspoon ground cinnamon**

1 **tablespoon salt**

1/8 **teaspoon freshly ground black pepper**

4 **cups vegetable stock or chicken stock, preferably homemade (recipes in Chef's Appendix)**

2 **cups heavy cream or half-and-half**

2 **apples, peeled and finely diced**

1 **tablespoon unsalted butter**

1 **teaspoon sugar**

Make the soup. Heat the canola oil in a large heavy stockpot over medium heat. Add the sweet potatoes, onions, celery, carrots, and garlic. Sauté until the onions are shiny—about 3 minutes. Add the cumin, cinnamon, salt, and pepper; stir and cook for 2 minutes (this will intensify the flavors of the spices). Add the stock and cream, raise the heat to medium, and bring to simmering. Lower the heat to medium-low and simmer until the sweet potatoes are cooked—30 to 40minutes.

Purée the soup. Working in batches if necessary, transfer the soup to the container of a blender. Process until smooth; pour through a fine mesh strainer back into the stockpot, pressing any solids through the mesh with a wooden spoon. Keep the soup warm.

Sauté the apples. Heat the butter and sugar in a medium sauté pan over medium-low heat, stirring until the sugar is melted. Add the apples and sauté just until they begin to soften—about 5 minutes. Ladle the soup into individual bowls, spooning some apples into each, and serve.

BEET AND RED CABBAGE BORSCHT

MAKES ABOUT 6 CUPS (6 TO 8 SERVINGS)

ELLEN: This is another food that came out of a jar, courtesy of Manischewitz, and onto the Kassoff family table. Todd's version is pure heaven, especially with a slice of toasted crusty bread to dip into it or with some pumpernickel croutons on top.

5 tablespoons canola oil

4 cups peeled, diced beets (about 2 pounds)

1 small Yukon Gold potato, peeled and chopped

1 shallot, chopped

1 garlic clove, chopped

1 teaspoon caraway seeds

4 cups vegetable stock or chicken stock, preferably homemade (recipes in Chef's Appendix)

1 cup water

1 bay leaf

1½ tablespoons salt

⅛ teaspoon freshly ground black pepper

3 cups thinly sliced red cabbage

1 large carrot, cut into ½-inch dice (1 cup)

½ tablespoon honey

2 tablespoons red wine vinegar

½ cup sour cream

1½ tablespoons capers, rinsed and drained

3 scallions, thinly sliced crosswise, including part of the green

Toast or pumpernickel croutons for serving

Make the soup base. Heat 3 tablespoons of the oil in a 4-quart saucepan over medium-low heat. Add 3 cups of the beets, the potatoes, shallots, garlic, and caraway seeds. Cook for 5 minutes, stirring often with a wooden spoon. Stir in the stock, water, bay leaf, salt, and pepper; lower the heat to low and simmer, covered, until vegetables are tender—about 30 to 40 minutes. Strain the soup base through a mesh strainer into a clean saucepan, pushing the solids with the back of a ladle or spoon; discard solids and keep the liquid warm.

Complete the borscht. Place the remaining 2 tablespoons of oil in the saucepan used to cook the base; heat over medium-low heat. Add the cabbage, the remaining 1 cup of beets and carrots and cook for 3 minutes, stirring often. Add the honey and vinegar and cook 3 minutes more to reduce the acidity of the vinegar. Pour the warm soup base into the pan; simmer until the vegetables are tender—about 20 minutes. Chill for two hours.

Arrange the condiments. Put the sour cream, capers, and scallions each into a small bowl or cup. Serve the borscht at the table, topping each bowl with a dollop of sour cream and a sprinkling of capers and scallions. Add croutons or pass toast at the table if you wish.

MAKE IT PARVE. *Omit the sour cream garnish, and be sure to choose vegetable stock, not chicken stock.*

CROSTINI WITH SMOKED TROUT AND SOUR CREAM

MAKES ABOUT 15 SLICES

TODD: This easy, quick snack calls for trout, but any cold-smoked fish you might find in a grocery store or deli, such as salmon, whitefish, sable, or bluefish, would work just as well. If you don't feel like making your own crostini, you can generally find them already made in grocery stores. It cuts out a step, but costs a lot more.

1 small baguette, cut diagonally into ⅓-inch thick slices

¼ cup olive oil

Salt

Freshly ground black pepper

½ cup sour cream

6 fresh chives, thinly sliced crosswise

¼ teaspoon freshly squeezed lemon juice

¼ pound smoked trout

Toast the bread. Preheat the oven to 350°F. Arrange the baguette slices on a baking sheet. Brush the tops of the slices with ⅛ cup of the oil, dividing equally, and sprinkle lightly with salt and pepper. Turn the slices over and season the other side in the same way. Toast in the oven until the bread is golden brown on the edges and slightly crunchy, turning once—about 4 minutes per side. Cool on the baking sheet on a wire rack.

Assemble the crostini. Stir together the sour cream, chives, lemon juice, ¼ teaspoon salt, and ⅛ teaspoon pepper in a small bowl. If you like, cut the toast slices in half for easier eating. Break the fish into pieces (use your fingers) and layer onto the toast, topping with the sour cream mixture, dividing equally. Arrange on a serving plate.

CHICKPEA SALAD WITH FETA CHEESE AND MINT

MAKES ABOUT 6 CUPS

TODD: Especially when fresh vegetables aren't plentiful, it is a great idea to use legumes and beans as the main ingredient for salads. The extra protein comes in handy to provide the energy our bodies need in cold weather months. Herbs like mint and parsley are easily found year-round, so I don't really consider using them in the winter to be a "seasonal violation." Here's a tip for shaving the red onion: If you don't have an inexpensive Japanese vegetable slicer, it's a good idea to invest in one. It's a great tool for easily slicing onions really thinly.

Two 15.5-ounce cans chickpeas, rinsed and drained

1 cup quartered cherry tomatoes

1 cup very thinly sliced red onion (about 1 small onion)

½ cup crumbled feta cheese (2 ounces)

¼ cup slivered black olives

2 scallions, thinly sliced crosswise, including part of the green (¼ cup)

2 teaspoons chopped fresh mint leaves

1 garlic clove, minced

¼ cup olive oil, preferably extra virgin

2 tablespoons freshly squeezed lemon juice

1 teaspoon salt

⅛ teaspoon freshly ground black pepper

Place the chickpeas in a medium-size bowl. Add the tomatoes (hold these aside if making ahead of time so they don't get mushy), onions, cheese, olives, scallions, mint, and garlic; stir to mix. In a small bowl or glass measuring cup, whisk together the oil, lemon juice, salt, and pepper. Pour over the chickpea salad and stir to mix well. Refrigerate for at least 30 minutes before serving; if you held the tomatoes aside, mix them in about 30 minutes before serving.

LUNCH

TODD'S FAVORITE PASTRAMI
SANDWICH 105

SALT COD FRITTERS 106

WHITEFISH SALAD ON TOASTED BAGEL
WITH HAVARTI CHEESE 110

ROASTED CHICKEN WITH ROSEMARY
AND LEMON 112

SWEET AND SOUR VEAL MEATBALLS 114

TODD'S FAVORITE PASTRAMI SANDWICH

MAKES 6 SANDWICHES

TODD: This recipe is certainly not kosher, but it was a staple from my childhood. (Leave the cheese off if you have an issue with it.) Every Sunday after church, my mom would make my brother and me pastrami and Swiss cheese sandwiches on Pepperidge Farm hamburger buns with Dijon mustard. We would have two apiece and watch World Championship Wrestling and then get on the floor and wrestle. It's ironic that Ellen and I were probably eating pastrami sandwiches at the same time as kids and didn't even know it.

6 sesame seed buns

⅓ cup whole grain mustard

12 slices havarti cheese

1 pound thinly sliced beef pastrami

2 tablespoons olive oil, more if needed

Dill pickles for serving (choose a good quality or make the recipe on page 275)

Assemble the sandwiches. Heat a panini press to medium-high. Open the buns and arrange them on a work surface; spread the mustard on each piece, dividing equally. Place a slice of cheese on the bottom half of each bun; top with the pastrami, the remaining 6 slices of cheese, and then the bun tops. Drizzle the oil over the sandwiches (turn over to drizzle both sides).

Cook the sandwiches. Working in batches as necessary, grill the sandwiches in the press until the cheese is melted and the buns are well toasted. (If you don't have a panini press, heat a little olive oil in a sauté pan over medium-low heat and cook the sandwiches in it until the buns are toasted and caramelized.) Cut each sandwich in half. Serve with dill pickles on the side.

SALT COD FRITTERS

MAKES ABOUT THIRTY-SIX 1½-INCH FRITTERS (6 SERVINGS)

TODD: Dried salt cod (bacalhau) has been a staple in Mediterranean and Scandinavian countries for centuries and fritters made from it are popular in many countries. Drying and salting fish was a way to preserve it indefinitely in the days before refrigeration. Specialty food stores carry it and it is certainly readily available online. You must soak it to eliminate the salt before you use it and it's crucial that you change the water several times to rid it of as much salt as possible, so factor in about 24 hours for this preparatory part of the cooking process.

ELLEN: Fritters are great as an appetizer or an hors d'oeuvre if you make the balls bite-size, but we like them as a light lunch in the winter. (Sometimes you just crave something fried!) Serve them with Red Cabbage Coleslaw (page 57) or a salad made with nice winter lettuces, like endive, frisée, and/or arugula.

2 pounds dried salt cod

3 medium Yukon Gold potatoes (about 1½ pounds), peeled and cut into chunks

2 cups whole milk

2 cups water

6 garlic cloves, crushed

2 large egg yolks

2 teaspoons salt

¼ teaspoon fresh coarsely ground black pepper

1 cup all-purpose flour

2 cups egg wash (see Chef's Appendix)

2 cups crushed panko bread crumbs

4 cups canola oil for frying, or as needed

Soak the salt cod. Cut the salt cod into 2-inch cubes. Place in a large bowl and cover with water. Set aside to soak for 18 to 24 hours, changing the water every 6 to 8 hours to remove the saltiness.

Prep the potatoes. Bring a medium saucepan of water to boiling over high heat; add the potatoes, cover, and boil until easily pierced with a fork—about 15 to 20 minutes. Drain in a colander. When cool enough to handle, put the potatoes through a food mill or the grating disc in a food processor.

Cook the cod. Drain the cod and place in a medium-size saucepan. Add the milk, water, and garlic. Cook over medium-low heat until the cod is tender and flakes apart when poked with a fork—for approximately 45 minutes. Drain cod in a mesh strainer, discard the liquid and garlic.

Mix the fritters. Transfer the cod to a large bowl. Break up the cod into very fine flakes with a wooden spoon; it should be "mealy" in appearance. Add the potatoes and stir to combine. Stir in the egg yolks, salt, and pepper, mixing well.

(recipe continues)

Cook the fritters. Put the flour, egg wash, and bread crumbs each into a shallow dish. Shape the cod mixture into small balls, approximately 1½ inches in diameter. Roll each in the flour, then dip into the egg wash and roll in the bread crumbs. Pour 4 inches of oil into a medium saucepan and heat over medium heat to 325° (measure on a candy thermometer). Working in batches and adding more oil if needed, add the fritters to the pan and cook until golden brown on all sides—about 3 minutes total. Transfer the fritters to a paper towel–lined plate to drain; keep warm. To serve, line a bowl with a kitchen towel and arrange the fritters in it.

CULTURAL ENRICHMENT

In 1971, I was living in Princeton, New Jersey, an idyllic environment with a storied university and a rich history. My then-husband was enrolled at the Woodrow Wilson School of Public Affairs and I was supporting us both through my work as a music teacher at Princeton Day School. Though just an hour from New York City, in those days Princeton had a very small-town feel. The main street was home to a grocery store, a barber, a bowling alley, and a Woolworth's. There were a luncheonette, a diner, and two independent cinemas. The malls and multiplexes of today were still far from being born.

My teaching activities kept me busy, but somehow I found the time to participate in the local community's "PJ&B" musical production. PJ&B stands for "Princeton Junction & Back," in reference to the two-car train, The Dinky, that connected the campus to the Amtrak station and thus the cities of the East Coast corridor. The musical that year was *Fiddler on the Roof*. I was given the part of Fruma Sarah, the butcher's dead wife, who rises from the grave to warn Tevye against his daughter's marriage to her widower. It makes me smile just to think of it: Me, an African American woman, playing the part of a crazed Jewish ghost, in preppy Princeton of the early 1970s! Inspired casting, to be sure. It was also tremendous fun.

In that same era, I was introduced to Jewish dishes by one of our best friends in Princeton, Jerry Goren, who revealed to me the wonders of lox, pastrami, challah, and bagels—even though, at the time, you had to drive half an hour to Hightstown to find them. Jerry and his wife became godparents to my children, who are now both out of college themselves. Sunrise, sunset, as Tevye sings; swiftly fly the years.

—SHEILA C. JOHNSON, co-founder of Black Entertainment Television & CEO of Salamander Hospitality

WHITEFISH SALAD ON TOASTED BAGEL WITH HAVARTI CHEESE

MAKES 6 OPEN-FACE SANDWICHES

TODD: I was introduced to smoked whitefish salad by Ellen's father, Ed, at the local deli. Any salad slathered on a bagel and toasted with melted cheese all over it is a winner in Ed's book and who could argue? The whitefish salad you buy in a store is usually over mixed and too mayonnaise-y—and you don't really know exactly what's in it, so this is one of those instances where making it yourself makes a huge difference. I can guarantee that there isn't any fennel in the store-bought stuff and probably no lemon zest, either. By the way, you can use any smoked fish you'd like, such as trout, carp, cod, pike, whiting, sturgeon, or halibut.

½ **pound smoked whitefish**

½ **cup sour cream**

½ **cup mayonnaise**

1 **teaspoon freshly grated lemon zest**

½ **teaspoon salt**

⅛ **teaspoon freshly ground black pepper**

¼ **cup finely minced celery**

¼ **cup finely minced red onion**

¼ **cup finely minced fennel bulb**

1 **tablespoon finely chopped fresh dill leaves**

4 **scallions, thinly sliced crosswise, including some of the green**

3 **bagels (sesame seed or your choice)**

6 **slices Havarti cheese**

Red onion slices

Tomato slices

Make the whitefish salad. Flake the whitefish into a medium bowl (use your fingers). Add the sour cream, mayonnaise, lemon zest, salt, and pepper; blend with a fork. Stir in the celery, onions, fennel, and dill. Taste the mixture and add salt and pepper if you wish. Cover and refrigerate for at least 1 hour.

Make the sandwiches. Heat the oven to 350°F. Slice the bagels in half and toast them in a toaster. Arrange them on a baking sheet, cut side up. Top each with one slice of cheese. Place in the oven to melt the cheese—about 3 minutes. Transfer the bagels to individual plates or a serving platter and top each with a few onion slices and tomato slices and a generous dollop of whitefish salad. Serve immediately.

ROASTED CHICKEN WITH ROSEMARY AND LEMON

SERVES 4

TODD: Every good cook should know how to roast a chicken properly. First of all, you have to start with a good product. The packaged, factory-produced, flavorless, chemical-laden birds you find in a traditional grocery store don't cut it. Spend the extra money on a farm-raised animal and then treat it with the respect that it, and you, deserve. Clean the bird, dry it, coat it with butter (or canola or olive oil, if keeping kosher), season it simply, and tie its legs together. Starting in a hot oven jumpstarts the caramelization process that results in a crispy skin. Serve the bird with lemon wedges; the citrus complements the sweetness of the flesh.

ELLEN: Roast chicken was pretty much a staple growing up. You could always open their refrigerator and tear off a little piece for a snack, slathering it in the juices and fat in the bottom of the pan. That was the best (see Roast Chicken When We Were Young, page 113).

One 3- to 4-pound whole chicken

1 lemon, cut in half crosswise

3 sprigs fresh rosemary

4 garlic cloves

¼ cup olive oil

1 tablespoon unsalted butter, softened, or canola or olive oil

Fresh coarsely ground black pepper

Lemon wedges for serving

Prep the chicken. Preheat the oven to 450°F. Trim any excess fat from the chicken. Rinse the chicken under cold water and pat dry with paper towels. Place the rosemary, garlic, and two lemon halves inside the cavity of the chicken and then rub the butter over its skin. Grind some pepper over the chicken and place it on a rack in a roasting pan.

Roast the chicken. Place the chicken in the oven; immediately lower the heat to 325°F. Roast for 20 minutes, then baste with the pan juices. Continue to roast, basting every 15 or 20 minutes and rotating the pan 180 degrees after 25 minutes (the second time you baste). Cook until done (the juices should run clear and the leg joints loose when moved)—45 to 60 minutes. Remove from the oven, cover loosely with foil, and set aside to rest 10 minutes. Carve the chicken as you wish, arrange on a platter, add lemon wedges along the edges, and serve immediately.

Roast Chicken When We Were Young

ELLEN: My grandmother, Rose Henkin, and Aunt Lil, my great aunt on my father's side, were champions of the roast chicken. They did not know from styrofoam packets of chicken parts in those days. They bought whole chickens from a butcher and then utilized every part of them. Going to a grocery store and buying packages of legs or breasts or thighs just would not have registered to them—it's not something that would have jibed with their sense that everything should have more than one purpose and offer possibilities for more than one meal.

They would roast chickens in their oval roasting pans and then carve them like you would Thanksgiving turkeys, making the breast the primary part of that day's meal. The legs and wings were utilized for everything from chicken salad to potpie. Or soup, because of course the carcass would wind up as the base for a broth, to which vegetables and whatever bits of chicken were still around were added. So that meant a chicken was good for three meals. Well, three and a half if you count the noshing. There was nothing better than sneaking into the fridge in the middle of the night and pulling a shred of chicken off and noshing on it. Or making a sandwich on Wonder Bread toast slathered with mustard and gelatinized pan juices.

In my mother's time, and thereafter, everyone went breast crazy. Nowadays, through farmers' markets, people are becoming reacquainted with whole chickens and their glories.

SWEET AND SOUR VEAL MEATBALLS

SERVES 6 TO 8

TODD: Meatballs have enjoyed a renaissance lately, be it in white-tablecloth restaurants or fast food joints. We serve them at Equinox as a lunch special over polenta or noodles or as an hors d'oeuvre for catering events. This dish combines the Kassoff penchant for things sweet and sour (in the Chinese food tradition) with elements of my mother's Swedish meatball recipe from the '70s. The recipe calls for ground beef and veal, but feel free to use beef only, or ground turkey or chicken.

½ cup whole milk or soy milk

¼ cup red wine

⅔ cup cubed white bread

1 pound ground veal

¼ pound ground beef

1 large egg, beaten

1 cup finely minced yellow onion (1 small onion)

2 garlic cloves, minced

1 teaspoon chopped fresh thyme leaves

¼ teaspoon dried oregano

¼ teaspoon smoked paprika

1 teaspoon salt

⅛ teaspoon freshly ground black pepper

¼ cup bread crumbs

Canola oil for frying

Sweet and Sour Sauce (recipe follows)

MAKE IT MEAT. *Substitute soy milk for the cow's milk.*

Mix the meatballs. Combine the milk and wine in a medium bowl; stir in the bread and let it soak until soft, stirring once or twice—for a few minutes. Place the veal and beef in a large bowl. With your hands, transfer the bread to the bowl with the meat, squeezing out as much liquid as possible. Add the egg, onions, garlic, thyme, oregano, paprika, salt, and pepper to the meat. Thoroughly mix together with your hands.

Cook the meatballs. Put the bread crumbs in a shallow dish. Shape the meat mixture into small balls, 1½ to 2 inches in diameter, and roll each in the crumbs. Pour 2 inches of oil into a large sauté pan and heat over medium heat. Working in batches, add the meatballs to the pan and cook until golden brown on all sides and cooked through— about 5 to 7 minutes total. Transfer the meatballs to a paper towel-lined plate to drain; keep warm. Taste a meatball and sprinkle more salt or pepper over the others if desired.

To serve, place the meatballs in a bowl, pour in the Sweet and Sour Sauce, and toss to mix. Serve immediately.

SWEET AND SOUR SAUCE

MAKES ABOUT 2 CUPS.

Stir together 1½ cups ketchup, ⅓ cup honey, ¼ cup apple cider vinegar, and 1 teaspoon soy sauce in a small saucepan. Cook over low heat, stirring frequently, until the sauce is shiny and smooth— about 10 minutes. Season to taste with a little salt and freshly ground black pepper.

DINNER

POTATO-CRUSTED COD FILLET 117

BEEF SHORT RIBS IN RED WINE 119

TODD'S MODERN DAY BRISKET 122

CABERNET-BRAISED LAMB SHANKS
WITH ROOT VEGETABLES 124

MATZO-STUFFED CORNISH
GAME HENS 126

POTATO-CRUSTED COD FILLET

SERVES 6

TODD: Using dehydrated potato flakes right out of a box is not something you'd think a chef would do, but it is in fact a very popular technique. You use the potato flakes like bread crumbs, attaching them to the fish's flesh with an egg wash. You then sauté the crust to brown it and finish cooking the fish in the oven. It's easy and elegant. I prefer Nordic cod because it's a tight, white, flaky fish, but halibut, hake, and cobia work well, too. Any sturdy white fish is fine, actually.

1 teaspoon salt

¼ teaspoon freshly ground black pepper

6 pieces cod fillet, about 5 ounces each

2 tablespoons canola oil

2 cups egg wash (see Chef's Appendix)

2 cups dehydrated potato flakes

6 lemon wedges for serving

Preheat the oven to 350°F. Sprinkle salt and pepper over the fillets, turning to season both sides. Place the egg wash and potato flakes each in a shallow dish. Heat the oil in an ovenproof sauté pan large enough to hold all six fillets. Dip one side of each fillet into the egg and then press into the potato flakes. Place the fillets in the pan crust-side down and cook for 4 minutes. Turn the fillets over and transfer the pan to the oven to bake until they easily flake with a fork—for 5 to 8 minutes more. Transfer the fillets to a paper towel-lined plate to drain briefly; serve immediately, adding a lemon wedge to each plate.

BEEF SHORT RIBS IN RED WINE

SERVES 6

TODD: Make sure you buy the American cut of short ribs, which each have a 2- to 3-inch wide bone in them with a big chunk of meat attached, rather than the flanken (or Korean) style short rib that is cut laterally into a long, thin strip with several bones. Use a deep, wide-bottom casserole or skillet, which can be used on top of the stove as well as in the oven. Brown the ribs in batches. Overcrowding the pan keeps the ribs from browning evenly (see On Braising, below).

2 cups all-purpose flour

¼ cup grapeseed oil

Salt

Freshly ground black pepper

12 beef short ribs, each 3 to 4 inches long

1 carrot, sliced into ¼-inch rounds

1 medium yellow onion, sliced

2 celery ribs, cut crosswise into ¼-inch slices

6 garlic cloves

1 tablespoon tomato paste

1 bottle Cabernet Sauvignon wine (750 milliliters)

8 cups veal stock (see About Veal Stock, page 47 and recipe in Chef's Appendix)

1 herb bouquet (see Chef's Appendix)

Sauté the meat and vegetables. Put the flour in a shallow dish. Heat the oil in a large flameproof casserole over medium-high heat. Sprinkle salt and pepper over the short ribs. Working in batches if necessary, dip the ribs in the flour, turning to coat and then shaking off the excess; transfer to the casserole. Sauté the ribs until golden brown—about 4 minutes per side; remove from the pan with tongs and set aside on a paper towel–lined plate. In the same pan, sauté the carrots, onions, celery, and garlic until lightly caramelized—about 10 minutes.

Braise the ribs. Preheat the oven to 350°F. Stir the tomato paste into the vegetables in the casserole and cook, stirring occasionally, for 5 minutes more. Lower the heat to medium; add the wine and cook until the liquid is reduced by half—about 10 minutes. Add the veal stock, herb bouquet, and ribs. Raise the heat to medium-high and continue to cook until the liquid is simmering; cover the casserole and place in the oven. Cook until the meat is pulling away from bone—approximately 1½ hours.

To serve, transfer the ribs to a platter. Pour the sauce from the pan through a mesh strainer and over the ribs; discard the vegetables.

On Braising

TODD: Searing meat, barely covering it with liquid, cooking it slowly to make it tender, and then thickening that liquid is all part of the braising process. The technique particularly lends itself to

(recipe continues)

the cooking of less expensive cuts of meat that contain a lot of connective tissue and collagen. The thickened gravies are fairly hearty, so you often find braises on wintertime tables.

ELLEN: My grandmother was a fan of anything that could be stewed or cooked for a long time because you could set it and forget it. That meant there was less margin for error. She would never have used the word braising, even though that is exactly what she was doing.

TODD: Beef stew, lamb shanks, short ribs, brisket—all of these dishes find their way onto the Jewish table and the tables of many other cultures as well. What separates something average from something really terrific is the care taken with every step of the process. Generally, this is how the braising process should go:

1. If your recipe calls for flouring the meat before you brown it, use flour seasoned with salt and pepper, and shake off excess. Brown the meat WELL on all sides and transfer it to a bowl. Remember, caramelization adds flavor, so DO NOT CROWD THE PAN. Cook in batches if necessary; you do not want to wind up with gray chunks of meat that boil in their own juices.

2. In the same pot in which you browned the meat, caramelize a combination of aromatic vegetables. If using tomato paste, add it to the caramelized vegetables and cook it briefly.

3. Deglaze the pan with wine and, using a flat-edged wooden spoon, scrape all the caramelized bits from the bottom of the pan. The wine adds acidity to the finished dish. Allow the alcohol to cook off (chefs' lingo for "cook until evaporated"), return the meat and any of its released juices to the pot.

4. Cover the meat and vegetables with stock. The better the stock, the better the braise.

5. Add flavor enhancers (herbs, spices).

6. Cook, covered, over low heat until the meat is fork-tender.

7. Strain and defat the cooking liquid. Reserve the cooked meat and discard all the other solids.

8. Return the cooking liquid to the pot and thicken it into a sauce, either by reducing it, adding puréed braised vegetables to it, or using a thickening agent, such as a slurry, roux, or beurre manié (as indicated in your recipe or explained in a basic cookbook). Add the reserved meat to the thickened sauce.

UNKNOWN HISTORY, SHARED TRADITIONS

I didn't grow up with Jewish families in northern Spain or with any kind of Jewish foods—or so I thought. These were mostly unknown to me until I arrived in America and settled at first in Manhattan, where I loved going to all the Jewish delis. Blintzes, pastrami, knishes, and matzo ball soup: To me this was super exotic food. I loved it but I had no reference for it. While Jewish culture was simply not present in the Spain I grew up in, I discovered that was not always so.

For many, to think of Spain is to think of Catholic kings and queens, the cathedrals, and the religious holidays. The history of Jewish culture on the Iberian Peninsula is largely unfamiliar. But Spain has long been a bridge between Europe and Africa and Asia, and the many peoples who passed through or settled there for a time all left traces of their architecture, technology, traditions, and ideas. Like the delta of a great river, Spain was enriched by their contributions. Although I did not realize it growing up, the legacy of the Sephardic Jews, who were forced from the Iberian Peninsula during the Spanish Inquisition, remains close to the surface.

Traces of Jewish culinary traditions are still to be found in Spain, particularly in Andalusia in the south, where my wife is from, and the use of almonds, honey, pine nuts, eggplant, and spices such as saffron, cumin, and coriander in Spanish cuisine is often attributed to Sephardic cooking. One explanation for the great number of pork dishes in Spanish cuisine is that at the time of the Inquisition, eating pork was an easy way to prove one was a good Christian. Indeed there are many Spanish dishes that are very similar to classic Jewish dishes except for the inclusion of pork or lard. The long-simmered legume stews or *cocidos* of Spain are remarkably similar to *adafaina*, a Jewish stew of chickpeas and lamb. Even the manner in which adafaina was eaten is similar to how Spaniards eat cocido: The stew is served in three courses: first the soup, then the meat, and finally the vegetables. Some argue that the Majorcan sweet bread *ensaimada* is actually a type of challah. The classic tapa of *boquerones en vinagre*—anchovies in vinegar—has even been said to be Jewish in origin.

Now that I live in the U.S. and have many friends from Jewish families, I love to cook for them the Sephardic dishes of my Spanish home and thus share with them a little of my own Jewish roots.

—JOSÉ ANDRÉS, chef and restaurateur

TODD'S MODERN DAY BRISKET

SERVES 6 TO 8

TODD: I took the traditional Jewish braised brisket (see The Jewish Brisket, Modernized, page 123) and added techniques from my French arsenal to come up with a modern, elegant version of this beloved meat dish. It must be made a day before you wish to serve it, but there's an extra plus with that—it lets all the flavors fully develop and frees you for other things.

2 tablespoons salt

1 tablespoon smoked paprika

1 tablespoon mustard seed

1 teaspoon freshly ground black pepper

One 3-pound beef brisket, trimmed of excess fat

2 tablespoons canola oil

2 sprigs fresh rosemary

2 sprigs fresh thyme

3 garlic cloves, crushed

1 carrot, chopped

2 celery rib, chopped

1 small onion, chopped

4 cups veal stock (see About Veal Stock, page 47, and recipe in Chef's Appendix)

2 cups dry red wine (such as Cabernet Sauvignon)

½ cup balsamic vinegar

Brown the brisket. Heat the oven to 325°F. Mix together the salt, paprika, mustard seed, and pepper in a small bowl. Rub the spice mixture all over the brisket. Heat the oil in a large heavy skillet over medium-high heat. Add the brisket and cook until brown on both sides, turning once—5 to 7 minutes per side.

Bake the brisket. Transfer the brisket to a baking dish just large enough to hold it. Then add the rosemary, thyme, and garlic. Add the chopped vegetables and pour in the veal stock, wine, and vinegar. Cover the dish with heavy-duty aluminum foil and bake until the brisket is fork-tender—3 to 4 hours. Transfer the brisket temporarily to a plate while you strain the liquid through a mesh strainer into a small saucepan (discard the herbs, vegetables, and garlic) and wash and dry the baking dish.

Press the brisket. Return the brisket to the clean baking dish. Place another heavy dish on top of it, directly on the meat, to weight it down. The ideal weight for this is 2½ pounds, so add some canned goods to the top dish. Then wrap the entire assemblage in foil (over weights and all) and refrigerate overnight and until shortly before ready to serve.

Make the sauce. Meanwhile, heat the strained braising liquid over medium heat until it is reduced to about 2½ cups—about 20 minutes. The finished sauce should have a glaze-like consistency. Taste the sauce and add salt or pepper if you wish. Refrigerate the sauce until ready to reheat the brisket.

Complete the brisket. Shortly before ready to serve, remove the brisket from refrigerator and transfer to a cutting board. Also remove the sauce. Cut the brisket into 3-inch cubes: You don't want to waste any of the meat, so the cubes don't need to be exactly this size or perfect along the edges. Place the brisket in a pan just large enough to hold it in a single layer. Pour in enough sauce to just cover the meat (you may add a little stock or water if there isn't enough sauce to do this). Heat over low heat until warmed through—about 10 minutes. Spoon the brisket onto a serving platter; pour the sauce over and serve.

The Jewish Brisket, Modernized

TODD: The exalted position that brisket holds in Jewish American cooking cannot be underestimated. My first exposure to it was interesting as well as inspirational.

ELLEN: He came over to our house for the holidays and had his first brisket, which (sorry Mom) was somewhat dry. Braising isn't her forte. Unfortunately, Todd met my grandmother and Aunt Lil in the last few years of their lives when they weren't cooking much anymore, so he never got to taste their brisket, which was glorious.

TODD: The thing about brisket is that it needs to be braised low and slow to keep it moist and then cut against the grain. The traditional way of making Jewish brisket is as a pot roast: searing it and braising for three hours or so in a fairly low oven, often with lots of onions.

I like a non-traditional version that utilizes French technique. You braise the meat (with red wine, veal stock, and balsamic vinegar), then remove it from the braising liquid once it's cooked, press it down with weights to compress it and then refrigerate it. This compacts the meat and presses excess fat out of it. Once the meat is cold, you cut it into 5-ounce blocks (known a *pavés* in French, which means cobblestones) and reheat them in strained and reduced braising liquid. It's an elegant, modern version of brisket.

CABERNET-BRAISED LAMB SHANKS

SERVES 4 TO 6

ELLEN: We knew lamb as a symbol of Passover—lamb shank was a dried-out bloody bone you'd only find on a Seder plate. I love how Todd took something that was largely symbolic and turned it into something edible.

TODD: Make sure you ask the butcher for foreshanks, because they are much meatier. This is just a terrific, hearty winter dish that relies on braising technique (see On Braising, page 119). We love to serve the shanks over couscous or Saffron Rice Pilaf (page 201).

2 cups all-purpose flour

¼ cup canola oil

1½ teaspoons salt

Freshly ground black pepper

6 lamb shanks

2 medium carrots, chopped

1 onion, chopped

2 celery ribs, chopped

4 garlic cloves, crushed

⅓ cup tomato paste

3 cups Cabernet Sauvignon wine

4 cups Roasted Chicken Jus (recipe in Chef's Appendix)

2 cups water

3 sprigs fresh thyme

2 cups mixed diced root vegetables, such as celery root, turnips, and carrots

12 roasted garlic cloves, halved lengthwise

Brown the shanks and vegetables. Put the flour in a shallow dish. Heat the oil in a large sauté pan over medium-high heat. Sprinkle the salt over the shanks and grind a little pepper over them, too. Dip them in the flour, turning to coat and then shaking off the excess; transfer to the pan. Sauté until golden brown on all sides—about 6 to 8 minutes total; remove from the pan with tongs and set aside on a paper towel-lined plate. In the same pan, sauté the chopped carrots, onions, and celery until slightly brown—about 5 minutes.

Braise the shanks. Preheat the oven to 325°F. Add the garlic to the vegetables in the sauté pan; stir in the tomato paste and cook for 2 minutes. Lower the heat to medium; add the wine and cook until the liquid is reduced by half—about 10 minutes. Taste the mixture and add salt or pepper if you wish. Place the shanks in a casserole large enough to hold them with room to spare. Pour the vegetable and red wine mixture over them; pour in the chicken jus and water and add the thyme. Cover the casserole and place in the oven. Cook until the meat is pulling away from bone—1½ to 2 hours.

Complete the sauce. Transfer the shanks to a plate and cover with foil to keep warm. Strain the liquid (we call this lamb jus) through a mesh strainer into a saucepan and discard the vegetables. Wash and dry the casserole and return the shanks to it; keep warm. Add the diced root vegetables and garlic to the lamb jus in the saucepan; heat over medium heat until simmering, lower the heat to medium-low, and simmer until the vegetables are soft—10 minutes. Pour the lamb jus and vegetables over the shanks and serve.

MATZO-STUFFED CORNISH GAME HENS

SERVES 4

TODD: My mom always chose to cook Rock Cornish game hens instead of large chickens. They were perfect for our family—with the four of us (my brother, mom, dad, and me) each getting a whole bird. Cornish hens have gotten a bad rap for some reason; you never see them in restaurants anymore. Too bad, because this recipe, stuffing the birds with matzo and chicken livers and serving them with braised cabbage and chicken jus, is a winner.

STUFFING:

1 cup chicken livers (about 7 ounces)

¼ cup canola oil

1 large yellow onion, cut into ¼-inch dice

3 celery ribs, cut into ¼-inch dice

3 garlic cloves, minced

2 teaspoons chopped fresh sage

½ teaspoon salt

⅛ teaspoon freshly ground black pepper

3 matzo crackers (full sheets), crushed into pieces

HENS:

4 Cornish game hens

2 tablespoons olive oil

4 tablespoons unsalted butter (½ stick), cut into small pieces

Salt

Freshly ground black pepper

2 carrots, coarsely chopped

2 celery ribs, coarsely chopped

Make the stuffing. Clean the livers (see Chef's Appendix or page 9), then coarsely chop them into ½-inch pieces. Heat the oil in a large sauté pan over medium heat. Add the onions, celery, and garlic, cook for 2 minutes; lower the heat to medium-low and continue to cook until the vegetables are translucent and begin to soften—6 to 8 minutes. Add the livers, sage, salt, and pepper; sauté until the livers are cooked—about 5 minutes. Transfer the mixture to a paper towel-lined plate to drain. Place the crushed matzos in a medium bowl; add the liver mixture and mix well with a wooden spoon. Taste the stuffing and add more salt or pepper if you wish.

Clean the hens. Trim any excess fat from the hens; wash them under cold water and pat dry with paper towels. Set aside.

Mix a mirepoix. Mix the carrots, celery, and onions in the bottom of a roasting pan large enough to hold all 4 hens.

Stuff the hens. Preheat the oven to 400°F. Loosely fill the cavity of each hen with stuffing. Drizzle 1½ teaspoons oil over each hen and rub into skin. Sprinkle each hen with salt and pepper. Truss the hens with twine (tie the legs together, tuck the wings under the backs). Place the hens, breast up, in the roasting pan, on the mirepoix. Dot each with the butter, dividing equally. (If there is extra stuffing, place it in an appropriate size casserole or ramekin; add it to the oven with the hens about halfway through the roasting time.)

1 medium yellow onion, coarsely chopped

1 cup Roasted Chicken Jus (recipe in Chef's Appendix)

Braised Cabbage for serving (recipe page 134)

MAKE IT MEAT. *Dot the hens with margarine instead of butter, or brush them with canola or olive oil.*

STUFF A CHICKEN INSTEAD

This stuffing is also an excellent choice when you feel like roasting a whole 3- to 5-pound chicken (or can't find any Cornish hens). Prepare the recipe as indicated here, but let the chicken roast at 400°F for 20 minutes before lowering the heat to 325°F, and allow more time overall for it to cook—60 to 80 minutes total, depending on size. Carve the chicken as you wish and serve as described for the hens.

Roast the hens. Place the pan in the oven and roast for 10 minutes, lower the heat to 325°F. Roast for 40 minutes more, until done (the internal temperature of the thigh should register 160° on an instant read thermometer),—checking from time to time that the hens are browning evenly and rotating the pan 180 degrees about halfway through the cooking time.

Make the sauce. Transfer the hens to a cutting board and cover with foil to keep warm. Transfer the mirepoix and pan juices to a small saucepan and add the Roasted Chicken Jus. Bring to simmering over medium heat; simmer for 10 minutes. Strain the sauce through a fine mesh strainer into another pan or serving pitcher; discard the mirepoix and keep the sauce warm.

Carve the hens for serving. Slice the thighs, legs, and breast meat from each hen—as you would when carving a turkey. Carefully spoon the stuffing from inside each hen and place on individual plates. Spoon some Braised Cabbage next to the stuffing. Arrange the meat from one hen on top of the stuffing and cabbage on each plate. Spoon the sauce over the top and serve.

SIDES

PICKLED HEIRLOOM BEETS WITH HARD-BOILED EGGS

SERVES 6

ELLEN: In Todd's early days with my family, there was always a selection of hard-boiled eggs and some kind of pickled vegetables as side dishes on the table, like pickles or pickled beets or giardiniera mix. So he got the inspiration to do a recipe combining beets and eggs. I have to say, the yolks of the hard-boiled eggs against the red of the beets make both those items look more inviting.

TODD: What you are basically doing here is poaching beets in a pickling brine (see Pickled Foods Belong in Your Repertoire, page 164) until they are barely tender, letting everything cool, and then refrigerating the beets overnight so they absorb the brine's flavor. This is why you have to start the dish at least the day before. Pickled beets will last at least a month in the refrigerator, so why not make a big batch and snack on them whenever you want?

2 bay leaves

1 star anise

2 sprigs fresh thyme, broken into short pieces

12 black peppercorns

1 teaspoon coriander seeds

1 teaspoon fennel seeds

Small piece of cheesecloth to make spice sachet

6 cups water

2 cups apple cider vinegar

1 cup sugar

1 tablespoon table salt

2 bay leaves

1 large red beet, peeled and cut into ½-inch dice (about 2 cups)

1 large yellow beet, peeled and cut into ½-inch dice (about 2 cups)

6 large eggs, preferably from your farmers' market

Coarse sea salt for serving

Make a spice sachet. Place the bay leaves, star anise, thyme, peppercorns, coriander, and fennel in the middle of the cheesecloth; fold up the cloth over the spices and tie closed or bind with kitchen twine.

Pickle the beets. Combine the water, cider vinegar, sugar, and salt in a medium pot. Bring to simmering over high heat, stirring to dissolve the sugar. Lower the heat to medium-low and add the bay leaves, spice sachet, and beets; simmer for 10 minutes. Remove the pan from the heat and let the beets cool in the liquid. Refrigerate the beets in the liquid until ready to serve—at least overnight.

Cook the eggs. Bring a medium pot of water to simmering over high heat; lower the heat to low. Gently add the eggs; simmer, uncovered, for 14 minutes. Drain the eggs and submerge in a bowl of ice water until completely cooled.

Arrange for serving. Peel the eggs and cut lengthwise into quarters. Drain the beets in a colander or large sieve; discard the sachet and bay leaves. Arrange the beets and eggs on a platter or individual plates; sprinkle with the sea salt or pass the salt at the table.

EQUINOX MAC AND CHEESE

SERVES 6 TO 8

ELLEN: Mac and cheese has been an American childhood favorite since Kraft put it on the table in 1937 and called it a Kraft Dinner. I think it was one of the first boxed convenience items that our grandmothers embraced. There was something intriguing and addictive about that neon-orange cheese powder, but Todd winces at the very thought of it. Here is his from-scratch version in all its glory.

TODD: This hearty and comforting dish has been on the Equinox menu since 1999. I make a classic béchamel sauce and then upgrade a combination of cheddar, Parmesan, and Gruyère cheeses with a dash of truffle oil. (A little goes a long way, so use it judiciously.) For kids, you can omit the truffle oil, but leave it in for adults—it adds extra dimension and earthiness.

½ **pound elbow macaroni**

½ **cup unsalted butter (1 stick), cut into pieces**

½ **cup all-purpose flour**

6 cups milk (any type)

1 cup shredded medium cheddar cheese (4 ounces; we like Tillamook All-Natural Cheddar)

1 cup shredded Gruyère cheese (4 ounces)

1 cup grated Parmesan cheese (4 ounces)

2 tablespoons salt

Pinch freshly ground black pepper

1½ teaspoons to 1 tablespoon truffle oil

1 cup dry bread crumbs, homemade from brioche bread or Panko (see Chef's Appendix)

Cook the macaroni. See "Cooking Pasta" in the Chef's Appendix. Preheat the oven to 350°F. Lightly oil an 8×10-inch baking dish (or six individual ramekins). Bring a large pot of salted water to boiling over high heat; stir in the macaroni and cook according to the package directions until al dente (done but still firm to the bite). Drain the macaroni in a colander and transfer to a large bowl.

Make the sauce. Meanwhile, melt the butter in medium-size sauté pan over medium-low heat; slowly add the flour, stirring until it forms a thin paste (this is a roux). Slowly whisk in the milk, cooking until well blended and slightly thickened—about 8 to 10 minutes (this is classic béchamel sauce). Stir ½ cup of the cheddar cheese, ½ cup of the Gruyère, and ½ cup of the Parmesan into the sauce, stirring constantly with a wooden spoon until the cheeses are melted and incorporated. Season with the salt and pepper; keep warm if the macaroni is still cooking.

Mix and bake the macaroni. Add the cheese sauce to the bowl with the macaroni; stir in the truffle oil to taste. Spoon about half of the macaroni-cheese mixture into the prepared baking dish (or divide among the ramekins), spreading evenly. Sprinkle half of the remaining cheddar, Gruyère, and Parmesan cheeses over the top. Repeat the layering with the remaining macaroni-cheese mixture and remaining cheeses. Sprinkle the bread crumbs evenly over the top. Bake until the sauce is bubbly and the topping is golden—for 12 to 15 minutes.

POTATO AND CHEESE KNISHES

MAKES THREE 8-INCH KNISHES

ELLEN: I had my first knish at a deli in New York when I was a child. So many cultures have versions of flaky pastry pies with savory fillings—who doesn't love them?

TODD: I like the dough as flaky as possible. Letting it rest for several hours gives the gluten a chance to relax and allows the butter to solidify well, so that when the dough is baked, it creates layers of flour and butter. You can make both the filling and the dough the day before.

2 cups all-purpose flour

2 teaspoons salt

1 cup cold unsalted butter (2 sticks)

3 teaspoons vegetable shortening

1 large egg yolk

¼ cup ice water

1 pound russet (Idaho) potatoes, peeled and cut into quarters

2 tablespoons canola oil

¼ cup diced yellow onions, sautéed

1 garlic clove, minced

½ cup ricotta cheese

¼ cup grated Parmesan cheese (1 ounce)

1 tablespoon chopped fresh parsley

⅛ teaspoon freshly ground black pepper

Egg wash (see Chef's Appendix)

Prepare the dough. Sift the flour and 1 teaspoon salt into a large bowl. Cut in the butter using two knives. Add the shortening and egg yolk, beating until blended with a hand-held electric mixer on low speed; add the water and continue beating until the dough comes together.

Transfer the dough to a lightly floured work surface and knead for 2 minutes. Wrap the dough in plastic wrap and refrigerate overnight.

Prep the potatoes. Bring a large pot of salted water to boiling over high heat. Drop the potatoes into the pot and cook until fork tender—20 to 30 minutes. Drain in a colander and set aside to dry (pat dry with a kitchen towel if they don't air-dry quickly). Put the potatoes through a food mill (or the ricing attachment on a food processor) into a large bowl. You need 2 cups; if there is more, reserve the excess for another use.

Make the filling. Heat the oil in a small sauté pan over medium-low heat. Add the onions and garlic and sauté until shiny and aromatic—3 to 4 minutes. Transfer the onion mixture to the bowl with the potatoes. Add the ricotta and Parmesan cheeses, the parsley, the remaining 1 teaspoon salt, and the pepper; mix together with a wooden spoon.

Fill the knishes. Preheat the oven to 350°F. Line a baking sheet with parchment paper (the paper will adhere better if you lightly spray the pan with nonstick cooking spray before laying the paper on it). Divide the dough into three equal pieces. Roll out each piece to a 6×8-inch rectangle on a lightly floured work surface. Cut each rectangle into two 3×8-inch strips. Spoon some of the filling along the center of three strips, leaving a 1-inch margin along each edge and at the ends. Brush some egg wash along the margins; lay one of the remaining strips on top of each filled strip and press together along the edges—forming a rectangular packet.

Bake the knishes. Arrange the knishes on the prepared baking sheet. Bake until golden brown—about 20 minutes. Cut the knishes into 2-inch lengths and serve immediately.

BRAISED CABBAGE

SERVES 6

TODD: This is the perfect companion for my Matzo-Stuffed Cornish Game Hens (page 126). And it couldn't be easier to make.

⅓ **cup canola oil**

One 1-pound head of green cabbage, quartered, cored, and very thinly sliced

1½ **tablespoons salt**

⅛ **teaspoon freshly ground black pepper**

2 tablespoons unsalted butter, softened

MAKE IT PARVE. *Substitute margarine or olive oil for the butter.*

Heat the oil in a medium sauté pan over medium heat. Stir in the cabbage; lower the heat to medium-low. Stir in the salt and pepper. Cook, uncovered, for 15 minutes, stirring frequently. Stir in the butter; continue to cook until the cabbage is wilted and golden—10 minutes more. Drain the cabbage in a colander. Return to the pan (or transfer to a serving bowl); taste the cabbage and add more salt and pepper if you wish. Keep warm until ready to serve.

CUCUMBER AND YOGURT SALAD WITH FRESH DILL

SERVES 4

TODD: This was one of the first dishes I was exposed to at La Petite Auberge in Fredericksburg, which was my first cooking job. I thought, "Cucumbers, yogurt, raisins, and dill? Really?" and then, of course, I came to discover that this salad is a Mediterranean staple. What's key here is to use Greek yogurt, which is strained and therefore less watery and much creamier than regular or low-fat yogurts; it's available in most grocery stores.

ELLEN: Yogurt is one of those staples in so many cuisines. The Sephardic version of yogurt is strained—also known as yogurt cheese. If you don't find Greek yogurt easily, it's worth the extra time to strain regular yogurt (through cheesecloth in a fine-mesh strainer over a bowl for an hour or so, depending on the quantity you're straining) as it will keep the salad thick and chunky.

½ **cup golden raisins**

2 **medium seedless (English) cucumbers, peeled, quartered lengthwise, and thinly sliced**

1 **small red onion, thinly sliced**

½ **tablespoon minced fresh dill leaves**

1 **cup plain Greek yogurt**

1 **teaspoon salt**

⅛ **teaspoon freshly ground black pepper**

Soak the raisins. Place the raisins in a small bowl. Add hot water to cover and set aside to soak for 1 hour. Drain in a mesh strainer.

Mix the salad. Place the cucumbers, onions, raisins, and dill in a medium bowl. Add the yogurt, salt, and pepper; stir with a wooden spoon until well combined. Taste the salad and add more salt and pepper if you wish. Cover and refrigerate; we prefer the taste when this is slightly chilled so if it becomes fully cold, remove it from the refrigerator about 15 minutes before serving.

MODERN-STYLE TZIMMES

SERVES 4 TO 6

ELLEN: Tzimmes is another one of those polarizing dishes. For many people the mere mention of prunes makes noses crinkle. Put them in a stew of sweet potatoes—the classic tzimmes mix—and you find yourself in real "love it or hate it" territory.

TODD: Plums don't seem to work people up as much as prunes do, which is why I use them here, but as a garnish, mostly. This dish is basically a compote of caramelized sweet potatoes, potatoes, and carrots—a simple, seasonal side dish for a winter meal.

1 tablespoon canola oil

1 tablespoon butter

1 large sweet potato (about 10 ounces), peeled and cubed

2 medium Yukon Gold potatoes (about 10 ounces), peeled and cubed

1 large carrot, chopped

1 teaspoon salt

⅛ teaspoon freshly ground black pepper

¼ cup honey

1 tablespoon apple cider vinegar

2 ripe black or red plums, pitted, quartered, and sliced

MAKE IT PARVE. *Substitute margarine for the butter.*

Cook the vegetables. Heat the oil and butter in a large sauté pan over medium heat until the butter is melted. Add the sweet potatoes, Yukon Gold potatoes, and carrots; stir to coat. Cook, stirring occasionally, until evenly caramelized—5 to 8 minutes. Lower the heat to low and stir in the salt and pepper. Cook until the vegetables are tender—6 to 8 minutes more.

Finish the tzimmes. Stir in the honey and cook until the vegetables become glazed—about 4 minutes. Stir in the vinegar and cook for 2 minutes to reduce its acidity. Transfer the tzimmes to a large platter. Arrange the plum slices on top and serve.

DESSERTS

DAIRY-FREE BROWNIES

MAKES EIGHTEEN 3×3-INCH BROWNIES

ELLEN: Our former pastry chef at Equinox, Tom Wellings, came up with this recipe because we wanted to offer a vegan-friendly sweet at our Muse Café in the Corcoran Gallery of Art. The flax seed acts as an egg substitute, providing oil and nutrients to the brownies as well as some binding power. Because there's no dairy in these treats, they're suitable for meat meals.

⅔ **cup lukewarm water**

½ **cup golden flax seed meal**

4¼ **cups all-purpose flour**

1 cup plus 2 tablespoons unsweetened dark cocoa powder

1¾ **teaspoons salt**

1¼ **teaspoons baking soda**

3 ounces unsweetened chocolate, chopped (see On Chocolate for Baking, page 217)

1¼ **cups boiling water**

3 cups sugar

1 cup canola oil

1¼ **teaspoons vanilla extract**

Mix the batter. Preheat the oven to 325°F. Spray two 9-inch square pans with nonstick cooking spray. Pour the lukewarm water into a large bowl; add the flax seed meal and stir together with a wooden spoon until combined. Sift together the flour, cocoa powder, salt, and baking soda into a medium bowl. Place the chopped chocolate in a small bowl; pour in the boiling water and whisk together until the chocolate is melted and incorporated into the water, forming a thick liquid. In a second medium bowl, stir together the sugar, oil, and vanilla until well combined. Stir the sugar mixture into the flax mixture; gradually add the flour mixture, folding together. Pour in the chocolate and fold together until the batter is evenly colored—it will be dense and dough-like.

Bake the brownies. Spoon the batter into the prepared pans, dividing equally and spreading to level. Bake until a paring knife inserted in the center of the pans comes out clean—for 40 minutes. Transfer the pans to wire racks to cool slightly; then cut each into nine brownies (or however many you wish), removing from the pan to another rack to finish cooling.

RICOTTA: THE TWIST ON DRAINING

To remove all excess liquid from ricotta, line a fine-mesh strainer with a double thickness of cheesecloth large enough to be able to pick up the ends. Suspend the strainer over a bowl and add the ricotta to the cheesecloth. Allow the cheese to drain for 30 minutes; bring the cloth ends together and twist gently to wring.

WARM LEMON-RICOTTA FRITTERS

MAKES TWELVE 2-INCH DIAMETER FRITTERS

TODD: This Italian-inspired dish is from my days at Galileo Restaurant. Make sure you use whole fat ricotta cheese (anything less would be too watery and vapid—the rich dairyness of the cheese makes all the difference) and wring excess water from it (see Ricotta: The Twist on Draining, opposite page). The drier the cheese, the lighter the fritter.

Peanut or grapeseed oil for frying

2 large eggs

1 cup ricotta cheese (drained in cheesecloth to remove any liquid)

2 tablespoons granulated sugar

2 teaspoons freshly grated lemon zest

½ teaspoon vanilla extract

¼ cup all-purpose flour

½ teaspoon baking powder

¼ teaspoon salt

Confectioner's sugar for coating the cooked fritters

Heat the oil for frying. Pour oil into a deep fryer to the maximum fill line and preheat to 350°F, or fill a deep saucepan no more than halfway with oil and heat over medium-low heat to 350°F (measure on a candy thermometer).

Mix the batter. Using a whisk, lightly beat the eggs in a large mixing bowl. Add the ricotta, granulated sugar, lemon zest, and vanilla, and whisk together until thoroughly combined. With a dry whisk, mix the flour, salt, and baking powder in a small bowl. Add the flour mixture to the egg mixture and fold together using a rubber spatula.

Cook the fritters. Pour a couple of inches of confectioner's sugar into a medium bowl. Carefully drop rounded tablespoonfuls of batter into the hot oil. They will float up quickly; if they don't, gently dislodge them from the bottom using a metal spoon or spatula. Pay close attention to the fritters as they cook, and as soon as each is golden brown on one side, turn it over. Cook until evenly golden on all sides—4 to 5 minutes total per fritter. As each is done, use tongs or a slotted spoon to transfer it to a paper towel-lined plate to drain briefly; add to the bowl with the confectioner's sugar. Roll the fritters in the sugar and serve warm.

PENNSYLVANIA DUTCH APPLE DUMPLINGS

MAKES 3 DUMPLINGS (6 SERVINGS)

TODD: Something we used to eat up in my childhood. Typically, my grandmother, who lived in Lancaster, didn't do a lot of her own cooking. She would take my mom and me to the Amish markets there and buy a lot of prepared foods. These apple dumplings were always a special treat, so good with those tart Pennsylvania apples. I don't know why they call them dumplings, though. They are really just apples baked in pastry. To do ahead, you could wrap the apples earlier in the day, refrigerate them, and bake them about an hour before dinnertime, so they can rest. Or, bake them off earlier in the day, do not refrigerate them, and then reheat them for a few minutes in a low-temperature oven just before serving.

3 cups all-purpose flour

1 teaspoon salt

1 cup cold unsalted butter (2 sticks), cut into pieces

⅓ cup ice water

3 baking apples such as Granny Smith or Honeycrisp

1 tablespoon freshly squeezed lemon juice

¼ cup light brown sugar

1 tablespoon unsalted butter, softened

½ teaspoon ground cinnamon

Granulated sugar for sprinkling

Make the pastry dough. Using an electric mixer on medium-low speed, mix the flour and salt with the butter until the butter is in pieces roughly the size of peas (you can alternatively use a food processor fitted with a metal blade, pulsing to cut and mix in the butter). With the mixer running, drizzle in just enough of the ice water to form a dough; then immediately turn off the mixer. Turn out the dough onto a lightly floured work surface and flatten it into a disk. Wrap the dough in plastic wrap and refrigerate until firm—2 hours or overnight.

Prepare the apples. Peel and core the apples. Brush them with the lemon juice. Using a fork, mix together the brown sugar, butter, and cinnamon in a small bowl or glass measuring cup, and rub all over the apples, pressing any leftover into the hollow centers.

Assemble the dumplings. Roll out the dough on a lightly floured work surface, forming an 8×24-inch rectangle a little less than ⅛-inch thick. Cut the dough into three 8-inch squares. Working with one at a time, place an apple in the center of each; fold up one corner of the dough to the top of the apple. Moisten the outside of the tip of the corner with a drop or two of water, then fold up the opposite corner and overlap the tip onto the first; press together (the water will help the dough adhere to itself). Repeat with the two remaining corners. Place the dumplings in a baking pan and refrigerate for at least 1 hour.

Bake the dumplings. Preheat the oven to 375°F. Sprinkle the dumplings with sugar. Use a small paring knife to poke a couple of small holes in the top of each dumpling to allow steam to escape during baking. Bake the dumplings until the pastry is golden and the apples are tender when pierced with a skewer—25 to 30 minutes. Cool in the baking pan on a wire rack for 20 to 30 minutes; serve warm, cutting each dumpling in half.

Apple Memories

ELLEN: Whenever Todd makes anything with apples, like strudel or dumplings, I always think of fall, the Shenandoah Valley and the Shenandoah Mountains. My dad built a little cabin on a couple of acres there in the '70s, right on the Shenandoah River. It was in a little village called Maureytown, 30 miles outside of Winchester.

Back then, Interstate 66 wasn't completed yet so you had to take Route 55 through Virginia's hills, heading toward Sky Line Drive. In the fall, the leaves would be turning mind-boggling shades of orange, sienna, and ochre, and apple trees were everywhere. We'd stop at our favorite spot, The Apple House in Linden, Virginia, and stuff ourselves with apple pie washed down with apple cider. The place is still there, I hear—known for apple doughnuts, apparently. But in my day, *way* back when, it was all about the apple pie, which was the best ever. A couple of those pies always found their way to the dinner table in the cabin that night.

TODD: I always think of apple dumplings in the fall. Going through a Pennsylvania Dutch cookbook researching a recipe for them induced a flashback of the big yellow refrigerator that sat in the corner of my grandmother's kitchen. Muzzie, that's what my brother and I called our grandmother, was such a good lady, but not really into cooking so much. Her refrigerator was filled with all the goodies she'd buy from the central market in downtown Lancaster where the Amish came to sell their wares. Whenever I opened the fridge, there would be containers of pickled eggs and pickled beans that held much less interest for me than the Amish desserts we'd find there, which often included apple dumplings ready to be baked.

FLOURLESS CHOCOLATE CAKE

MAKES TWO 10-INCH CAKES

ELLEN: This recipe has a lot going for it. It has fewer carbohydrates than a regular cake might, it's gluten-free, and it's suitable for holiday baking. If two cakes is too much, you can halve the recipe to make just one.

TODD: The key to the best flavor is to use bittersweet chocolate, which we define as between 65 and 75 percent cocoa solids (see On Chocolate for Baking, page 217).

2½ cups bittersweet chocolate, chopped

2½ cups unsalted butter (5 sticks), cut into pieces

18 large eggs, separated

1 cup sugar

Melt the chocolate. Preheat the oven to 300°F. Butter two 10-inch cake pans and lightly dust with cocoa or flour, shaking out the excess. Place the chocolate and butter in a large bowl and set it over a pan of simmering water. Keep the water simmering and stir the chocolate and butter occasionally, until melted and combined. Lift the bowl away from the pan and set aside to cool slightly (don't let it firm up).

Make the batter. Beat the egg yolks and sugar in a large bowl with an electric mixer on high speed until light and doubled in volume. In a second bowl, whisk the egg whites by hand until semi-stiff peaks form. Gradually add the egg yolk-sugar mixture to the melted chocolate, gently folding together with a rubber spatula. Fold in the egg whites until just combined.

Back the cakes. Pour the batter into the prepared pans, dividing equally. Bake until the cakes are set (a small jiggle in the centers is okay)—for 20 to 30 minutes. Cool the cakes in the pans on wire racks.

UPSIDE-DOWN PINEAPPLE CAKE

MAKES ONE 10-INCH CAKE

ELLEN: This is one of my favorite desserts, so I asserted my spousal rights and insisted Todd include a recipe for it.

TODD: The gold pineapples you find in grocery stores these days are terrific because they are always perfectly ripe and sweet and take the guesswork out of the selection process. I like to bake the cake in a cast-iron skillet because it looks rustic and makes a nice presentation if you turn the warm cake out in front of your guests. (You could also use a cake pan with deep sides.) I omitted the maraschino cherry garnish that was popular when we were kids; they are soaked in food dye and I just find them unpleasant.

1 ripe large pineapple

3½ cups sugar

2 cups unsalted butter (4 sticks), cut into pieces

4 cups all-purpose flour

2 tablespoons baking powder

Pinch of salt

3 large eggs

Seeds from 2 vanilla beans (see Chef's Appendix)

Whipped cream for serving (optional)

Peel and cut the pineapple. Use a strong sharp knife to cut away the peel: Take the top off first, and then stand the fruit upright and slice down the sides, then remove any eyes. Slice it horizontally into rounds about ⅓ inch thick. Use a paring knife or a small round cutter to remove the core from each round. Cut the rounds into wedges.

Make the pineapple "bottom." Butter a 10-inch cast-iron skillet or deep regular cake pan. Combine ½ cup sugar with 1 tablespoon water in a small saucepan; place over medium-high heat and cook without stirring until an amber caramel develops—5 to 10 minutes. Carefully pour the hot caramel into the prepared pan, using only as much as is needed to form a ⅛-inch thick layer over the bottom. Arrange the pineapple on the caramel, placing the pieces very close together (it's okay for them to overlap slightly) and completely covering the caramel. Set aside.

Make the batter. Preheat the oven to 375°F. Melt the butter in a small saucepan over low heat; let cool to room temperature. Whisk together the flour, baking powder, and salt in a medium bowl. In a large bowl whisk together the eggs, remaining 3 cups sugar, and vanilla bean seeds until combined. Gradually add the flour mixture to the egg mixture, stirring until smooth. Stir in the butter until incorporated.

Bake the cake. Pour the batter into the pan, covering the pineapple and stopping when the batter is 1 inch below the top. (If there is excess batter, bake it in a small buttered pan or in muffin tins.) Bake until a cake-tester inserted in the center comes out clean—30 to 40 minutes. Transfer the pan to a wire rack to cool slightly—about 15 minutes. Then, while still warm, invert a cake plate over the pan and turn the pan and plate over together—the caramel and pineapple will release from pan bottom. Serve the cake warm or at room temperature, accompanied by whipped cream if you wish.

SEMOLINA HALVAH CAKE

MAKES ONE 9×3-INCH CAKE

ELLEN: Halvah, that sesame- and honey-based confection, is something I always had a love/hate relationship with. A mountain of it, usually marbled, invariably sat front and center at the deli and looked so enticing surrounded by almonds and looking all chocolaty. Sadly, though, it often turned out to be pasty and dry.

TODD: That's why Ellen was adamant that we come up with a version that was more cakelike. Semolina, a durum wheat flour that works well with the toasted sesame halvah flavor, creates an interesting cake.

1 cup all-purpose flour

1 cup semolina flour

3 teaspoons baking powder

1 teaspoon salt

½ cup butter

½ cup sugar

3 eggs, separated

½ cup honey

1 teaspoon vanilla extract

1 teaspoon fresh lemon zest

1 cup milk

SESAME STREUSAL TOPPING

½ cup flour

¼ cup brown sugar

½ cup butter, melted

1 teaspoon sesame seeds

Make the batter. Preheat the oven to 325°F. Butter a 9 by 3-inch cake pan. Whisk together the flour, semolina, baking powder and salt in a medium size bowl. Using an electric mixer on low speed, cream the butter in a large bowl, add the sugar, then the egg yolks one at a time, beating until the mixture becomes golden and creamy—about 2 minutes. Add the honey, vanilla and lemon zest to the bowl, then the milk, beat until incorporated. Add the flour mixture to butter mixture, and fold in until incorporated.

Make the topping. Using a fork, mix together the flour, brown sugar, butter, and sesame seeds in a small bowl. Mash ingredients lightly with the fork until just combined and chunky.

Bake the cake. Spoon the batter into the prepared pan, spreading evenly. Sprinkle ⅓ of a cup sesame streusel topping over it; save any extra topping for another use (it can be frozen). Bake the cake until a tester inserted in the center comes out clean—40 minutes. Cool the cake in the pan on a wire rack. When completely cool, unmold and serve.

SPRING

TODD: Of course, it's only a matter of time before our winter cravings for stews and root vegetables give way to a vague feeling of monotony. In Washington, we always get a good bout of weather around the second or third week of February. It's kind of like a postcard of spring and our thoughts start turning to ramps, peas, asparagus, and spring lamb. It's also a bit of a cruel hoax, though, because those things aren't really in season yet.

ELLEN: So we ease our way out of winter with transitional foods, like kugel, egg salad, matzo brei, and some of the dishes that evoke my Mediterranean yearnings: sautéed spinach with sesame seeds, eggplant caviar, chickpea salad, quinoa salad with dried figs and mint. Mint and chives pop up early in the garden and find their way into many of our dishes.

TODD: Then our farmers start calling. Steve Turnage will show up at the back door of Equinox with the first crate of asparagus from the Nothern Neck, and sugar snaps and English peas aren't far behind.

ELLEN: For us Jewish folk, spring means Passover. We began offering a Seder for friends and family in our private wine room at Equinox in 2000. (We call that the Obama Room now because that's where the Obamas celebrated the First Lady's forty-forth birthday during their first Inauguration weekend.)

TODD: It was a steep learning curve for me that first year, not mixing milk and meat, the whole flour thing. I think I tried to put a pasta dish on the menu and Ellen just rolled her eyes at me.

ELLEN: And now he's a brisket maven!

BRUNCH

MATZO BREI 153

MORRISON STREET SOUR CREAM
COFFEE CAKE 154

POACHED SALMON MOUSSE
WITH CUCUMBER SALAD 157

TUNA NOODLE KUGEL 158

TODD'S DEVILED EGG SALAD 160

MATZO BREI

SERVES 4 TO 6

ELLEN: Every year around Passover, Mom would go crazy cleaning out the pantry, purging the house of anything with flour in it and replacing it with every "kosher for Passover" product she could get her hands on. Needless to say, there were boxes and boxes of matzo (we were a Manischewitz family) and that meant we had to figure out what to do with all of it, because you know we weren't going to throw any of it out. Matzo brei is a great brunch dish in general because kids love to help prepare it. The fried little cakes are so versatile—you can treat them like you would French toast, pancakes, or latkes. We particularly like them at Passover brunch. Our parents would sleep in and we kids would make matzo brei and eat half of them before they even got up.

6 matzo crackers (full sheets)

2 large eggs

¼ teaspoon salt

⅛ teaspoon freshly ground black pepper

½ cup unsalted butter (1 stick)

½ cup Strawberry Compote (see page 211)

MAKE IT PARVE. *Use margarine instead of butter to fry the matzo brei.*

Prep the matzos. Break the matzos into large pieces. Whisk together the eggs, salt, and pepper in a medium bowl. Submerge the matzos in the egg mixture.

Cook the matzos. Melt the butter in a large cast-iron skillet over medium-high heat, cooking until the butter foams and begins to turn light brown (chefs call this color *noisette*). Using a slotted spoon so the excess egg mixture drains, transfer the matzos to the butter and cook without stirring until lightly browned on the bottom—1 minute; turn and cook the other side for 1 minute. Taste the matzo brei and sprinkle with additional salt if you like. Transfer to a paper towel–lined plate to drain briefly. Serve warm with strawberry compote.

MORRISON STREET SOUR CREAM COFFEE CAKE

MAKES ONE 9-INCH SQUARE CAKE

ELLEN: Pretty much everyone has a recipe for sour cream coffee cake with a streusel topping. My mother clipped hers out of the newspaper in the early 70's. She became famous for her coffee cake—all of Morrison Street was abuzz about it in our Chevy Chase neighborhood growing up (see Mothers and Cakes: Lisa Kassoff, opposite page). The recipe doubles, even triples, well, but if you're making it with kids, prepare extra steusel topping because it seems to disappear before it even hits the cake.

2 cups all-purpose flour

1 teaspoon baking powder

¼ teaspoon baking soda

½ teaspoon salt

½ cup unsalted butter or margarine (1 stick), softened

1 cup sugar

2 large eggs

1 cup sour cream or plain yogurt

TOPPING:

½ cup light brown sugar

3 tablespoons unsalted butter, melted

2 teaspoons ground cinnamon

2 teaspoons vanilla extract

1 cup chopped pecans

Make the batter. Preheat the oven to 350°F. Butter a 9-inch square pan; dust with flour, shaking out the excess. Whisk together the flour, baking powder, baking soda, and salt in a medium bowl. Using an electric mixer on low speed, cream the butter in a large bowl; add the sugar and then the eggs, beating until the mixture becomes golden and creamy—about 2 minutes. Add the flour mixture to the butter mixture in three additions, alternating with the sour cream, beating until blended after each addition.

Make the topping. Using a fork, mix together the brown sugar, melted butter, cinnamon, and vanilla in a small bowl. Stir in the pecans.

Bake the cake. Spoon the batter into the prepared pan, spreading evenly, and sprinkle a generous layer of the topping over it; reserve any extra topping for another use (it can be frozen). Bake the cake until a tester inserted in the center comes out clean—25 to 30 minutes. Cool the cake in the pan on a wire rack for 10 to 15 minutes. Serve warm, right from the pan.

MOTHERS AND CAKES: LISA KASSOFF

My mother, Lisa Kassoff, did not do a lot of baking, but in our neighborhood in Washington, DC, she was known for her sour cream coffee cake. She clipped the recipe out of the *Washington Post* in 1972 and would bring it out in the three or four weeks leading up to the holidays every year for the next ten years. The recipe became yellow and faded over time—you'd think we'd have memorized the recipe by the seventh or eighth year, but no. There was something ritualistic about that little square recipe making its way out every year. In my mind, mom and coffee cake will always go hand in hand.

I must say, it is a killer recipe. It has everything you want in a coffee cake: moistness, an airy crumb, and lots of crumbly, streusel-y pecans on top. Mom and I would bake fifteen of them every year for holiday gift-giving. I remember marching into school with coffee cakes in my hand, fresh out of the freezer and wrapped in tin foil, and offering them to some of the staff and teachers. Then Mom and I would walk around the neighborhood and give away the rest of the cakes. That was a time when people didn't mind if someone rang their doorbell—and actually opened the door without asking who was there.

POACHED SALMON MOUSSE WITH CUCUMBER SALAD

SERVES 6

TODD: The salmon mousse recipe familiar to most people is the kind made with canned salmon, cream cheese, and gelatin set in a fish-shaped mold—served cold. This recipe, a puree of salmon, cream, and egg whites baked into a fluffy mousse, is much more refined and looks beautiful on a brunch table. We like this version, which is garnished with a lightly dressed cucumber salad.

2 pounds salmon fillets (skin removed)

4 large egg whites

2 cups heavy cream

2 teaspoons salt

¼ teaspoon freshly grated lemon zest

⅛ teaspoon freshly ground black pepper

Cucumber Salad (recipe below)

Make the mousse. Preheat the oven to 325°F. Cut the salmon into 2-inch chunks. Place the salmon and egg whites in the container of a food processor and process until pureed. Add the cream and pulse to incorporate; do not over mix. Transfer the salmon mixture to a medium bowl and fold in the salt, lemon zest, and pepper.

Cook the mousse. Butter a 8×4×3½-inch-deep terrine mold or 6-inch square baking dish; spoon the mousse into the dish and cover with foil. Place the mold in a baking pan somewhat larger than it, and place on the middle rack in your oven. Pour water into the pan to come halfway up the sides of the mold. Cook until a fork or skewer inserted in the middle of the mousse comes out clean—about 45 minutes for the terrine mold or 30 minutes for the square dish. Lift the mold out of the water bath and transfer to a wire rack to cool slightly. Run a paring knife around the inside of the mold to loosen the mousse and then carefully invert it onto a plate. Serve the mousse warm, thinly sliced, with Cucumber Salad as a topping or on the side.

CUCUMBER SALAD

MAKES ABOUT 2 CUPS

Peel 2 medium cucumbers; cut each in half lengthwise and then into thin slices. Thinly slice half a red onion. Chop enough fresh dill leaves to equal 1 tablespoon. Whisk together ½ cup plus 2 tablespoons olive oil and ¼ cup freshly squeezed lemon juice in a medium bowl. Add the cucumber and onion slices and dill and toss to mix. Taste the salad and season with salt and pepper if you wish.

TUNA NOODLE KUGEL

SERVES 8 TO 10

TODD: The Kassoffs introduced me to the kugel (see Kassoffs and Kugels, below), which my mother would just have called a casserole. This recipe is really just a tuna noodle casserole. Use good quality canned tuna—I particularly like Italian Cento brand tuna packed in olive oil.

½ pound extra-wide egg noodles

½ cup unsalted butter (1 stick), softened and cut into pieces

2 cups finely diced yellow onion (2 small onions)

2 tablespoons canola oil

3 large eggs

1 cup ricotta cheese, softened

1 cup cream cheese (8 ounces), softened

8 ounces good quality canned tuna fish, drained and flaked

1 cup whole or 2% milk

½ cup toasted pine nuts (see Chef's Appendix)

Freshly grated zest of 1 lemon

¼ teaspoon ground nutmeg (preferably freshly grated)

1 tablespoon salt

⅛ teaspoon freshly ground black pepper

Cook the noodles. Preheat the oven to 350°F. Lightly butter a 3-inch-deep, 10-inch rectangular baking dish. Bring a large pot of salted water to boiling over high heat; stir in the noodles and cook according to the package directions, until tender. Drain the noodles in a colander and transfer to a large bowl. Add the butter and toss until the butter is melted and the noodles are coated.

Mix the kugel. Heat the oil in a medium sauté pan over medium heat. Add the onions and sauté until shiny—about 3 minutes. Whisk together the eggs, ricotta, and cream cheese in a large bowl. Pour the egg mixture into the bowl with the noodles and toss to mix; stir in the tuna. Add the milk, onions, pine nuts, lemon zest, nutmeg, salt, and pepper to the bowl you mixed the eggs in and stir until combined; pour into the noodle mixture and stir to mix well.

Bake the kugel. Spoon the noodle mixture into the prepared baking dish. Bake until the kugel has risen slightly and is beginning to turn golden brown on top—about 20 minutes. Then raise the oven temperature to 450°F and bake until the top is caramelized—for 5 to 7 minutes more (the total baking time should be about 30 minutes, you can also caramelize the top under the broiler, but you'll only need 1 to 2 minutes to do that). Transfer the kugel to a wire rack to cool for 5 minutes before serving.

Kassoffs and Kugels

ELLEN: Kugel is one of those things that is just part of a Jewish upbringing. It's one of those not quite sweet, not quite savory dishes that is irresistible to me. My grandmother had a knack for making it just right, so that the wide noodles and cheese melded into fluffiness with raisins suspended all the way through it. In my mother's kugel, the raisins always made their way to the top, where they and the noodles wound up burning.

TODD: To be honest, the first time I had kugel at the Kassoffs it was something I wasn't familiar with. It was a little sweet, creamy, and full of noodles, kind of like a dessert but served at brunch along with all the savory deli items. So I started making kugels at home, using crème fraîche and golden raisins in the sweet version and then making a savory version as a form of tuna noodle casserole, substituting ricotta for cottage cheese. It's like a tuna gratin with a creamy interior.

ELLEN: Sweet or savory, you have to use broad noodles. They stand up to the baking process better than the small noodles do.

TODD: Even Italian pappardelle would be a good noodle to use here or in the Kassoff-Style Sweet Noodle Kugel on page 181.

TODD'S DEVILED EGG SALAD

SERVES 4 TO 6

TODD: We all grew up with deviled eggs and now they are making a big comeback. You see them on just about every restaurant menu in town these days, including mine. So I just took that idea and turned it into a salad.

ELLEN: Egg salad was always part of our deli order growing up and Harrison loves egg salad. It's so simple to make, yet Todd and I seem to argue about exactly how to do it. I like to use an egg slicer and rotate the eggs to get a fine dice and Todd prefers the eggs coarsely chopped and chunky. Plus, I like it kind of sweet, with sweet relish, and he likes it tangy, with cornichons. The one thing I don't compromise on is the mayonnaise: My Duke's wins out over his Hellman's, but you can use whatever brand you prefer.

6 large eggs, preferably from your farmers' market

¼ cup mayonnaise

1 tablespoon whole grain mustard

4 cornichon pickles, finely chopped

½ teaspoon salt

⅛ teaspoon freshly ground black pepper

Paprika for sprinkling

¼ cup minced fresh chives

2 scallions, finely sliced crosswise, including part of the green (2 tablespoons)

Cook the eggs. Bring a medium pot of water to simmering over high heat; lower the heat to low. Gently add the eggs; simmer, uncovered, for 14 minutes. Drain the eggs and rinse under cold water to stop the cooking.

Make the salad. Peel the eggs and coarsely chop them. Mix the mayonnaise, mustard, cornichons, salt, and pepper in a medium bowl; gently fold in the eggs. Transfer the salad to a serving bowl; sprinkle lightly with paprika and then scatter the chives and scallions over the top.

STARTERS

COUSCOUS SALAD 163

SPRING ASPARAGUS AND PICKLED RED
ONION SALAD 164

SWEET RED PEPPER HUMMUS 168

EARLY SPRING PEA SOUP 169

QUINOA SALAD WITH FIGS AND MINT 171

EGGPLANT CAVIAR WITH PITA CHIPS 172

COUSCOUS SALAD

MAKES 3½ TO 4 CUPS

ELLEN: Couscous is so easy to prepare—it's a one-to-one ratio of liquid and couscous, boiling the water or stock and pouring it over the couscous, covering it and letting it steam for several minutes. For this recipe, we add lots of roasted veggies and dress everything with a citrusy vinaigrette.

TODD: We love to use our panini press, George Foreman grill, or cast-iron grill pan in the cold weather months when we can't cook outside because we like the charred flavor that cooking process imparts.

2 cups quick-cooking couscous

2 cups vegetable stock (recipe in Chef's Appendix) or water

1 large zucchini, cut into ¼-inch rounds

1 large red onion, cut in half crosswise and each half quartered

6 shitake mushrooms (about 2 ounces), stems removed

6 tablespoons olive oil

1 roasted red bell pepper (see Chef's Appendix), diced

4 scallions, thinly sliced crosswise, including part of the green (½ cup)

2 tablespoons freshly squeezed orange juice

1 teaspoon freshly grated orange zest

1 tablespoon champagne vinegar

1 tablespoon chopped fresh mint

¼ teaspoon ground cumin

½ teaspoon salt

⅛ teaspoon freshly ground black pepper

½ cup toasted slivered almonds (see Chef's Appendix)

Steam the couscous. Place the couscous in a large heatproof bowl. Bring the stock to boiling in a small saucepan over high heat; pour over the couscous. Cover the bowl with plastic wrap and set aside for 10 minutes to let the couscous steam. Then uncover the bowl and fluff the couscous with a fork. Keep in a warm place.

Grill the vegetables. Meanwhile, heat a panini press or gas or charcoal grill to high. Toss the zucchini, onions, and mushrooms with 2 tablespoons of the oil. Grill the vegetables until they are tender and slightly charred—6 to 8 minutes. Cut the vegetables into bite-size pieces and add to the bowl with the couscous; add the roasted peppers and scallions and toss to mix well.

Dress the salad. To make a vinaigrette, whisk together the orange juice, orange zest, vinegar, and remaining 4 tablespoons oil until well combined and then stir in the mint. Pour the vinaigrette over the couscous, mixing well. Mix in the cumin, salt, and black pepper. Taste the salad and add more cumin, salt, or pepper if you wish. Sprinkle the almonds over the top and serve.

SPRING ASPARAGUS AND PICKLED RED ONION SALAD

SERVES 6

TODD: This is an excellent starter for a Shabbat or holiday dinner. There is just something so elegant about asparagus stalks, with their bright green color and tight, floral-like tips. It's a good idea to go the extra mile, as we do in restaurants, and peel the asparagus. The outside of the stalks can be fibrous, so that step ensures that every bite will be tender and that the presentation as a whole will look refined (see Thoughts on Asparagus, page 165).

36 jumbo asparagus spears, peeled

2 cups Pickled Red Onions (recipe follows)

3 cups mixed baby salad greens, such as mache, frissée, and red oak leaf lettuce, washed and spun dry

1 teaspoon salt

⅛ teaspoon freshly ground black pepper

1 cup Sherry Mustard Vinaigrette (recipe follows)

Parmesan cheese to shave over salad

MAKE IT PARVE. *Omit the Parmesan shavings; the salad won't be the same but it still will be tasty.*

Cook the asparagus. Bring a medium saucepan of lightly salted water to simmering over high heat. Add the asparagus and boil until al dente (firm to the bite)—3 to 4 minutes. Using tongs, transfer the asparagus to a bowl of ice water and allow to chill completely (add more ice if you need to). Then transfer the asparagus to paper towels or kitchen towels to drain.

Arrange the salad. Lay six asparagus on each of six plates. Divide the Pickled Red Onions equally over the asparagus. In a large bowl, toss the salad greens with Sherry Mustard Vinaigrette to taste; mound them on top of the onions and asparagus, dividing equally. Using a vegetable peeler or cheese plane, shave eighteen very thin slices of Parmesan cheese and lay three on top of each plate of salad. Drizzle with additional Vinaigrette if desired.

PICKLED RED ONIONS

MAKES ABOUT 2½ CUPS

Thinly slice enough red onion to equal 4 cups (about 2 red onions). Combine 2 cups water, 1 cup red wine vinegar, 1 cup sugar, 1 teaspoon salt, and ½ teaspoon freshly ground black pepper in a medium saucepan; bring to simmering over medium-high heat, stirring to dissolve the sugar. Wrap ¼ teaspoon mustard seeds, ¼ teaspoon coriander seeds, and 1 bay leaf in a small piece of cheesecloth, tying closed with kitchen twine. Add this spice sachet and the onions to the sugar mixture and bring to boiling over high heat; immediately remove the pan from the heat and set aside to let the onions reach room temperature in the pickling liquid. Discard the spice sachet and if not ready to use the onions, transfer them with the pickling liquid to a food storage container and refrigerate for up to 3 weeks.

SHERRY MUSTARD VINAIGRETTE

MAKES ABOUT 1 CUP

This simple, versatile vinaigrette gets a little edge from sherry vinegar and adds a distinctive accent to green or vegetable salads. I particularly like it with ripe juicy tomatoes and also with roasted artichokes. You can add a teaspoon or so of fresh herbs if you like— oregano is nice with the asparagus.

Whisk together ¼ cup good quality sherry vinegar, 2 tablespoons red wine vinegar, 1½ teaspoons whole grain mustard, 1 teaspoon Dijon mustard, and 1 teaspoon honey in a small bowl. Add ¼ cup canola oil and ¼ cup olive oil and whisk until well combined. Season with salt and freshly ground black pepper to taste.

THOUGHTS ON ASPARAGUS

Asparagus is one of the vegetables that really signals the coming of spring and that our winter dependence on root vegetables is coming to an end. If you're willing to have them come from outside the US or from faraway states, they are available pretty much year-round these days. We, however, only use locally grown varieties.

Asparagus season starts sometime in early May in North Carolina and then spreads its way up the coast into Virginia. Steve Turnage of Rappahannock Fruits and Vegetables starts bringing us local asparagus around Memorial Day.

Once our Virginia farmers are exhausted of their supply, asparagus grown by the Pennsylvania Mennonites and other farmers becomes available through Tuscarora Organic Farmers Cooperative and Path Valley Growers. That keeps us in the asparagus game pretty much through July.

One side note about asparagus: Many wine aficionados are adamant about not having asparagus on wine-dinner menus; they claim the vegetable's "greenness" is a wine killer but I just don't agree with that. Especially in risotto, white wine's floral tones complement the grassy nature of asparagus. For drinking, Rieslings and Gewürztraminers pair excellently with asparagus.

Pickled Foods Belong in Your Repertoire

TODD: All good cooks should have a basic pickling recipe in their repertoires; to me it is as essential as using good salts and olive oils. Pickled foods bring so much to the plate: acid, salinity, sweetness, texture. They go particularly well with rich or fried foods because they cut through the fat. That's why, when Ellen started making falafel at home all the time and serving it with pickled vegetables like in Israel, it was just natural for us to put the combo on the menu at Muse Café.

For my brine, I like a foundation of water, apple cider vinegar, sugar, and salt (in the proportions given with the Pickled Heirloom Beets recipe, page 129), to which I add various aromatics: coriander seeds, fennel seeds, bay leaves, peppercorns, and garlic make a great foundation. Red pepper flakes, mustard seeds, cinnamon stick, cloves, and/or star anise can be good additions. Basically, cooks should try different combinations and adjust the recipe to suit their tastes.

SWEET RED PEPPER HUMMUS

MAKES 4 CUPS

TODD: Of course there are all kinds of prepared hummuses on the market nowadays, but there is really nothing like making homemade chickpea puree, starting with dried chickpeas and cooking them with aromatics. I really learned a lot about cooking with chickpeas from Ellen, who got turned onto them in Israel. Give yourself some plan-ahead time, because the chickpeas have to be soaked overnight. We roast our own red peppers, too, but you could easily prepare this hummus with canned chickpeas and/ or peppers. It just wouldn't be as good as ours, of course!

1½ cups dried chickpeas, soaked in water overnight

2 bay leaves

3 whole garlic cloves

2½ teaspoons salt

1 roasted red bell pepper (see Chef's Appendix), diced

2 tablespoons tahini (sesame paste)

2 tablespoons freshly squeezed lemon juice

½ cup good quality olive oil

⅛ teaspoon freshly ground black pepper

Pita chips or crudités for serving

Cook the chickpeas. Drain the soaking water from the chickpeas and place them in a medium saucepan; add 2 of the garlic cloves, the bay leaves, and 1½ teaspoons of the salt. Cover with 4 inches water. Bring to boiling over high heat; lower the heat to medium and simmer, uncovered, until the chickpeas are cooked (chewable but not mushy)—about 1 hour.

Purée the hummus. Drain the chickpeas in a colander; discard the garlic and bay leaves and transfer the chickpeas to the container of a food processor fitted with a metal blade. Add the roasted pepper, tahini, and lemon juice. Mince the remaining garlic clove and add to the processor along with the remaining 1 teaspoon salt and the black pepper. Process until the mixture is smooth. Then with the machine still running, slowly add the oil until incorporated. Transfer the hummus to a serving bowl. Serve with pita chips or crudités.

EARLY SPRING PEA SOUP

SERVES 4

TODD: Peas are synonymous with springtime. Their lovely green color and subtle sweetness have such a nice delicateness that you just shouldn't mess with them too much. Some stock, some onion and garlic, and a garnish of crème fraîche and mint—that's really all you need. We serve this soup chilled, but you can absolutely serve it warm.

SOUP:

¼ cup canola oil

1 medium yellow onion, minced

1 large garlic clove, minced

1 pound fresh or thawed frozen shelled English peas (petit pois)

6 cups vegetable or chicken stock (recipes in Chef's Appendix)

1 teaspoon salt

$\frac{1}{16}$ teaspoon freshly ground white pepper

½ teaspoon sugar (if needed)

GARNISH:

2 cups fresh or thawed frozen shelled peas

¼ cup crème fraîche or sour cream

4 mint leaves, very finely and neatly diced

MAKE IT PARVE. *Omit the sour cream or crème fraîche garnish.*

Cook the soup. Heat the oil in a medium saucepan over medium heat. Stir in the onions and garlic. Sauté until the onions are shining and garlic is aromatic—for 3 minutes. Add the peas, vegetable stock, salt, and pepper. If your peas are sweet you shouldn't need the sugar, but sugar will help boost the flavor, so if you need it, stir it in now. Bring the soup to simmering, lower the heat to low and let the soup simmer until the peas are tender—about 20 minutes.

Puree the soup. Working in batches, transfer the soup to the container of a food processor fitted with a metal blade and process to a smooth purée. Pour the soup through a fine mesh strainer into a medium bowl. Cover and refrigerate until chilled and you are ready to serve it—at least 60 minutes (you can alternatively place the bowl over another bowl filled with ice). Taste the soup and add more salt or pepper if you wish.

Blanch the peas for the garnish. If using fresh peas for the garnish, bring a medium pot of water to boiling over high heat, add the peas, and cook until crisp-tender—2 to 3 minutes. Drain in a colander and rinse under cold water to stop the cooking.

To serve, ladle the soup into individual bowls and top each with some peas, 1 tablespoon of crème fraîche, and a sprinkling of mint.

QUINOA SALAD WITH FIGS AND MINT

MAKES 4 CUPS

TODD: Even though quinoa is a South American grain, we love to use it as you would Mediterannean grains, like farro or couscous. It's a grain that you don't see enough of on menus and tables in my opinion. It has a wonderful, nutty taste and it is gluten-free, which is something for which we are getting more and more requests at our restaurants. The red wine vinaigrette (store any extra in the fridge; it will last for weeks and is good to have on hand for quick salads) complements the sweetness of the figs, a favorite fruit of mine from my Italian cooking background.

12 dried figs

2 cups quinoa

4 cups vegetable stock (recipe in Chef's Appendix)

½ cup Red Wine Vinaigrette (recipe follows)

¼ cup toasted pine nuts (see Chef's Appendix)

2 scallions, thinly sliced crosswise including part of the green (2 tablespoons)

1 tablespoon chopped fresh mint

1 teaspoon freshly grated lemon zest

¾ teaspoon salt

Sprinkling of freshly ground black pepper

Soak the figs. Place the figs in a medium heatproof bowl. Add boiling water to cover; set aside until plump.

Cook the quinoa. Rinse the quinoa in water and drain. Combine the quinoa and stock in a medium saucepan. Bring to boiling over high heat; lower the heat to low, cover and simmer until the liquid is absorbed—about 30 minutes. Transfer to a large bowl and fluff with a fork.

Mix the salad. Drain the figs in a colander; transfer to a cutting board and cut into quarters. Pour ½ cup of the Red Wine Vinaigrette over the quinoa and toss to mix. Add the figs, pine nuts, scallions, mint, lemon zest, salt, and pepper; toss to mix. Taste the salad and add more salt or pepper if you wish.

RED WINE VINAIGRETTE

Place ¾ cup reduced red wine (see Chef's Appendix), ¼ cup red wine vinegar, 1 large egg yolk, 1 tablespoon whole grain mustard, and 1½ teaspoons honey in a blender. Pulse to combine and then slowly drizzle in 1 cup canola oil and 1 cup olive oil, pulsing every so often to combine; run the blender for 30 seconds to fully emulsify. Transfer to a storage jar; season with salt and pepper to taste. (This vinaigrette will keep for two weeks in the refrigerator.)

EGGPLANT CAVIAR WITH PITA CHIPS

MAKES ABOUT 4 CUPS DIP

TODD: Roasting really rounds out the natural sweetness of eggplant, whose seeds have a caviar-like appearance and texture, in my opinion. This purée with roasted garlic and lemon juice is like baba ghanouj, but without the tahini. It's just so simple and fresh—a perfect spring starter.

3 medium eggplants

2 tablespoons olive oil (use a good quality to mix into the caviar)

3 garlic cloves, roasted or fresh and not peeled (to roast, see page 173)

1 teaspoon freshly squeezed lemon juice

1 teaspoon ground cumin

½ teaspoon salt

⅛ teaspoon freshly ground black pepper

Pita breads

Ground smoked paprika for dusting pitas

Roast the eggplants. Preheat the oven to 350°F. Pierce each eggplant in several places (use a fork or skewer) and place them on a baking sheet. Drizzle the eggplants with 1 tablespoon of the olive oil. Roast until the skins are blistered and the flesh is soft—about 60 minutes. (If your garlic is not already roasted, add it to the oven during the last 20 minutes of baking time.) Transfer the baking sheet to a wire rack and let the eggplants cool for 20 minutes. Keep the oven on.

Make the dip. Cut the eggplants in half and scoop out the flesh from the skins. Transfer to the container of a food processor fitted with a blade and process until smooth. Add the remaining 1 tablespoon oil, the garlic, lemon juice, cumin, salt, and pepper and pulse to combine.

Make pita chips. Cut the pitas into wedges. Arrange on a baking sheet and place in the oven until lightly toasted, golden, and crispy—15 to 20 minutes. Lightly sprinkle the pitas with the smoked paprika.

ROASTED GARLIC

Preheat the oven to 350°F. Separate the cloves from a garlic bulb but do not peel them. Scatter them in a pie pan or small roasting pan. Sprinkle with salt and pepper, drizzle with olive oil, and toss to mix. Roast until the skins begin to pop and the flesh is soft—about 20 minutes. The roasted cloves can be refrigerated in a food storage container for up to 1 week. To use, squeeze the flesh out of the skins.

TO ROAST A WHOLE GARLIC BULB, simply slice off and discard the top; sprinkle the cut surface with salt and pepper and drizzle with olive oil. Wrap bulbs in foil and roast for 30 to 40 minutes; when bulbs are ready the tops should be golden brown and lightly caramelized and the cloves should be tender.

LUNCH

BASIL-CRUSTED BREAST OF CHICKEN 175

GRILLED LAMB BURGERS WITH OLIVE TAPENADE 177

GRILLED VEGETABLE WRAP 178

KASSOFFS' SWEET NOODLE KUGEL 181

CURRIED CHICKEN SALAD WITH GOLDEN RAISINS AND SLIVERED ALMONDS 183

BASIL-CRUSTED BREAST OF CHICKEN

SERVES 6

TODD: This is an awesome technique, rendering the panko crumbs bright green and full of explosive flavor with fried basil leaves. It's a great recipe for people who like to make dishes and who have a bit of extra time to cook, say on weekends. The recipe calls for breast halves with the first joint of the wing still attached to them because the bone helps retain moisture and makes a nice presentation. Using wing-free breast halves is fine, too.

4 bunches fresh basil

Canola oil for frying

6 chicken breast halves, wing on (about 5 ounces each)

Salt

Freshly ground black pepper

3 cups panko bread crumbs

2 cups egg wash (see Chef's Appendix)

Fry the basil. Cut the basil leaves from their stems, you should have about 4 cups. Pour 3 inches of oil into a heavy saucepan. Place over medium heat and bring to 325°F measured on a candy thermometer. Working in batches, add the basil leaves and fry until they stop sizzling and darken slightly. Using tongs, transfer the basil to paper towels to drain.

Sauté the chicken. Preheat the oven to 350°F. Wash the chicken under cool water and pat dry. Season with a little salt and pepper. Heat ¼ cup canola oil in a large sauté pan over medium heat. Working in batches if necessary, sauté the breast halves, turning once, until they are golden brown on both sides and about 20 percent cooked—about 4 minutes total. Transfer to a paper towel-lined plate to drain and cool.

Crust the chicken. Working in batches if necessary, place the bread crumbs and basil in the container of a food processor fitted with a metal blade. Pulse until finely ground and the crumbs become green. Transfer the crumb mixture to a shallow dish. Place the egg wash in a second shallow dish. Dip each breast in the egg and then roll in the crumbs to coat both sides. Arrange the chicken in a baking dish large enough to hold the pieces in one layer.

Bake the chicken. Bake the chicken until fully cooked (to an internal temperature of 145°F measured on an instant-read thermometer) and the crust is firm and lightly browned—10 to 12 minutes. Remove from the oven and let rest for 10 minutes. Serve the breast halves as they are, or cut the wing from each and slice the meat; arrange on individual plates.

GRILLED LAMB BURGERS WITH OLIVE TAPENADE

MAKES 5 TO 6 BURGERS

TODD: We buy whole lambs at Equinox, which means we have to come up with ways to use up scraps and ground meat, so making burgers was a natural solution. The customers love them. They make a nice change of pace from traditional beef burgers and have that extra kick to them that lamb meat imparts. Lamb can stand up to bold flavors, so olive tapenade makes a perfect condiment. I like these burgers done medium rather than rare, so I cook them for an extra minute or so on each side.

2 pounds ground lamb (preferably shoulder cut)

1 small yellow onion, finely chopped

½ cup tomato sauce

1 teaspoon Worcestershire Sauce

¼ teaspoon Tabasco Sauce

2 garlic cloves, minced

1 tablespoon chopped fresh mint

½ teaspoon ground cumin

½ teaspoon ground fennel

1 teaspoon salt

⅛ teaspoon freshly ground black pepper

Brioche or potato buns

½ cup thinly sliced roasted red bell peppers (see Chef's Appendix) and Romaine lettuce for serving

Mix the burgers. Preheat a gas or charcoal grill to high. Place the meat and onions in a large bowl. Whisk together the tomato sauce, Worcestershire Sauce, Tobasco Sauce, garlic, mint, cumin, fennel, salt, and pepper in a glass measuring cup; pour into the bowl with the meat and mix well using your hands. Shape the mixture into 5 or 6 patties, each about 1-inch thick and 4 inches in diameter, dividing equally.

Grill the burgers. Place the patties on the grill and cook until done, turning once—about 4 minutes per side for medium-rare. Meanwhile, toast the rolls or warm them over the grill. Serve the burgers on the rolls, dolloped with Olive Tapenade (or pass the Tapenade around the table) and topped with crunchy lettuce and a few roasted pepper slices.

OLIVE TAPENADE
MAKES ABOUT 2½ CUPS

Finely chop 2 cups pitted black olives (Kalamata and Nicoise olives are good choices). Place in a small bowl. Add ½ cup diced fresh tomatoes (drain any juices), 2 teaspoons olive oil, 1 finely chopped medium shallot, and ¼ teaspoon chopped fresh thyme leaves. Stir together. Season the tapenade with salt and pepper to taste. Refrigerate in a food storage container up to one week.

GRILLED VEGETABLE WRAP

MAKES 6 WRAPS

ELLEN: Since these days I'm vegetarian, Todd makes sure that vegetarian dishes are well represented on all of our menus. We serve this wrap at Muse Café at the Corcoran Gallery of Art. It has a lot of my favorite vegetables in it—squash, eggplant, shiitakes—plus avocado and arugula. When we get them from our local farmers, we like to add grilled asparagus, too.

1 zucchini, cut lengthwise into ¼-inch thick slices

1 yellow summer squash, cut lengthwise into ¼-inch thick slices

1 small eggplant, peeled and cut lengthwise into ¼-inch thick slices

Half a small butternut squash, peeled, seeded, thinly sliced, and cut into 1-inch wide strips

1 medium yellow onion, peeled and cut into ¼-inch thick slices

12 shiitake mushrooms, stems removed

Salt

Freshly ground black pepper

1 roasted red bell pepper, cut into 1-inch wide strips (see Chef's Appendix)

1 roasted yellow bell pepper, cut into 1-inch wide strips

¼ cup olive oil

Six 12-inch spinach wraps

Tarragon Mayonnaise (recipe follows)

2 cups arugula leaves

2 avocados, thinly sliced

Roast the vegetables. Preheat the oven to 350°F. Place the zucchini, yellow squash, butternut squash, eggplant, onions, and mushrooms in a large bowl; pour in the olive oil and toss to coat. Spread on a baking sheet and sprinkle with salt and pepper. Roast until tender—15 to 20 minutes. Remove from the oven and stir in the roasted pepper strips. Transfer to a wire rack to cool.

Make the sandwiches. Preheat a panini press to 350°F (if you don't have a press, you can cook these on a grill pan). Lay the wraps flat on a work surface. Using a rubber spatula or small spoon spread the Tarragon Mayonnaise over the wraps, dividing equally. Arrange the grilled vegetables in layers in the middle of each wrap. Top with some avocado slices and arugula leaves. Sprinkle with salt and pepper. Fold up two opposite edges of each wrap to cover the filling, then fold up one of the remaining edges and roll each sandwich into a large cylinder. Heat a grill pan if using; spray the panini press or grill pan with canola or olive oil and grill the wraps, pressing lightly, just until nice grill marks form on them and they become slightly crispy—about 4 to 5 minutes in the press or, on the grill pan, about 4 minutes per side turning once. Cut each wrap in half and serve.

TARRAGON MAYONNAISE
MAKES ABOUT 1¼ CUPS

Whisk together 1 cup mayonnaise, 1 tablespoon chopped fresh tarragon leaves, 1 tablespoon chopped fresh chives, and ½ teaspoon freshly grated lemon zest in a small bowl. Taste the mayonnaise and season with salt and freshly ground black pepper if you wish. Cover and refrigerate until ready to use.

KASSOFFS' SWEET NOODLE KUGEL

SERVES 6

ELLEN: We Kassoffs love our kugels (see Kassoffs and Kugels, page 158). At Passover time, we serve this sweet kugel for a light lunch, especially the day after the large Seder meal. If you'd like to do this, too, make sure to buy noodles that are Kosher for Passover.

½ cup golden raisins

½ pound broad egg noodles

4 tablespoons unsalted butter (½ stick), melted

16 ounces cottage cheese

2 cups crème fraîche

4 large eggs, beaten

1 teaspoon vanilla extract

½ cup sugar

1 teaspoon ground cinnamon

1 teaspoon ground nutmeg

Soak the raisins. Place the raisins in a small bowl. Add warm water to cover and set aside to soak for 1 hour. Drain in a mesh strainer.

Cook the noodles. Preheat the oven to 375°F. Lightly butter a 9×13-inch baking dish. Bring a large pot of salted water to boiling over high heat; stir in the noodles and cook for 6 minutes. Drain the noodles in a colander and transfer to a large bowl. Pour in the butter and toss until the noodles are coated.

Mix the kugel. Mix the cottage cheese, crème fraîche, eggs, and vanilla in a medium bowl; stir in the sugar, cinnamon, and nutmeg. Add to the noodles and stir until combined; stir in the raisins. Spoon the noodle mixture into the prepared baking dish. Bake until the filling is set and the top is golden brown—30 to 45 minutes.

LET MY PEOPLE GO

I'm no foodie. When I told Todd and Ellen that I have to really restrain myself from going to McDonald's more than once a week, my brain was almost melted by lasers shot from their eyes, emanating from their inner souls. What can I say. I like a Number 2 Combo with bacon, Dr. Pepper, and hot mustard sauce.

Whether you believe it or not, when you are a culinary genius and a passionate restaurant guru, you need friends like me to create a balance with the real world. Friends who not only love McDonald's but find happiness in any and all drive-throughs. Todd and Ellen need friends like me, if only to make them feel better about the career path they have chosen. At least that's how I look at it. That's how I justify my involvement with this book.

In all seriousness, I am honored to share my experience with Jewish food with Todd and Ellen and all the smart/healthy people who are reading this book. I'm not Jewish but my brother-in-law is. My one memorable experience with Jewish food was a meal we had called a seder. (Which, if you are not Jewish or up on the Book of Exodus, is a meal that celebrates the Jews being freed by Charlton Heston from Pharoah in *The Ten Commandments*.) We ate matzo, a flat bread—the Jews were fleeing and couldn't wait for it to rise. We had lamb to represent the lamb's blood that was put on the Jews' doors so the Angel of Death would pass over their homes on the night of the tenth plague, when the firstborn sons of all Egyptians were killed. We ate bitter herbs to remind us of their slavery, salt water to remind us of their tears, egg to represent their rebirth as free men. And we drank lots and lots of wine to celebrate their freedom. My family takes the last part very seriously as we are very proud and happy that my brother-in-law's (and obviously Ellen's) ancestors were freed. Thanks Charlton/Moses.

—KELLER WILLIAMS, musician

CURRIED CHICKEN SALAD WITH GOLDEN RAISINS AND SLIVERED ALMONDS

TODD: When you go to the deli nowadays, you usually see bright yellow curried chicken salad with raisins and almonds right alongside the regular white chicken salad we're all used to. It has become part of the culinary lexicon—people just love it. My mom used to make curried chicken salad at lunchtime all the time because my dad asked for it. At the French restaurant where I had my first cooking job, the chef served it scooped into an avocado half.

¾ cup golden raisins

One 3-pound roasted chicken (such as Roasted Chicken with Rosemary and Lemon, page 112)

1 small red onion, minced

¾ cup toasted slivered almonds (see Chef's Appendix)

2 scallions, chopped, including part of the green (about ¼ cup)

1 cup mayonnaise

1 teaspoon curry powder

1 teaspoon salt

⅛ teaspoon freshly ground black pepper

Soak the raisins. Place the raisins in a small bowl. Add very hot water to cover and set aside to soak for 1 hour. Drain in a mesh strainer.

Make the salad. Pull the chicken meat from the bones, tearing into bite-size pieces and placing in a large bowl. Add the onions, raisins, almonds, and scallions. Mix the mayonnaise with the curry powder, salt, and pepper in a glass measuring cup; spoon into the bowl with the chicken. Stir together until combined. Cover and refrigerate for 30 minutes; serve.

DINNER

BAKED CHICKEN LEGS IN WHITE
WINE 185

GRILLED NEW YORK STRIP STEAK WITH
CARAMELIZED ARTICHOKES 186

PISTACHIO-CRUSTED LOIN OF LAMB
WITH ROASTED GARLIC JUS 189

PANKO-CRUSTED FLOUNDER
WITH PESTO BUTTER SAUCE 190

CABBAGE STUFFED WITH GROUND
BEEF AND ONIONS 192

BAKED CHICKEN LEGS IN WHITE WINE

SERVES 6

TODD: Chicken baked with white wine and chicken broth was a favorite of my mother's when I was growing up, but she always made breasts and legs together. Because those parts cook at different rates of speed, some of it was always kind of dry. This recipe uses dark meat only. By cooking the chicken on a bed of onions, you are half-braising and half-roasting the parts, so the skin remains golden brown and slightly crisp.

1 medium yellow onion, thinly sliced

6 chicken legs (about 6 ounces each), thighs and drumsticks separated

1½ teaspoons salt

½ teaspoon ground cumin

¼ teaspoon freshly ground black pepper

¼ teaspoon crushed fennel seeds

2 tablespoons olive oil

2 cups dry white wine (such as Chablis or Sauvignon Blanc)

1 cup chicken stock (recipe in Chef's Appendix) or water

2 bay leaves

1 garlic clove, minced

Season the chicken. Preheat the oven to 350°F. Arrange the onions in the bottom of a flameproof baking dish large enough to hold the chicken in one layer. Mix the salt, cumin, pepper, and fennel seeds in a cup. Drizzle the oil over the chicken pieces and sprinkle them with the spice mixture, rubbing it in with your hands. Arrange the chicken over the onions in the baking dish and add the wine, stock, bay leaves, and garlic.

Bake the chicken. Place the dish in the oven and bake until the chicken is cooked (160°F measured on an instant-read thermometer) and the skin is golden brown—about 45 minutes. Transfer the dish from the oven to the stove top and remove the chicken to a platter; leave the onions in the pan but discard the bay leaves. Skim the excess fat from the pan juices; bring them to boiling over medium heat, scraping up any browned bits. Spoon the onions and pan juices over the chicken legs and serve.

GRILLED NEW YORK STRIP STEAK WITH CARAMELIZED ARTICHOKES

SERVES 6 TO 8

TODD: Steak continues to cook after it's removed from its heat source (this is known as residual cooking) so it is vital to take it off the grill before it has reached your desired degree of doneness. If you want medium-rare meat, remove it from the heat when it is rare and let it rest for 10 minutes or so.

ELLEN: Couscous Salad with roasted vegetables (page 163) is a great starter for this dish because it goes so well with artichokes. Love the ones in this dish because they are a version of *carciofi alla giudia*, or Jewish-style artichokes that date back to Roman imperial times. They are really nothing more than artichokes fried in oil until brown and crispy. Todd adds garlic and shallots, which make them much tastier.

TODD: At Equinox we don't use frozen artichokes, but for the home cook it does save a lot of time not having to peel, core, and poach fresh artichokes in acidulated water. I think frozen artichokes are a great product.

1½ teaspoons salt

½ teaspoon freshly ground black pepper

2 tablespoons BBQ Spice Mix (see Chef's Appendix)

3 large New York strip steaks (about 16 ounces each)

One 9-ounce bag frozen artichoke hearts, thawed

Canola oil for frying

2 tablespoons unsalted butter

¼ cup olive oil

2 shallots, thinly sliced

1 garlic clove, minced

1 tablespoon chopped parsley

MAKE IT PARVE. *Substitute margarine or olive oil for the butter.*

Season the steaks. Mix ¾ teaspoon salt, ¼ teaspoon pepper, and the BBQ Spice Mix in a cup. Lay the steaks on a work surface, sprinkle with half the seasoning; turn the steaks over and sprinkle the remaining seasoning on the other side. Let rest at room temperature for 30 minutes.

Fry the artichokes. Meanwhile, preheat a gas or charcoal grill to high. Pour 2 inches of the oil into a heavy saucepan. Place over medium heat and bring to 325°F measured on a candy thermometer. Add the artichoke hearts and fry until they turn light golden brown—3 to 4 minutes. Use tongs or a slotted spoon to transfer the artichokes to a paper towel-lined plate to drain.

Season the artichokes. Heat the butter and olive oil in a large sauté pan over medium heat, stirring until the butter is melted. Add the shallots and garlic; cook, stirring several times, until aromatic and shiny—1 minute. Add the artichokes to the pan, stirring until they are lightly coated with butter mixture. Stir in the remaining ¾ teaspoon salt and ¼ teaspoon pepper, and the parsley. Keep warm.

Grill the steaks. Grill steaks to the desired doneness—about 5 minutes per side for medium-rare. Slice the meat into ½-inch thick slices and serve with a spoonful of the artichokes on the side.

WHEN RED MEAT WAS A TREAT

Food is often a statement of love and comfort but can sometimes be an indulgence, an expression of lavishness. The New York strip is one of those dishes that represented certain financial well-being when I was growing up. When steak was in the house—life was good.

My father, Ed Kassoff, was a real estate developer and you could always tell when things were going well for him because he'd come home with a big smile on his face and a bag from the butcher containing big, thick steaks wrapped in brown paper. Steaks were very much a treat, not a right, for us; in our house, the New York strip was definitely the cut of choice.

PISTACHIO-CRUSTED LOIN OF LAMB

SERVES 4

TODD: My mother, Weezie Gray, was from Lancaster County, known for its tremendous Amish lamb, so she exposed us to lamb at an early age. This recipe calls for the loin, the thick meaty section you see in a loin chop or the eye of a rack of lamb, but without bones. You may have to request your butcher to cut a loin roast for you. In this dish, the loin is completely defatted and covered with a lovely pistachio crust.

4 lamb loins (about 5 ounces each), trimmed of all fat

Salt

Freshly ground black pepper

2 tablespoons canola oil

1 cup all-purpose flour

1 cup egg wash (recipe in Chef's Appendix)

1 cup Pistachio Crust (recipe follows)

4 sprigs fresh thyme

1 cup Roasted Garlic Jus for serving (recipe in Chef's Appendix)

Additional roasted garlic for garnish (optional)

Brown the lamb. Preheat the oven to 350°F. Season the meat all over with salt and pepper. Heat the oil in a large sauté pan over medium heat. Add the meat and cook until golden brown on all sides—about 4 minutes. Transfer the meat to a plate to cool slightly.

Crust the lamb. Lay the thyme in the bottom of a baking dish large enough to hold the loins in one layer. Put the flour, egg wash, and Pistachio Crust each into a shallow bowl. One at a time, roll the loins first in the flour, then the egg wash, and then in the Pistachio Crust, pressing the crust securely to the meat with your hands. Arrange the meat on the thyme in the baking dish.

Roast the lamb. Roast the loins until they are medium rare (130°F on an instant-read thermometer) and the crust is firm and lightly browned—about 15 minutes. Remove from the oven and let rest for 5 minutes. Warm the Roasted Garlic Jus while the lamb rests. Slice the lamb into medallions, arrange on individual plates with extra roasted garlic if you like, and serve drizzled with Roasted Garlic Jus.

PISTACHIO CRUST

MAKES ABOUT 4 CUPS

Lightly toast 2 cups of pistachios (see Chef's Appendix). Cool and place them in the container of a food processor fitted with a metal blade. Add 1½ cups panko bread crumbs, 1 tablespoon chopped fresh parsley, 1 tablespoon chopped fresh thyme, ½ teaspoon salt, and ⅛ teaspoon freshly ground black pepper. Pulse until finely ground and well mixed—about 30 seconds. Store in an airtight container in the refrigerator for up to 2 weeks.

PANKO-CRUSTED FLOUNDER WITH PESTO BUTTER SAUCE

SERVES 6

ELLEN: Every now and then, my mother, like all Jewish mothers, felt it was necessary for us kids to eat some fish. But what was readily available in the grocery store were those Styrofoam boxes of flounder fillets that had been there who knows how long. Baking in a Pyrex dish with lemon slices, salt, pepper, and paprika was the preferred method of cookery. Consequently, it took years for me to develop a taste and appreciation for fish. Todd really opened my eyes to the wonders of fresh fish handled with care and expertise.

TODD: This dish appeared on the menu for a private party to rave reviews. We pair it there with potato purée and collard greens. It's basically a fish schnitzel with a basil beurre blanc stabilized with a touch of cream (that's a fried breaded cutlet with a basil wine-butter sauce). For the sauce, we use a homemade pesto (make it in advance to give the flavors a chance to meld), often using basil we grow at home. We always encourage using components made with fresh herbs (see Herb Power, page 191), but you can use store-bought pesto if you must.

PESTO BUTTER SAUCE:

1 cup packed fresh basil leaves

⅛ cup toasted pine nuts (see Chef's Appendix)

1 garlic clove

½ cup olive oil

¼ teaspoon salt

¼ cup freshly grated Parmesan cheese (1 ounce)

Pinch freshly ground black pepper

1 cup dry white wine (such as Chablis or Sauvignon Blanc)

1 shallot, minced

½ cup heavy cream

½ cup cold unsalted butter (1 stick), cut into cubes

Make the pesto. Place the basil, pine nuts, and garlic in the container of a mini food processor fitted with a metal blade. Pulse together, slowly drizzling in the oil; stop a few times to scrape down the sides of the container. Add the salt and pepper; pulse to combine. Transfer the pesto to a small bowl, fold in the Parmesan; cover and refrigerate until chilled so that the flavors meld—45 to 60 minutes.

Make the sauce. Place the wine and shallots in a small saucepan. Bring to simmering over medium heat. Simmer until the liquid has been reduced by three-quarters (so ¼ cup remains)—8 to 10 minutes. Stir in the cream and simmer for 2 minutes; lower the heat to low and add the butter cubes one at a time, slowly whisking until each is melted before adding the next. Remove the sauce from the heat and stir in ½ cup of the pesto. (Reserve any remaining pesto for another use.) Taste the sauce and add more salt or pepper if you wish. Keep warm.

FISH:

2 cups egg wash (see Chef's Appendix)

2 cups dry bread crumbs (preferably panko)

1½ cups all-purpose flour

½ teaspoon salt

⅛ teaspoon freshly ground black pepper

6 flounder fillets, about 5 ounces each

½ cup canola oil

1 tablespoon unsalted butter, softened

Crust the fish. Place the egg wash and bread crumbs each in a shallow dish. Mix the flour, salt, and pepper in a third shallow dish. Sprinkle the flounder with salt and pepper. Then, one at a time and being sure to coat both sides, dip them first into the flour, shaking off the excess, and then into the egg wash and finally into the bread crumbs.

Sauté the fish. Heat the oil in a large sauté pan over medium heat. Add the fish and cook, turning once, until the flesh begins to flake and is no longer translucent—5 to 6 minutes total. To enrich and help caramelize, add the butter 1 minute before the fish is done, stirring to melt; tip the pan so the butter runs into the rest of the juices and then spoon the juices over the fish. Serve immediately (use a slotted spatula to transfer the fillets to individual plates), with the Pesto Butter Sauce on the side.

Herb Power

TODD: When we were growing up, fresh herbs were not part of the culinary vernacular. You could readily buy curly parsley in the grocery store, but no one had even heard of Italian flat-leaf parsley, which is what most cooks prefer to use these days.

ELLEN: Thyme was something that was dried and sage was powdered and both came in a little red and white tins (the old McCormick tins from the 70's).

TODD: My mother would put those awful dried rosemary leaves on a rib roast—they were like little sticks and didn't even have much flavor at all. Today, mercifully, fresh herbs are readily available, so there is every reason to use them abundantly.

In our backyard in Washington, D.C., we grow rosemary, mint, sage, thyme, basil, chives, tarragon, parsley, and dill. There is nothing better than being able to walk outside and pick whatever you need. There is no denying that a stock made with fresh thyme, with its grassy, earthy quality, makes a vastly better stock than one made with the dried variety.

And dishes just come alive when finished with fresh herbs. A sprinkle of chives can be the difference between everyday mashed potatoes and something fit for company. The same is true for risotto—pretty much any dish you can think of.

If you don't have a garden, cultivate some herbs on your windowsill. And be sure to include a bay leaf plant (bay laurel). Fresh bay leaves add boosts of flavor to stocks, sauces, and soups, and the difference between fresh and dried is enormous.

CABBAGE STUFFED WITH GROUND BEEF AND ONIONS

SERVES 4 TO 6

ELLEN: This dish was the first meal I put together completely on my own, greatly influenced by Grandma Rose, whom I probably called several times while I was making it. It must have turned out all right, because it seems my attachment to cooking started that day and has only grown since. Todd's recipe pretty much remains faithful to mine, but he adds cumin, an integral spice in our Mediterranean palate, and some chili powder, for some zing.

8 green cabbage leaves

1 pound ground beef (ground chuck is good for this)

2 tablespoons canola oil

1 small yellow onion, finely diced

3 garlic cloves, minced

1 teaspoon ground cumin

1 teaspoon chili powder

½ cup water

2 tablespoons tomato paste

Salt

Freshly ground black pepper

2 tablespoons olive oil

Soften the cabbage leaves. Bring a medium saucepan of salted water to simmering over medium-high heat. Add the cabbage leaves and cook for 1 minute. Drain in a colander and rinse under cold water to stop the cooking. Transfer the cabbage leaves to a paper towel-lined plate to drain; cover with paper towels and set aside.

Make the filling. Heat 1 tablespoon of the canola oil in a heavy medium skillet over medium heat. Add the beef, stirring to break up. Cook, stirring occasionally, until the fat has been released from the beef—8 to 10 minutes. Drain the fat from the skillet and transfer the beef to a plate. In the same skillet, heat the remaining 1 tablespoon canola oil over medium heat; add the onions and garlic and sauté until translucent—about 5 minutes. Return the beef to the skillet and stir in the cumin and chili powder. Mix the water and tomato paste in a glass measuring cup and then stir into the beef mixture. Lower the heat to low and cook until any visible liquid has evaporated. Season the filling with salt and pepper to taste; transfer to a medium bowl, cover, and refrigerate until slightly chilled—about 45 minutes.

Stuff and bake the cabbage. Preheat the oven to 350°F. Butter a 10×12-inch baking dish. Lay the cabbage leaves on a work surface (if they are cupped, orient them to accept the filling). Spoon some filling onto the center of each leaf, dividing equally. Fold up the edges to enclose the filling. Arrange the stuffed leaves (with the loose edge down) in the prepared dish. Sprinkle with salt and pepper and drizzle the olive oil over the top. Cover the dish with foil and bake for 20 minutes. Remove the foil and continue to bake until the edges of cabbage begin to turn golden brown—10 minutes more. Serve immediately.

SIDES

WILTED SPINACH WITH SESAME SEEDS 195

STRING BEANS WITH SHALLOTS AND
TOASTED HAZELNUTS 196

PAN-ROASTED PEARL ONIONS AND
TURNIPS WITH LEMON THYME 199

SAFFRON RICE PILAF WITH
SPRING PEAS 201

CARAMELIZED CAULIFLOWER 202

WILTED SPINACH WITH SESAME SEEDS

SERVES 4

TODD: Chefs love to cook with spinach because it's packed with nutrients, has such a vibrant green color, and complements dishes without dominating them. Spinach pairs wonderfully with sesames, those tiny grainlike, protein-filled seeds packed with distinctive, nutty flavor. As side dishes go, this one is as easy as it gets.

2 tablespoons olive oil

2 shallots, thinly sliced

2 garlic cloves, finely minced

4 cups packed spinach leaves

½ teaspoon salt

⅛ teaspoon freshly ground black pepper

1 teaspoon sesame oil

½ teaspoon toasted sesame seeds (see Chef's Appendix)

Heat the olive oil in a large sauté pan over medium heat. Add the shallots and garlic and sauté until shiny and aromatic—2 minutes. Stir in the spinach, salt, and pepper, and cook until the spinach is wilted—2 minutes. Drizzle with the sesame oil. Transfer the spinach to a paper towel–lined plate to drain briefly, then place in a small serving bowl and sprinkle the sesame seeds on top.

STRING BEANS WITH SHALLOTS AND TOASTED HAZELNUTS

SERVES 6 TO 8

TODD: Blanch the beans ahead of time, even the day before, to make putting this dish together a snap. It's string beans almondine, except with hazelnuts. (You could use just about whatever nut you prefer: crushed macadamias, pecans, almonds, cashews, etc.)

1 pound fresh string beans

2 tablespoons canola oil

2 tablespoons unsalted butter

1 cup sliced shallots

2 garlic cloves, minced

2 cups toasted chopped hazelnuts (see Chef's Appendix)

1 teaspoon salt

⅛ teaspoon freshly ground black pepper

MAKE IT PARVE. *Use margarine or olive oil instead of butter.*

Blanch the beans. Bring a large pot of salted water to boiling over high heat, add the beans and cook until crisp-tender—3 to 4 minutes. Drain in a colander and rinse under cold water to stop the cooking.

Cook the beans. Heat the oil and butter in a large sauté pan over medium heat. Add the shallots and garlic and sauté until shiny and aromatic—2 minutes. Stir in the beans, hazelnuts, salt, and pepper. Sauté until the beans are warmed through and nuts are evenly distributed. Transfer to a platter and serve immediately, family style.

FORGET THE ETHNIC DIVIDE

Growing up, I never knew the difference between Jewish food and Italian food. Seriously, I had no idea there was a distinction between the two and not for reasons you might think. Yes, I'm a Jew-talian; Jewish on my dad's side and Sicilian on my mom's. But it does not matter what your religion or ethnicity is if you live in New York—you are surrounded by this mysterious blend that breaks any faith-based barriers or cultural divide.

This meshing via food is prevalent in almost every corner of the state from Buffalo to Albany, Binghamton to New Rochelle: at the Jewish deli, the Italian bakery, the bagel place, or the pizza place, a mix-and-match happens without one even realizing the lack of distinction. For instance, you can go into any bakery and get a great rugelach or hamantaschen in the mix of Italian cookies—you know, the ones piled high on those trays, the ones you buy by the pound. Yes, cannoli, Napolean, sesame, anisette, and the Christmas mix are right there with the Hanukah and Passover favorites. Often to be found among the lox, cream cheese, chopped liver, and onions at most bagel places are mixed olives, gardinera, and roasted peppers: At our house, this assortment is simply known as Sunday Brunch.

I lived on the Lower East Side for a stint, next door to one of the last standing bialy bakeries, and across the street from a pickling joint. Guess what I ate every day? And where can you get the best knish? At the pizza place, silly, that's where. Oh, are they out? Then check the Sicilian grocery, because they always have Coney Island's best knish. And the biggest arancini you have ever seen.

In New York, this lack of culinary distinction is so normal, so everyday, that it wasn't until I moved to D.C. that I realized its strangeness. This matter-of-course combo I grew up with was nowhere to be found, and I was in culture shock. I still am at times. Thinking of what awaits me at home, I can never leave New York without a detour through Howard Beach for salt bagels and Sicilian olive salad. Heaven.

—DORON FRANCESCA GREENBLATT PETERSAN, owner of Sticky Fingers Vegan Bakery in Washington, D.C.

PAN-ROASTED PEARL ONIONS AND TURNIPS WITH LEMON THYME

SERVES 6 TO 8

TODD: Late spring means onions to me and I go crazy for those sweet little pearl onions. You can find them already peeled in the grocery store sometimes (or good quality frozen ones), but knowing how to peel them is a good technique to have in your repertoire. There are many kinds of turnips available nowadays other than the large white ones we know from years ago. I especially love baby turnips, about the size of radishes, either the white ones or the purplish pink ones. They are sugary and earthy at the same time and look so elegant.

4 cups pearl onions, preferably a mix of red and white

2 cups baby turnips, tops removed

2 tablespoons canola oil

2 tablespoons unsalted butter

1 tablespoon chopped fresh lemon thyme leaves

1 tablespoon chopped fresh chives

Salt

Freshly ground black pepper

MAKE IT PARVE. *Substitute margarine or olive oil for the butter.*

Blanch and peel the onions. Bring a medium saucepan of salted water to boiling over medium heat. Trim off the root end of the onions. Add the onions to the water, return the water to simmering, and simmer for 1 minute. Drain the onions in a colander and rinse under cold water; pat dry on paper towels. Peel the skins from the onions (use a paring knife if you need it).

Peel and blanch the turnips. Bring a medium saucepan of salted water to boiling over medium heat. Use a vegetable peeler to peel the turnips; cut each in half. Add the turnips to the simmering water, return the water to simmering and simmer for 2 minutes. Drain in a colander and rinse under cold water; pat dry on paper towels.

Pan-roast the vegetables. Heat the oil and butter in a large sauté pan over medium heat; allow the butter to foam. Add the onions, lower the heat to medium-low, and cook for 5 minutes, stirring occasionally to brown evenly. Stir in the turnips and cook until lightly caramelized—6 to 8 minutes. Sprinkle the lemon thyme, chives, and a little salt and pepper over the top and stir to mix. Transfer to a deep bowl and serve immediately, family style.

SAFFRON RICE PILAF WITH SPRING PEAS

SERVES 4 TO 6

TODD: Rice was big in our family. We had rice two or three times a week and I still can't get enough of it. My mother was into the Uncle Ben's Long Grain and Wild Rice mix that she prepared with canned cream of mushroom soup. All of her casseroles had rice in them, usually those steam-in bags you could buy at the store. She still makes a rice dish with canned mushrooms that rocks.

ELLEN: Who doesn't love rice with goodies in it? Growing up we were big Rice-a-Roni fans. It was all about the San Francisco treat.

TODD: In a pilaf, rice is sauteed with onions (or shallots and/or garlic) and baked—or cooked on the stove top—in stock. Once the rice is cooked, other ingredients get added in: in this case spring peas and scallions. Saffron gives the rice a pleasant yellow hue, which really makes those spring peas pop.

2 cups shelled spring peas or English peas

1 tablespoon unsalted butter

1 tablespoon canola oil

1 medium yellow onion, minced

2 cups long grain white rice (not quick-cooking or instant)

¼ teaspoon saffron threads

4 to 5 cups vegetable stock or chicken stock

1 bay leaf

1 teaspoon salt

⅛ teaspoon freshly ground black pepper

2 scallions, thinly sliced on the diagonal, including part of the green

MAKE IT PARVE. *Substitute margarine or olive oil for the butter.*

Blanch the peas. Bring a medium pot of water to boiling over high heat, add the peas and cook until crisp-tender—2 to 3 minutes. Drain in a colander and rinse under cold water to stop the cooking.

Cook the rice. Preheat the oven to 350°F. Heat the butter and oil in a 4-quart ovenproof saucepan (or flameproof casserole) over medium heat. Add the onions and sauté until shiny and translucent—2 minutes. Stir in the rice and saffron; add 4 cups of the stock, bay leaf, salt, and pepper. Cover the pan with a tight-fitting lid. Raise the heat to high and bring the stock to simmering. Transfer the pan to the oven and bake until almost all the liquid has been absorbed and the rice is just cooked (chewable but still firm)—about 20 minutes. Add more stock if needed. Remove the pan from the oven. Stir in the peas and scallions until warmed through by the heat of the rice (place on a burner over low heat if necessary). Serve immediately.

CARAMELIZED CAULIFLOWER

SERVES 4 TO 6

TODD: This dish has been a signature at my restaurants for many years. These days there are many varieties of heirloom cauliflower available, like pointy Romanesco or mustard-colored and green cauliflower. Already delicious from being caramelized, it is paired here with almonds and raisins.

1 cup golden raisins

2 tablespoons canola oil

1 tablespoon unsalted butter

1 head cauliflower (or the equivalent mix of several heirloom varieties), cut into ½ -inch florets

½ cup toasted slivered almonds (see Chef's Appendix)

1 tablespoon chopped parsley

¾ teaspoon salt

⅛ teaspoon freshly ground black pepper

MAKE IT PARVE. *Substitute margarine or olive oil for the butter.*

Soak the raisins. Place the raisins in a small bowl. Add hot water to cover and set aside to soak for 1 hour. Drain in a mesh strainer.

Cook the cauliflower. Heat the oil and butter in a large sauté pan over medium heat. Add the cauliflower and cook without stirring until caramelized on the bottom—2 to 3 minutes (the less the cauliflower moves in the pan, the more evenly it will caramelize). Turn florets over and caramelize the other side in the same way, cooking until the cauliflower is crisp-tender and its edges are golden brown. Add the raisins, almonds, parsley, salt, and pepper. Toss well to combine. Taste and add more salt and pepper if you wish. Serve immediately.

HOME COOKING IN ISRAEL

Growing up in Israel food was a major part in my life. My mother cooked in a traditional Polish-Jewish way. I can still remember everything she served. One dish that I always adored was cauliflower latkes, which she would serve during the week, not on the Sabbath. Here is the recipe:

Take a head of cauliflower, cut it in sections, and boil in water until very tender; then drain. With a fork, mash the cauliflower and add bread crumbs and an egg or two depending on the amount, plus salt to taste. Make into burger-size patties. Melt some butter in a skillet and fry till brown on both sides.

She used a similar recipe with zucchini, except she grated the zucchini and did not cook it before frying. Nothing better than food one remembers enjoying as a child—of course there is chopped liver . . .

—ITZHAK PERLMAN, violinist and conductor

DESSERTS

MANGO, PINEAPPLE, AND
POMEGRANATE SALAD 205

CHOCOLATE HAZELNUT RUGELACH 206

WEEZIE'S SOUR CREAM CHEESECAKE
WITH STRAWBERRY COMPOTE 209

APRICOT HAMANTASCHEN 213

HONEY CAKE WITH CHOCOLATE
DRIZZLE 216

MANGO, PINEAPPLE, AND POMEGRANATE SALAD

SERVES 6

TODD: This is just a clean, light, and refreshing dessert. It's lovely at brunch (which is when we offer it at the Muse Café in the Corcoran Gallery of Art in Washington). It's also a great dessert after a big meal.

ELLEN: And it's obviously perfect for Passover. Pomegranates add the Middle Eastern touch that I adore and the tart, ruby-like seeds look so festive.

1 small golden pineapple

2 medium mangos

1 pomegranate

½ cup sugar

⅔ cup passion fruit juice

6 mint leaves, finely chopped

Prep the pineapple and mangos. Use a strong sharp knife to cut away the peel from the pineapple: Take the top off first, and then stand the fruit upright and slice down the sides remove any eyes. Slice it horizontally into rounds about ½ inch thick. Use a paring knife or a small round cutter to remove the core from each round. Cut the slices into ½-inch cubes and place in a large bowl. Peel and pit the mangos and cut the flesh into dice; add to the bowl with the pineapple and stir together.

Mix the salad. Cut the pomegranate in half and take out enough seeds to equal ½ cup (discard the membrane that divides the interior of the fruit). Whisk together the sugar and juice in a small bowl. Pour the sugar mixture over the pineapple mixture; stir to mix well. Stir in the pomegranate seeds and mint. Refrigerate at least 1 hour to meld the flavors.

CHOCOLATE HAZELNUT RUGELACH

MAKES 24 TO 30 COOKIES

ELLEN: These sweet pastries of rolled, filled crescent dough are another Ashkenazi dish that became popular among American Jews. Growing up, they were the ultimate impulse buy, because they'd be piled up on a cake stand near the cash register, inducing every child to nag her mother into buying a few.

TODD: To this rugelach, I added the love for hazelnuts I acquired working at Galileo for so many years. Rather than adding hazelnut-infused chocolate (gianduja), we opted to use bittersweet chocolate, chopped hazelnuts, and praline paste. This last really kicks up the nut flavor; look for it at a gourmet market or online. Make sure to clear room in the fridge and freezer large enough to fit your baking sheet.

2 cups all-purpose flour

3 tablespoons granulated sugar

Pinch kosher salt

1 cup cold unsalted butter (2 sticks), cut into pieces

10 tablespoons cold cream cheese (5 ounces), cut into pieces

1 cup bittersweet chocolate, chopped (see On Chocolate for Baking, page 208)

¼ cup hazelnut praline paste

1 cup toasted, coarsely chopped hazelnuts (see Chef's Appendix)

Cream for brushing

Turbinado sugar for sprinkling

Confectioners' sugar for dusting (optional)

Make the dough. Place the flour, granulated sugar, and salt in the container of a food processor fitted with a blade; pulse to mix. Add the butter and cream cheese and pulse until just combined and a dough forms. Scoop the dough into a ball and wrap it in plastic wrap; refrigerate for at least 2 hours (preferably overnight).

Roll out the dough. Lightly flour a work surface. Divide the dough into 2 pieces and roll out each to a 10-inch diameter round about ¼-inch thick. Cut each round into 12 to 15 equal wedges. Cut a very small vertical slit at the base of each wedge—this will help the dough roll into a cresent shape, like a croissant. Transfer the wedges to a baking sheet and cover with plastic wrap; refrigerate while you make the filling.

Make the filling. Combine the chocolate and praline paste in the top of a double boiler over (not in) simmering water. Stir occasionally to combine as they melt. Stir in the hazelnuts. Remove the top pan from over the water and set aside until the chocolate mixture cools to room temperature.

Fill the cookies. Line a second baking sheet with parchment paper (the paper will adhere better if you lightly spray the pan with nonstick cooking spray before laying the paper on it). Remove the baking sheet with the dough from the refrigerator. Working with

one wedge at a time, spread some of the filling over each wedge and then, starting at the base, roll it up and shape it into a crescent. Transfer the crescents to the prepared baking sheet. Transfer the baking sheet with the crescents to the freezer. Preheat the oven to 375°F.

Bake the cookies. When the oven is heated, remove the baking sheet with the crescents from the freezer. Brush the crescents with a little cream and sprinkle with turbinado sugar. Bake until golden brown—about 35 minutes. Transfer to a wire rack to cool on the baking sheet (crumbs would make a mess on your countertop). When ready to serve, dust the rugelach with confectioners' sugar if you wish.

ON CHOCOLATE FOR BAKING

Chocolate nomenclature can be confusing, so I think it's best to stick with percentages (the percent of cocoa solids). I find that chocolate in the 50 to 65 percent range provides the best overall flavor in most recipes, so semisweet would generally be the way to go, sticking as close to the upper range of that as possible.

PERCENT COCOA SOLIDS

Below 50 = milk chocolate

50-65 = semisweet

65-75 = bittersweet

above 75 = bitter

MELTING CHOCOLATE

Chocolate melts faster if you chop it first.

Microwave method: Place the chocolate in a small microwave-safe bowl and microwave on high for 30 seconds; remove and stir. If not completely melted, repeat the microwaving. Stir until smooth. Set aside.

Stovetop method: Place the chocolate in the top of a double boiler, over (but not in) boiling water. Stir occasionally until the chocolate is melted. Melted chocolate will "seize" (separate and become grainy) if even a drop of moisture mixes with it and there's no fix for this, so be careful that no steam or water falls into the pan with the chocolate. Set aside.

WEEZIE'S SOUR CREAM CHEESECAKE WITH STRAWBERRY COMPOTE

MAKES ONE 9-INCH ROUND CAKE

TODD: My mother was famous for her cheesecakes; she used to make them for the chef at the first restaurant where I worked, who in turn sold them and turned a profit (see Mothers and Cakes: Weezie Gray, page 211). I substituted mascarpone for some of the cream cheese she uses in this recipe, just to add an extra note of richness, but you could use all cream cheese if you prefer. The cake and compote must be made a day ahead to give it a chance to set. When serving, dip the blade of your knife into hot water and wipe it clean after cutting each slice. This gives you neat slices with crisp edges.

2 cups cream cheese (1 pound)

1¼ cups mascarpone cheese (10 ounces)

¼ cup sugar, more for optional brûlé

1 teaspoon grated lemon zest

½ teaspoon vanilla extract

3 large eggs

½ cup sour cream

2 cups crushed graham crackers (about 30 crackers)

2 to 4 tablespoons unsalted butter, melted

Strawberry Compote (recipe follows)

Mix the filling. Using an electric mixer fitted with a paddle on low speed, beat the cream cheese, mascarpone, and ¼ cup of the sugar, the zest and vanilla in a large bowl just until smooth—about 3 minutes. Beat in the eggs one at a time, scraping the sides of the bowl after each addition. Beat in the sour cream until the mixture is smooth.

Prepare the crust. Preheat the oven to 325°F. Butter a 9-inch springform pan and lightly dust with flour, shaking out the excess. Place the crushed graham crackers in a medium bowl and gradually stir in the melted butter, adding only enough butter to coat all the crumbs. Press the crumb mixture into the bottom of the prepared pan, covering completely. Spoon the batter over the crumb crust, spreading to level.

Bake the cheesecake. Place the cake pan in a slightly larger baking pan, and place on the middle rack in your oven. Pour water into the baking pan to come halfway up the sides of the cake pan. Bake until the cake is set—it should jiggle ever so slightly when gently shaken— for 30 to 40 minutes. Lift the cake pan out of the water bath and transfer to a wire rack to cool completely; refrigerate overnight.

(recipe continues)

To serve, run a knife around the inside of the springform pan to loosen the crust and then remove the sides from the pan. Slice the cake. If you wish, brûlé each slice by sprinkling the top with 2 tablespoons of sugar and then burning carefully with a blow torch just until a glaze forms; let cool for 2 minutes. Top each slice with a generous spoonful of Strawberry Compote and serve.

STRAWBERRY COMPOTE
MAKES ABOUT 2½ CUPS

This recipe works with Bing cherries and many other fresh fruits, too; experiment! To learn about using vanilla beans, see the box at right.

Hull 2 cups of strawberries and cut them in half. Combine them with ½ cup sugar in a medium saucepan. Split 1 vanilla bean lengthwise in half and scrape the seeds into the pan; stir to combine and then add the pod halves. Bring to simmering over medium-high heat and cook until the sugar is melted and the berries are softened—for 5 to 10 minutes. Remove from the heat, remove the vanilla pods, and transfer the compote to a small bowl (or food storage container); cover and refrigerate until chilled.

Mothers and Cakes: Weezie Gray

TODD: I owe a great deal to my parents, Bradley and Louise (Weezie) Gray. You could easily say that my culinary career took the path it did because of them, with my mother's cakes playing a prominent role in the scenario.

I had left the University of Richmond in 1985 and returned to my parents' home in Fredericksburg, Virginia, with the vague idea of going to culinary school. The Culinary Institute of America required two years of previous restaurant experience before they would accept me. I was a rowdy twenty-year-old chasing the Grateful Dead and I loved the restaurant business—especially the socializing. Well, my folks got their fill of that pretty fast, so they hatched a scheme, unbeknownst to me.

VANILLA BEANS ARE SOMETHING TO LOVE

Vanilla beans and vanilla extract have different applications. For baked goods—both batters and icings—extract is often the right choice. But when you are looking for a more intense vanilla flavor, for instance for ice cream or a savory dish, the fresh bean is a better choice and will add terrific flavor. The beans can vary in size depending on type, of which there are three main options: Bourbon, Madagascar, and Tahitian. I prefer Tahitian, but they can be expensive. Vanilla beans should be moist, not dried out. Store them in a cool dry place—not the fridge, which dries them out—I use airtight containers.

To use, split the pod lengthwise and scrape the tiny vanilla seeds into whatever you are making. For syrups and sauces, sometimes you will add the pod, too, in order to maximize the flavor, and then remove it when finished simmering. Your recipe will indicate which method to use.

Every Friday night, Mom and Dad ate at a little French restaurant called La Petite Auberge. Seven-thirty, Table 12 in the corner, Dr. Gray and Nurse Gray. Dad was the town urologist and Mom was his nurse. The owner, Christian Renault, was also the chef and the three had become friendly.

Well, Mom is a great baker and had a reputation in town for her killer cakes, baked in springform or bundt pans: German chocolate cake; blueberry, strawberry and cherry cheesecakes; all sorts of coffee cakes. She would take those cakes down to La Petite Auberge and give them to Christian, who would say, "Weezie, I'm going to put some crème anglaise on this cake and sell it." He just loved the idea of making an extra hundred dollars off those cakes he got for free and it delighted my mother that they were good enough for people to pay money for.

After dinner one night, my parents brought up the idea of my working for him. Now, Christian was not some easygoing, pushover guy, so it wasn't like he was going to give me a free ride. (He's also a sweetheart and a ridiculous classical guitarist—traits I came to know and appreciate over time.)

Christian's plan was this: I'd have to cook for free, but he would teach me enough of the basics to make me fit for culinary school. To earn enough money to pay rent and bills, I'd have to wait tables in the dining room.

Christian really put the screws to me, but looking back, I wouldn't change a minute of it. Sure, he was tough. But this is what he taught me: You cook, you inspire, you teach your people, and you run your business—the rest of it is a bunch of BS. To this day I consider him the model for how to operate a business as a chef/owner and in my heart I know that the way he and I do things is the right way.

It all comes full-circle. When Christian's twenty-one-year-old son, Raymond, graduated from Johnson and Wales College of Culinary Arts in 2003, Christian asked if I would take him for a year and I was honored to say yes. So Raymond came to work for me at Equinox. After that year, he returned to La Petite Auberge as the chef.

APRICOT HAMANTASCHEN

MAKES ABOUT 30 COOKIES

ELLEN: These filled pastries, tri-cornered to mimic Haman's hat and served during Purim celebrations, were a source of conflict in the Kassoff family growing up. Mom didn't give in to her children's entreaties not to buy any filled with prunes or poppy seeds, so a grabfest would occur amongst my brothers and me to see who could get to the apricot-filled ones first.

4 cups dried apricots

3½ cups all-purpose flour

1½ teaspoons baking powder

2 large eggs

1½ cups sugar

1 teaspoon freshly grated lemon zest

1 teaspoon freshly grated orange zest

¾ cup chopped walnuts (optional)

1 cup egg wash (see Chef's Appendix)

Soak the apricots. Place the apricots in a medium bowl. Add boiling water to cover and set aside to soak for 1 hour.

Mix the dough. Whisk together the flour and baking powder in a medium bowl. Whisk together the eggs, 1 cup of the sugar, and the lemon zest and orange zest in a large bowl, whisking until the sugar is dissolved and the mixture is creamy and foamy. Sift the flour mixture into the egg mixture, stirring together with a wooden spoon until combined and a dough forms. Wrap the dough in plastic wrap and refrigerate for 1 hour.

Make the filling. Drain the apricots in a colander, stirring to eliminate the surface water, and then blot dry on paper towels. Transfer them to a chopping board or bowl and finely chop. Mix the apricots, walnuts if using, and the remaining ½ cup sugar in a medium bowl, stirring until well combined.

Make the cookies. Preheat the oven to 350°F. Spray two baking sheets with nonstick cooking spray. Roll out the dough on a lightly floured board to ¼-inch thickness. Cut out 3-inch circles (use a biscuit cutter). Place a generous spoonful of filling in the center of each circle, then fold up three sides so the cookie looks like a 3-cornered hat, pinching the dough edges together but leaving the center open as shown in the photo. Gather the dough scraps and reroll; cut and fill in the same way. Arrange the cookies on the prepared baking sheets and lightly brush with the egg wash, which will give them a nice color. Bake until the pastry is golden brown—20 to 25 minutes. Transfer the cookies from the baking sheets to wire racks to cool.

SANDWICH COOKIES ARE NICE, TOO

For a different presentation (especially if you like to save the hat shape for Purim), make these into sandwich cookies. Use a small cutter to remove the centers from half the circles you cut out. Spread the filling over the whole circles and place a cutout circle on top of each one. Bake as above. You can dust the cooled cookies with confectioners' sugar if you wish.

USE ALMONDS FOR PASSOVER

This recipe can easily be transformed for serving at Passover. Simply substitute ground blanched almonds for the flour and omit the baking powder, and mix as directed for the Hamantaschen. The dough will be too sticky to roll out so choose one of the following options to shape and bake the cookies.

THUMBPRINT COOKIES. Wrap the dough in plastic wrap and refrigerate for 2 hours. Pinch off walnut-size pieces, roll into balls, and arrange on a baking sheet, pressing a hollow into the center of each with your thumb. Fill the hollows with the apricot filling and bake for 15 minutes.

SLICE-AND-BAKE COOKIES. Shape the dough into a log about 2 inches in diameter and wrap in plastic wrap; freeze overnight. Slice ¼-inch thick and bake for 12 minutes. Make into sandwich cookies with the apricot filling if you wish.

HONEY CAKE WITH CHOCOLATE DRIZZLE

MAKES TWO 4×8-INCH LOAF CAKES

ELLEN: I love this spice cake with raisins and chocolate because it's so versatile. It's a lovely dessert, but cut into little squares it goes nicely with an afternoon cup of tea. I also serve this cake at Rosh Hashanah, which I always associate with honey.

TODD: Make the glaze just before you're ready to top the cooled cake; if you make it too far ahead of time it will thicken and be too difficult to drizzle easily.

¾ cup raisins (optional)

Whisky or hot water, as needed to soak raisins if used

2¾ cups all-purpose flour

2½ teaspoons baking powder

2 teaspoons ground cinnamon

1 teaspoon salt

½ teaspoon baking soda

½ teaspoon ground cloves

¾ cup lightly toasted chopped nuts, such as almonds (optional, see Chef's Appendix)

3 large eggs

1 cup honey

1 cup canola or grapeseed oil

1 cup freshly brewed strong coffee

1½ teaspoons vanilla extract

Chocolate Drizzle (recipe follows)

Soak the raisins. Place the raisins in a small bowl. Add whisky or hot water to cover and set aside to soak for 1 hour. Drain the raisins in a mesh strainer before using.

Mix the batter. Preheat the oven to 350°F. Spray two 4×8-inch loaf pans with nonstick cooking spray and line the bottoms with parchment paper, or rub the pans with butter and dust them with flour, shaking out the excess. Sift together the flour, baking powder, cinnamon, salt, baking soda, and cloves in a large bowl. Stir in the nuts if using. In a second large bowl, lightly whisk the eggs to break them up; then, whisking after each addition to incorporate, add the honey, oil, coffee, and vanilla. Stir in the raisins if using. Make a well in the center of the flour mixture and pour in the egg mixture, stirring gently until combined.

Bake the cakes. Pour the batter into the prepared pans, dividing equally, and bake until a tester inserted in the centers comes out clean—45 to 55 minutes. Cool the cakes in the pans on wire racks for about 20 minutes; turn them out onto the racks to cool completely. Transfer the cakes to a platter and ladle the Chocolate Drizzle over the tops; let the glaze cool before slicing the cakes.

MAKE IT PARVE. *Skip the Chocolate Drizzle. It won't be so magical but the honey cake is delightful on its own.*

CHOCOLATE DRIZZLE

Chop 6 ounces of good quality dark chocolate (see On Chocolate for Baking, page 208). Put it in a bowl large enough to hold it and about a cup of liquid with room for stirring with a rubber spatula. Bring ¾ cup heavy cream and 1 tablespoon corn syrup to boiling in a small saucepan over low heat, stirring to combine, and immediately pour the mixture over the chocolate. Let stand until the chocolate is fully melted—for 1 minute. Then use a rubber spatula to gently stir the mixture together, starting in the center and using a folding motion. When you see an emulsification begin to form in the center, begin stirring in from the edges of the bowl. This will, with a little patience, result in a very smooth, shiny ganache that you can then drizzle over cakes or other baked goods while it is still warm. If you don't mind a few air bubbles in your glaze, you can simply use a whisk to bring the glaze together, which works faster.

SUMMER

ELLEN: I think more than any other season, summer exemplifies a true blending of the table for me and Todd, my experiences on a kibbutz in Israel when I was young solidified my Jewish connection to agriculture—understanding that agriculture is survival. To be able to farm is to be able to feed your community and that's what makes a culture survive. For centuries, Jews weren't allowed to own land, so the idea of cultivating land is not something to be taken for granted. When you add to that all the obstacles that Jews overcame to make the land in Israel productive, the significance of being at one with the land cannot be underestimated. That's why I am so dedicated to the cause of supporting farmers in general. In Israel it was all about the figs and avocadoes and apricots. Here it's berries, corn, and tomatoes.

TODD: By the time Memorial Day rolls around and the days start to heat up in Washington, Ellen and I are already craving tomatoes and corn even though we know those things are still a ways away. We know it's only a matter of time before we'll be picking plump, juicy figs from the backyard tree of our Crestwood rowhouse, but, man, it's hard to be patient.

ELLEN: Early June strawberries are what really kick off the season in our garden. We love to macerate them with a bit of sugar and a few drops of balsamic vinegar and spoon them over my homemade vanilla ice cream.

TODD: In addition to berries and figs, we also grow baby carrots, cherry and green zebra heirloom tomatoes, and every herb you can think of, all of which we have coming out of our ears come August. It's hard to imagine that a small plot the size of half a bowling lane yields so much bounty. Friends who come for dinner are always amazed at what our tiny plot of land produces, prompting Ellen to embark on one of her soapbox speeches about the virtues of growing your own food.

ELLEN: And I can't miss the chance to reiterate how important it is to support the farmers who grow food. That's why I make Todd stop at every farm stand we pass when we go on summer road trips to visit his parents on the Chesapeake Bay and my brother's family on the Jersey Shore.

TODD: Oh, those road trips. Ellen cannot bring herself to part with a plastic food container. We have drawers and drawers full of them in every size. She calls it "recycling," but hoarding is more like it if you ask me. "For the summer," she always says as she soaps up the empty containers from a Chinese take-out dinner. She packs them with ratatouille, Greek salad, succotash, panzanella, fried green tomato sandwiches, strawberry rhubarb cobbler—you name it. It always seems like more than the three of us could ever eat, yet somehow all of those containers are empty whenever we get to where we're going.

ELLEN: And ready to be washed out and used again! That's the Kassoff way.

BRUNCH

CHILLED SUMMER BORSCHT 221

SMOKED SALMON AND SWEET CORN
BEIGNETS 222

HEIRLOOM TOMATO GREEK SALAD 224

LOX, ONIONS, AND EGGS
WITH RYE TOAST 226

FRIED GREEN TOMATO SANDWICH 230

GRUYÈRE CHEESE PUFFS 233

CHILLED SUMMER BORSCHT

SERVES 6

ELLEN: My grandfather came over from Russia at a young age. His family brought a few borscht recipes with them. He ate it all the time—fall, winter, spring, summer, hot, cold, and any way in between. Beets were inexpensive and available even in the winter for Russians, so borscht was something directly linked to subsistence and an integral part of the cooking Jewish immigrants brought to America.

TODD: Beets are one of those dream ingredients for chefs. They are savory and sweet at the same time and are so versatile—they can be eaten hot, cold, pickled—and that color!

1 tablespoon canola oil

2 medium red beets, peeled and chopped

1 small Vidalia onion, thinly sliced

2 garlic cloves, chopped

1 cup freshly squeezed orange juice

1 cup port wine

4 cups vegetable stock or chicken stock, preferably homemade (recipes in Chef's Appendix)

1 teaspoon salt

⅛ teaspoon freshly ground black pepper

Extra virgin olive oil for drizzling

Peach Relish (recipe follows)

Cook the soup. Heat the canola oil in a large saucepan over medium heat. Stir in the beets, onions, and garlic; cook until the onions are shiny and aromatic—for 3 to 4 minutes. Add the orange juice and port and bring the liquid to boiling. Stir in the stock, salt, and pepper, and bring to simmering; lower the heat to medium-low and simmer the mixture until the beets are tender—for 30 to 40 minutes.

Puree the soup. Working in batches if necessary, transfer the soup to a food processor fitted with a metal blade and process until the mixture is smooth; pour the soup through a fine mesh strainer into a large bowl or food storage container. Cover and refrigerate until thoroughly chilled—for 4 to 6 hours or overnight.

To serve, ladle the soup into six chilled bowls, dividing equally. Spoon the Peach Relish equally onto each serving and drizzle with just a little extra virgin olive oil (about 1 tablespoon total).

PEACH RELISH
MAKES ABOUT 1 CUP

Make this relish shortly before serving the soup and make sure to use ripe, juicy peaches. If you wish, peel 2 medium peaches. Pit them and then cut them into ⅓-inch dice; add to a medium bowl. Thinly slice 2 scallions crosswise, including some of the green part, and add to the peaches. Pluck enough leaves from some sprigs of fresh lemon thyme to equal a little more than ½ teaspoon; mince them and stir into the peaches and scallions. Season the relish to taste with a little salt and freshly ground black pepper.

SMOKED SALMON AND SWEET CORN BEIGNETS

MAKES 24 BEIGNETS

TODD: We love serving corn fritters at Equinox, either plain or with an interior garnish, be it crabmeat, other vegetables, or, in this case, smoked salmon. We call for cold-smoked salmon here, but hot-smoked would work well, too. Smoked trout would also be terrific (see Of Kipper Snacks and Cured Salmon, page 16).

2 medium ears fresh corn, husked

3 cups all-purpose flour

1 teaspoon baking powder

1 teaspoon salt

⅛ teaspoon freshly ground black pepper

2 large eggs

¾ cup sour cream

¾ cup whole milk

1 cup finely diced cold-smoked salmon (about 4 ounces)

2 scallions, thinly sliced crosswise, including part of the green (¼ cup)

Canola oil for frying

Lime Sour Cream (recipe follows)

Blanch the corn. Place the corn in a steamer basket over boiling water; cover and steam for 5 minutes. Lift the basket and rinse the corn under cold water. When cool enough to handle, slice the kernels from the cobs (you should have about 1 cup) and set aside.

Mix the batter. Whisk together the flour, baking powder, salt, and pepper in a large bowl. Add the eggs and sour cream and whisk to combine. Whisk in the milk. Using a spatula or wooden spoon, fold in the corn, salmon, and scallions. Cover the batter and refrigerate for at least 30 minutes.

Fry the beignets. Pour 4 inches of oil into a heavy saucepan. Heat the oil to 350°F (measure on a candy thermometer) over medium heat. Using two soup spoons or an ice cream scoop, gently drop balls of batter into the oil; work in batches and don't crowd the beignets. Fry the beignets, turning as needed to cook and color evenly, until they are golden brown on all sides—about 2 minutes total. Transfer the beignets to a paper towel-lined plate to drain. Serve with Lime Sour Cream on the side.

LIME SOUR CREAM

MAKES ABOUT 1 CUP

Whisk together 1 cup sour cream, 1 tablespoon mayonnaise, and 1½ teaspoons freshly squeezed lime juice in a small bowl. Add ¼ teaspoon freshly grated lime zest and 1 tablespoon finely chopped chives; stir to combine. Cover and refrigerate until ready to serve.

HEIRLOOM TOMATO GREEK SALAD

SERVES 4 TO 6

TODD: In the summertime, I take every opportunity I can find to serve tomatoes, especially all the different kinds of heirloom varieties available in farmers' markets these days (see Say Yes to Heirloom Tomatoes, below). A Greek salad, with chunks of feta cheese, briny Kalamata olives, and colorful peppers always looks great on a brunch or lunch buffet.

1 head Romaine lettuce, separated into leaves, washed, dried, and cut into bite-size pieces

2 ripe medium-large tomatoes, preferably Green Zebra and Purple Cherokee, cut into chunks

1 medium cucumber, peeled and cut into 1-inch cubes

1 small green bell pepper, cored, seeded, and cut into 1-inch cubes

1 small red bell pepper, cored, seeded, and cut into 1-inch cubes

1 small red onion, thinly sliced

1 cup pitted black olives (such as Kalamata or Nicoise)

½ cup crumbled feta cheese, plus more for serving

Pita breads, to toast for serving

Sherry Mustard Vinaigrette (see recipe page 306)

Prepare the salad. Preheat the oven to 350°F. Combine the lettuce, tomatoes, cucumbers, green and red peppers, onions, ½ cup of the cheese, and the olives in a large bowl, gently tossing to mix.

Make pita chips. Cut the pitas into wedges. Arrange on a baking sheet and place in the oven until lightly toasted, golden, and crispy—15 to 20 minutes.

Complete the salad. Drizzle Sherry Mustard Vinaigrette over the salad and toss to mix (add as much dressing as you like). Transfer the salad to a platter and sprinkle more cheese over the top. Arrange the pita chips around the edges or on a separate plate. Serve immediately.

Say Yes to Heirloom Tomatoes

TODD: You will see a lot of tomatoes in my recipes, especially in the summer. Around tomato season, you always come across people who claim that the best tomatoes ever come from their region: "You never had Jersey tomatoes!" or "These Blue Ridge tomatoes are like nothing you ever had." Well, I'm sorry, folks, but I don't think there is anything as good as the Purple Cherokees, Green Zebras, or peach tomatoes that come from Virginia. Or the Sun-Gold 100s I get from Steve Turnage.

It used to be that all you could get were vine ripe tomatoes that you'd order from your vegetable supplier, who was getting them from California, Florida, or South America. Waxy, pale, flavorless, mealy . . . every restaurant in town was using the same tomatoes. So to be honest, I never really liked tomatoes very much, but they were a necessary evil. I worked in an Italian restaurant, for goodness sake.

I'd say it was around the mid-'90s that things started to change. Famed chef Jean-Louis Palladin, may he rest in peace, is largely responsible for encouraging a whole generation of chefs to acquire a seasonal consciousness. A main source of this inspiration was his book, *Jean-Louis Palladin: Cooking for the Seasons* (Thomasson-Grant, Inc., 1989). My copy, signed by its photographer, Fred Maroon, is well worn and something I still consult to this day.

Palladin was the one who got all of us to chase farmers down and buy things in season. He simply refused to use tomatoes in the winter, something that was unheard of back then but which is the norm for many chefs today. And the public, largely, gets this.

The variety of tomatoes that come from the mid-Atlantic region is vast. If there's something you don't recognize in the store, buy it. Taste it. Expand your mind and repertoire. Here are some of my favorites:

- Juicy Purple Cherokees have a higher level of acidity and tartness, but an underlying sweet flavor.

- Green zebras (technically not an heirloom) are an early-breed and tart. They add a nice color contrast to red and yellow tomatoes.

- Sun-Golds are a breed of cherry tomatoes that are bright orange, ultra juicy and bursting with sweetness. They are especially terrific in couscous or lentil salads or a Greek salad or simply tossed with some olive oil, salt, pepper, and a splash of white balsamic vinegar.

- We would buy Jersey tomatoes at the shore when we went to Long Beach Island in the summer. They are big, sweet, firm, juicy tomatoes with that bright summer boldness that makes you want to pile up slices of them on white bread, slather them with mayonnaise, season them with salt and pepper, and eat them right at the kitchen counter.

LOX, ONIONS, AND EGGS WITH RYE TOAST

SERVES 6

ELLEN: Whenever there were leftover bits of lox from a deli spread in a Kassoff house, there was likely a platter of lox, onions, and eggs not far behind (see White Paper Sundays: The Kassoff Deli Experience, page 228). This was especially true when visiting my brother, Eric, and his family at the Jersey Shore. Eric's father-in-law, Herb Iris, would go out and buy enough deli food to feed an army, so this breakfast dish made regular appearances.

TODD: The onions add some body and sweetness—it's like a scrambled omelet. You can use lox (which is not smoked) or cold-smoked salmon for this recipe, especially since the salmon gets cooked in with the eggs (see Of Kipper Snacks and Cured Salmon, page 16).

ELLEN: But you have to add the salmon right at the end so it doesn't get *too* cooked.

1 dozen large eggs

1 cup half-and-half

1 tablespoon salt

⅛ teaspoon freshly ground black pepper

½ tablespoon butter

¼ cup canola oil

1 medium yellow onion, thinly sliced

2 tablespoons unsalted butter

1 cup coarsely chopped lox (about 4 ounces)

¼ cup finely chopped scallions (include some of the greens)

6 slices toasted rye bread

MAKE IT PARVE. *Use water instead of milk and margarine instead of butter.*

Prep the eggs. Whisk together the eggs, half-and-half, salt, and pepper in a medium bowl.

Sauté the onions. Heat the butter and oil in a large cast-iron skillet over medium heat. Stir in the onions; cook for 5 minutes. Lower the heat to medium-low and cook until the onions are soft and shiny—3 to 4 minutes more.

Scramble the eggs. Raise the heat to medium again and add the butter to the skillet with the onions; stir until melted. Pour the egg mixture into the skillet and mix together with a fork to scramble. When the eggs begin to set, stir in the smoked salmon and scallions. Serve immediately, family-style, arranging the toast around the edge of the skillet, and passing additional salt and pepper at the table.

White Paper Sundays: The Kassoff Deli Experience

ELLEN: At the Kassoff home growing up, anytime there was white paper, that meant deli time, and deli time was happy time. Hearing the masking tape tearing off and seeing the white paper unfolding are emblazoned memories of my childhood.

Two or three times a month, my dad would announce on a Sunday morning that he was going to Posen's Deli. My three brothers and I would get very excited, because we all wanted to go with him, but he never took all of us at the same time.

Posen's was on Georgia Avenue, just over the Maryland line. It was right next door to a Mr. Wash, so getting the car washed was always part of the ritual. Posen's was an old-fashioned deli, with salamis, piles of halvah and rugelach by the cash register, the briny smell of pickles, smoked fish, deli meat, and people yelling out their orders and demanding that their corned beef better be extra lean!

If we weren't among the chosen ones to go on the run with Dad, we'd wait at home anxiously, setting the table with plates, silverware, napkins, and condiments not so much to be helpful as to while away some time. Then Dad would come home with four or five brown grocery bags filled with goodies.

Loaves of freshly sliced rye, marbled, and challah bread came out first. Then came the packets of wrapped delicacies, taken from the bag one after the other. The ones with grease seeping through indicated that sablefish or lox were on the menu that day. *RIP—RIP* the sounds of the tape being torn off the packages as we opened them. Corned beef! Pastrami! Tongue! Rare roast beef! Muenster cheese! Pickles! Then there were all the side containers: chopped liver, macaroni salad, whitefish salad, cole slaw, egg salad, potato salad, tuna salad, chicken salad. Then the sodas: root beer and cream soda (Dad was a Brooklyn boy). And finally the sweets: all kinds of Danish and, if whatever kids went with him that day were particularly adept at nudging, a marble cake. It's too bad that delis seem to be going to the wayside these days, because the days of white paper are still among my most cherished memories.

TODD: And don't forget the Jersey Shore.

ELLEN: That was the deli experience writ large, thanks to Herb Iris, who was my brother, Eric's, father-in-law. Eric married Herb's daughter, Kerry, in the early '90s and we started visiting the Iris family at their Jersey Shore beach house on Long Beach Island every summer for twenty-some years.

TODD: Herb Iris made the Kassoff's brunch look like a light snack. He would go out to the casinos in Atlantic City until 5 a.m. and not get up until noon. We'd all be out on the boat or at the beach, but by the time we got home, Herb would have hit the deli and all his favorite local markets.

ELLEN: When we walked in the door, there would be this unbelievable spread on the dining room table: bagels, meats, cheeses, pickles, every kind of smoked fish with every conceivable mayonnaise-based salad, pastries—enough food for at least twenty-five people and there were only maybe ten of us on any given weekend.

FRIED GREEN TOMATO SANDWICH

MAKES 6 SANDWICHES

TODD: We make these for brunch on Sundays when there is a little extra time to perform the breading process. These sandwiches are a wonderful way to use ripe heirloom and firm green tomatoes at their peak. They give you a real burst of summer between two slices of bread and taste especially good accompanied by Shaved Radish Salad (see Say Yes to Heirloom Tomatoes, page 224).

1½ cups all-purpose flour

½ teaspoon salt

⅛ teaspoon freshly ground black pepper

1½ cups egg wash (see Chef's Appendix)

2 cups panko bread crumbs

3 green tomatoes, cut into ⅓-inch thick slices

½ cup canola oil

6 ciabatta rolls, split in half

Tarragon Mayonnaise (see recipe page 178)

Tender arugula or spinach leaves, washed and dried

2 ripe yellow or red tomatoes, thinly sliced

Shaved Radish Salad for serving (optional, recipe follows)

Fry the tomatoes. Whisk together the flour, salt, and pepper in a shallow bowl. Put the egg wash and bread crumbs each into a shallow bowl. One at time, dip each green tomato slice first in the flour mixture, shaking off the excess, then into the egg wash, and then coat generously with bread crumbs. Heat the oil in a large skillet over medium heat. Working in batches if necessary, fry the slices until golden brown, turning once—about 2 minutes per side. Transfer the slices to a paper towel-lined plate to drain. Sprinkle with salt and pepper.

Make the sandwiches. Toast the rolls in a toaster oven until just warmed through. Arrange them on a work surface. Spread some Tarragon Mayonnaise over the cut side of each piece. Place a layer of arugula on six of the pieces, then top it with a few slices of red or yellow tomato. Cut the fried tomato slices in half and overlap them on the layered fresh vegetables. Invert the remaining six pieces of roll on top to complete the sandwiches. Serve with a taste of Shaved Radish Salad on the side if you wish.

SHAVED RADISH SALAD

MAKES ABOUT ½ CUP

Use the large cutter on a box grater or a mandoline to slice 3 red radishes into 1/16-inch shavings. Do the same with one-quarter of a red onion. Mix together 1 teaspoon mustard seeds, 1 teaspoon apple cider vinegar, and 1 teaspoon olive oil in a small bowl. Add the radishes and onions; mix well. Season with salt and freshly ground black pepper to taste. Cover and refrigerate for 2 hours before serving to allow the flavors to meld. Then taste the salad and add more salt or pepper if you wish.

GRUYÈRE CHEESE PUFFS

MAKES ABOUT 4 DOZEN 2¼-INCH PUFFS

TODD: For cocktail parties, my mother would either buy frozen cheese puffs or bake little rectangles of Pepperidge Farm puff pastry brushed with egg wash and sprinkled with Parmesan cheese. To make these puffs, known as gougères, you take classic French cream puff dough (pâte à choux) and add grated cheese to it. Gruyère has a rich, nutty finish, but the puffs are also very tasty made with sharp cheddar cheese. Warm out of the oven, gougères make an elegant start to a summer brunch—actually, they're very good year round.

1 cup water

1 cup whole milk

1 cup unsalted butter (2 sticks), cut into pieces

1 tablespoon salt

1¾ cup all-purpose flour

8 to 10 large eggs

1½ cups grated Gruyère cheese

Mix the batter. Preheat the oven to 400°F. In a medium saucepan, bring the water, milk, butter, and salt to simmering over medium heat; stir to completely melt the butter. Raise the heat to medium-high and bring the mixture to boiling; then add the flour all at once, stirring with a wooden spoon until the mixture is smooth, a film forms on bottom of pan, and the dough pulls away from sides of pan. Transfer the dough to the bowl of an electric mixer fitted with a paddle. Mix on low for 2 to 3 minutes to release moisture. Then beat in 8 eggs one at a time—the mixture should be shiny, golden, and slightly sticky; if it looks dry, add another egg, and then another if it still looks dry. When the mixture is smooth, beat in the cheese.

Bake the puffs. Line a baking sheet with parchment paper (the paper will adhere better if you lightly spray the pan with nonstick cooking spray before laying the paper on it). Spoon the dough into a pastry bag fitted with round tip about ⅓-inch in diameter (if you don't have a pastry bag, use a sturdy plastic food storage bag with one corner cut off). Pipe the dough onto the prepared baking sheet in a spiral motion, forming rounds about 1½ inches in diameter spaced 3 inches apart. Place in the oven and bake for 5 minutes; then lower the heat to 350°F and bake until the puffs have risen and turned a deep golden brown—15 to 20 minutes more. Serve warm.

STARTERS

QUICK SUMMER SQUASH RATATOUILLE 235

SUMMER TOMATO SALAD WITH CRISPY ONIONS 237

JOAN NATHAN'S ROMANIAN ZUCCHINI POTATO LATKES 239

SALAD OF ROASTED HEIRLOOM BEETS WITH CAPERS AND PISTACHIOS 240

CORN CHOWDER WITH SHIITAKE MUSHROOMS 243

QUICK SUMMER SQUASH RATATOUILLE

SERVES 8 TO 10

ELLEN: Making ratatouille is a good way to use up all that squash and peppers you wind up with in the summer. It's a very forgiving dish in that it doesn't get totally messed up by adding too much of anything or shifting ingredients to use up whatever vegetables you have on hand. Without the cheese, it's a nice vegan dish and can be eaten cold, but we often put it in a gratin dish, melt cheese on top, and offer it as a starter with grilled country bread.

2 ripe tomatoes

¼ cup olive oil

1 medium red onion, cut into medium dice

2 garlic cloves, finely minced

1 small eggplant, peeled and cut into 1-inch cubes

1 medium zucchini, cut into 1-inch cubes

1 medium yellow squash, cut into 1-inch cubes

1 red bell pepper, cored, seeded, and cut into 1-inch cubes

2 cups V-8 juice

1 tablespoon chopped fresh thyme leaves

2 teaspoon salt

½ teaspoon freshly ground black pepper

2 cups grated Gruyère or Swiss cheese (8 ounces)

Garlic Toast (see recipe page 27) for serving

Prep the tomatoes. Bring a medium-size pot of water to boiling over high heat. Drop the tomatoes into the water and cook for 1 minute. With a slotted spoon, transfer the tomatoes to a bowl of ice water to stop the cooking. Use a paring knife to peel the tomatoes; then core each one and squeeze out the seeds. Chop the tomatoes.

Cook the ratatouille. Heat the oil in a large ovenproof sauté pan over medium heat. Stir in the onions and garlic, cook until shiny—2 minutes. Stir in the eggplant, cook for 3 minutes. Stir in the zucchini, yellow squash, peppers, and tomatoes; cook until they are shiny and slightly softened—3 to 5 minutes. Add the juice and thyme; bring the mixture to simmering. Lower the heat to low; cover the pan and simmer until the mixture has thickened and the vegetables are cooked through—30 minutes.

Add the topping. Preheat the oven to broil. Stir the salt and pepper into the ratatouille; taste the mixture and add more seasoning if you wish. Sprinkle the cheese over the ratatouille and place the pan under the broiler until the cheese is melted and lightly browned—2 to 3 minutes. Serve immediately, family style, with Garlic Toast if you wish.

SUMMER TOMATO SALAD WITH CRISPY ONIONS

SERVES 4

TODD: This is another great way to take advantage of summer's heirloom tomatoes: marrying them with fresh goat cheese, basil, and shaved onions and then topping them with lightly fried, sweet Vidalia onions, which can be made a couple of hours ahead of time (see Say Yes to Heirloom tomatoes, page 224).

CRISPY ONIONS:

1 cup buttermilk

1 medium Vidalia onion, sliced into ⅛-inch thick rounds

2 cups all-purpose flour

½ teaspoon chili powder

¼ teaspoon smoked paprika

1 teaspoon salt

⅛ teaspoon freshly ground black pepper

Canola oil for frying

SALAD:

3 ripe tomatoes, preferably an heirloom variety, cut into ⅓ inch thick slices

Salt

Freshly ground black pepper

1 small red onion, very thinly sliced

¼ cup crumbled goat cheese (preferably a fresh, local variety that has aged for 1 month)

6 fresh basil leaves, coarsely chopped

½ cup Balsamic Vinaigrette (recipeopposite)

Fry the onions. Put the buttermilk in a small bowl and add the onions. Mix the flour, chili powder, paprika, salt, and pepper in a medium bowl. Pour 3 inches of oil into a heavy saucepan. Heat the oil to 350°F (measure on a candy thermometer) over medium heat. Drain the onions in a mesh strainer and then add them to the flour mixture, tossing to coat. Using your hands or tongs, lift the onions from the flour, shaking off the excess, and gently add them to the oil; fry until they turn golden brown—2 to 3 minutes. Use a slotted spoon to transfer the onions to a paper towel–lined plate to drain. Taste the onions and sprinkle with more salt or pepper if you wish.

Make the salad. Arrange the tomatoes on four individual plates, dividing equally. Sprinkle with salt and pepper. Scatter the red onions evenly over the tomatoes and then top with the cheese, dividing equally. Drizzle some Balsamic Vinaigrette over each serving; divide the crispy onions and the basil on top. Serve immediately.

BALSAMIC VINAIGRETTE

MAKES ABOUT 1 CUP

Whisk together ¼ cup balsamic vinegar, 2 tablespoons sherry vinegar, 1 teaspoon honey, and I teaspoon whole grain mustard in a small bowl. Add ¼ cup olive oil and ¼ cup canola oil and whisk until well combined. Season with salt and freshly ground black pepper to taste.

FRENCH FOR LATKE

I was raised in Nice, France, in the 1950s. I spent eight months of the year in school; my summers were spent at my Grandmother Jeanne's in the Morvan region of Burgundy. So, my taste buds were mainly Niçoise for most of the year and at my grandmother's they turned to the local produce, game, and fish of the French countryside. Once in a while in the summer, my grandmother would make *la rappé*. She would grate old starchy potatoes and onion and bind them with flour and egg and shape the mixture into patties, which she would cook in a cast iron skillet until golden brown. You could smell it from a mile away. We would eat that with a small garden salad for dinner. In the early 1970s, after I had moved to the U.S., I was invited to a party. I noticed a memorable smell. I ate one of the potato latkes they were making and I thought "well this is *la rappé*, from my childhood," and they were delicious.

—CHRISTIAN RENAULD, chef and restaurateur

JOAN NATHAN'S ROMANIAN ZUCCHINI POTATO LATKES

MAKES TWELVE SMALL LATKES

TODD: Cookbook author and dear friend Joan Nathan has really been an inspiration to Ellen and me over the years, especially for the development of this book. I wanted to have a summer latke recipe that used zucchini in it because we always have so much of the squash to use up in the summer, thanks to our farmer friends like Steve Turnage (see Steve Turnage and Virginia Produce, page 264). Try though I did, I could not come up with a recipe that surpassed Joan's and she was gracious enough to let me include this recipe from *Joan Nathan's Jewish Holiday Cookbook* (Schocken Books, 2004).

2 pounds zucchini, peeled

2 large Yukon Gold potatoes, peeled

1 medium yellow onion

3 large eggs

Canola oil for frying

¾ cup matzo meal or dry bread crumbs

1 teaspoon salt

⅛ teaspoon freshly ground black pepper

Applesauce or sour cream for serving

Mix the latkes. Grate the zucchini down to the seeds on the large-mesh side of a box grater; discard the seeds. With your hands, squeeze out any liquid and transfer the zucchini to a medium bowl. In the same way, grate and add the potatoes and the onion to the bowl with the zucchini. Mix the eggs and 1 teaspoon of the oil in a small bowl; stir into the zucchini mixture. Add ½ cup of the matzo meal, mixing with your hands. If the mixture is loose, add more matzo meal. Mix in the salt and pepper.

Cook the latkes. Preheat the oven to 250°F. Heat a large heavy skillet over high heat; add ¼ cup of the oil and heat until it begins to smoke. Working in batches as necessary, shape the mixture into latkes by the soup-spoonful, flattening each slightly with your hands and gently adding to the pan. Lower the heat to medium-low and cook the latkes without moving them until brown on one side—3 to 4 minutes; turn them over and cook until the other side is brown—3 to 4 minutes more. Remove the latkes from the pan and transfer to a paper towel-lined plate to drain. Meanwhile, heat another ¼ cup oil in the pan and shape and cook another batch of latkes. When the first batch has drained, transfer them to a serving plate and keep warm in the oven. Serve hot with applesauce or sour cream.

SALAD OF ROASTED HEIRLOOM BEETS WITH CAPERS AND PISTACHIOS

SERVES 6

TODD: I just love the combination of red and golden yellow beets in salads, but you have to be careful to bake the two separately so the former don't bleed into the latter. It doesn't affect the taste if they do, just the appearance, so try not to let the salad sit very long after you've added the dressing. For a bigger salad, you can mix this with baby salad greens and top with shaved Parmesan cheese.

2 medium red beets

2 medium golden beets

1 tablespoon olive oil

Salt

Freshly ground black pepper

¼ cup golden raisins

½ cup toasted chopped pistachios (see Chef's Appendix)

3 tablespoons capers, rinsed and drained

1 medium red onion, thinly sliced

1 small bunch fresh chives, cut into ½-inch pieces

½ cup Lemon Vinaigrette (recipe follows)

Bake the beets. Preheat the oven to 325°F. Rub the olive oil over the beets and sprinkle them with salt and pepper. Loosely wrap each type in a separate aluminum foil packet. Place them in the oven and roast until the beets are tender and can be easily pierced with a sharp knife—about 60 minutes. Transfer the packets to a wire rack, unfold the foil, and let the beets cool. Peel the beets (use rubber gloves to keep your hands from staining) and cut them into bite-size chunks; place in a large bowl.

Soak the raisins. Meanwhile, place the raisins in a small bowl. Add hot water to cover and set aside to soak for 1 hour. Drain the raisins in a mesh strainer before using.

Mix the salad. Add the pistachios, capers, raisins, and onions to the bowl with the beets. Pour in the Lemon Vinaigrette and toss to mix. Taste the salad and add more salt or pepper if you wish.

LEMON VINAIGRETTE

MAKES 1 CUP

Squeeze enough lemons to produce ⅓ cup juice (about 2 medium lemons) and strain it into a small bowl. Add ⅓ cup olive oil, ⅓ cup canola oil, 1 teaspoon salt, and ⅛ teaspoon freshly ground black pepper. Whisk together until combined.

CORN CHOWDER WITH SHIITAKE MUSHROOMS

SERVES 6

TODD: People always anticipate the arrival of corn soup at Equinox in mid-summer (see Summer Gold: Corn, page 267). To extract maximum flavor from the corn in this dish, we simmer the cobs directly in the soup so their "milk" leaches out. You can use your time effectively by making the crouton and corn/shiitake garnishes while the soup is simmering. If you feel like splurging, use chanterelle mushrooms instead of shiitakes. Their meaty texture really adds body to the soup.

5 medium ears of fresh sweet corn

5 tablespoons plus 1½ teaspoons canola oil

1 medium yellow onion, coarsely chopped

2 celery ribs, chopped

3 garlic cloves, crushed

¼ teaspoon fresh vanilla bean seeds (see page 211) or vanilla extract

4 cups vegetable stock or chicken stock, preferably homemade (recipes in Chef's Appendix)

2 cups heavy cream

2 teaspoons salt

¼ teaspoon freshly ground black pepper

1½ cups ½-inch cubes brioche bread, for croutons

2 cups sliced shiitake mushrooms

Prep the corn. Husk the corn. Slice the kernels from the cobs; do not discard the cobs.

Cook the soup. Heat 2 tablespoons of the oil in a medium stockpot over medium heat. Stir in the onions, celery, and garlic; cook for 3 minutes. Measure 2 cups of the corn kernels and set them aside; add the rest of the kernels, the cobs, and vanilla bean seeds to the stockpot; stir. Cook for 2 minutes. Add the stock and cream. Bring the soup to simmering; lower the heat to medium-low and simmer, stirring occasionally, until the kernels are tender—about 30 minutes.

Toast the croutons. Meanwhile, preheat the oven to 350°F. Place the bread cubes on a baking sheet; drizzle with 2 tablespoons of the canola oil and toss to coat; spread evenly. Bake the croutons for 10 minutes; stir. Continue to bake until they are toasted and crunchy—about 10 minutes more. Remove from the oven and cool on the baking sheet on a wire rack.

Make the garnish. Heat 1 tablespoon oil in a medium sauté pan over medium-low heat. Stir in the reserved corn kernels and sauté until soft and slightly shiny—4 to 5 minutes; transfer to a small bowl and keep warm. Place the sauté pan back on the burner, raise the heat to medium, and add the remaining 1½ teaspoons oil. When hot, stir in the mushrooms, ½ teaspoon salt, and ⅛ teaspoon pepper. Cook until the mushrooms are tender—3 to 4 minutes.

(recipe continues)

Transfer to paper towel–lined plate to drain; cover with a paper towel and keep warm.

Puree the soup. Using tongs, remove and discard the corncobs. Working in batches, transfer the soup to the container of a blender or food processor and process until smooth. Return the soup to the stockpot (pouring through a fine mesh strainer if you prefer a very fine texture). Keep warm over low heat and stir in the remaining 1 teaspoon salt and remaining ⅛ teaspoon pepper (taste the soup and adjust the seasoning if you wish). Ladle the soup into six individual bowls. Add a spoonful each of the sautéed corn and mushrooms and scatter a few croutons on top. Serve immediately.

About Soup Making

TODD: Making soup is easy; making soup well takes talent. It's all about building a foundation and adding layers of flavor at every step. Start with local vegetables that are pesticide-free. Their flavor is key because they often will wind up being pureed into the body of soup. The stock or broth must have depth. Seasonings must be balanced and yet have complexity. Bundling herbs together and letting them infuse into the base is always a good idea. The garnish is the last opportunity to introduce flavor and texture elements: don't squander it. Make it eye-appealing and texturally interesting, but always bear in mind they must make sense in the context of the finished product. So no rosemary sprigs on an Asian-inspired soup, for example, just because they are pretty.

ELLEN: To me, soup is a code word for leftovers. Both my grandmother and my aunt would take whatever they had in the fridge and create something from nothing—there was always something simmering on the stove it seems. Maybe I'm hard-wired that way. Whenever we go on vacation, I'll clean out the refrigerator to make a big pot of something to take with us and Todd will say, "Stop using your soup pot as a trash can. Some things you just can't put in soup."

TODD: I'm all for using things up, but still I don't want eggplant skins in my gazpacho. Every ingredient has to have a good reason for being there. Soup has always been something I was known for and I always have two soups on the menu at Equinox: one cream-based, one not. At the turn of each season, the conversation comes up in the kitchen: What soups would we run for the next month that were really exemplary of the season? So, you see gazpacho at the beginning of the fall because of all the late summer tomatoes, then squash or sweet potato soup as the weather gets colder. Chicken soup is just one of those winter cure-alls that everybody relates to. In the spring, pea soup; in the summer, it's all about corn and then back to tomatoes. And so the cycle continues.

LUNCH

TRI-COLOR LENTIL SALAD WITH BALSAMIC
VINEGAR AND PINE NUTS 247

HANDMADE ORECCHIETTE WITH
SAUTÉED CORN AND SWISS CHARD 248

BBQ WILD KING SALMON
WITH SWEET CORN 251

GRILLED WILD ROCKFISH FILLETS
WITH AVOCADO SALSA 254

HARRI'S SARDINE SANDWICH
WITH MUSTARD BUTTER 256

RYE BREAD SALAD WITH CUCUMBER
AND ASPARAGUS 258

TRI-COLOR LENTIL SALAD WITH BALSAMIC VINEGAR AND PINE NUTS

MAKES ABOUT 10 CUPS

TODD: This is a great dish for a summer party. It's an inexpensive, colorful, peasant-driven dish with the Mediterranean influences that Ellen loves so much. We like using the little red and yellow tomatoes for this, but you could use large ones and simply dice them (see Say Yes to Heirloom Tomatoes, page 224).

1 cup dried green lentils

1 cup dried red lentils

1 cup dried yellow lentils

3 garlic cloves, crushed

3 bay leaves

3 springs fresh thyme

1½ cups minced red onion (about 1 large onion)

½ pint miniature yellow tomatoes (such as teardrop or Père Gialle), halved

½ pint miniature red tomatoes (such as cherry, grape, or teardrop), halved

1 to 2 bunches scallions, thinly sliced crosswise, including part of the green (1 cup)

1 cup toasted pine nuts (see Chef's Appendix)

¼ cup Roasted Garlic Paste (recipe follows)

1½ cups Balsamic Vinaigrette (see recipe 237)

1 teaspoon salt

¼ teaspoon freshly ground black pepper

Cook the lentils. Place each color lentils in a separate small saucepot. Cover with 2 to 3 inches water. Add the garlic, bay leaves, and thyme to each pot, dividing equally. Bring the pots to boiling over high heat (don't cover them), lower the heat to medium low, and cook until the lentils are tender—about 30 minutes. Drain one pot of lentils in a strainer, discard the garlic and herbs, and transfer the lentils to a large bowl. Repeat with the remaining lentils, adding each color to the same bowl.

Mix the salad. Add the onions, yellow and red tomatoes, scallions, and pine nuts to the bowl with the lentils. Stir in the Roasted Garlic Paste, Balsamic Vinaigrette, salt, and pepper. Taste the salad and add more salt or pepper if you wish. Serve at room temperature.

ROASTED GARLIC PASTE

The yield on this varies a bit depending on the size of your garlic cloves, but it's such a snap to make you can easily adjust the amount. For each ¼ cup paste you want, start with 12 roasted garlic cloves (see the Chef's Appendix).

If not yet peeled, squeeze the garlic cloves out of their skins. Place them on a cutting board. Using the back of a knife or metal spatula, press down on the cloves until they form a paste—work the knife back and forth to do this. Transfer the paste to a small dish, sprinkle with salt and pepper, and stir to mix. The paste can be stored, covered, in the refrigerator for up to 3 weeks.

HANDMADE ORECCHIETTE WITH SAUTÉED CORN AND SWISS CHARD

SERVES 4

TODD: Orecchiette was one of the first pastas we taught our son, Harrison, to make at home—it's that easy. You just press the dough between your thumb and forefinger and voilà—you have ear-shaped pasta. (The word means "small ears" in Italian.)

ELLEN: I love it because it's filled with vegetables. Todd just uses the tips of the asparagus and saves the bodies for vegetable stock, soup, or risotto.

PASTA:

2 cups semolina flour

¾ tablespoon kosher salt

1½ teaspoons olive oil, more to toss with cooked pasta

¾ cup warm water

SAUCE:

2 medium ears fresh sweet corn

1½ teaspoons canola oil

1 cup packed Swiss chard leaves, coarsely chopped

8 asparagus spears, cut into 1-inch lengths

⅓ cup chopped carrots

1½ tablespoons unsalted butter

1½ teaspoons olive oil

2 garlic cloves, minced

2 shallots, thinly sliced

½ cup heavy cream

Salt

Freshly ground black pepper

Make the pasta dough. Place the flour and salt in the bowl of a stand mixer fitted with a dough hook attachment. With the mixer on low speed, slowly drizzle in the 1½ teaspoons oil and some of the warm water, adding only as much water as needed for a dough to form and come together. Transfer the dough to a lightly floured work surface and knead with your hands for 2 minutes. Shape the dough into a ball and wrap in plastic wrap; refrigerate at least 1 hour.

Shape the orecchiette. Bring a large pot of salted water to boiling while you shape the dough. Unwrap the dough onto a lightly floured surface. Cut off a fist-size piece and roll it into a log about 1 inch in diameter. Cut the log into ½ -inch slices. Shape each slice into a little "ear" by pressing not-quite-flat with your thumb.

Blanch the pasta. Add the shaped pasta and boil for 4 minutes. Drain the pasta in a colander and then submerge it in a bowl of ice water to stop the cooking. When the pasta is cool, drain it again; transfer to a large bowl and toss with a little oil to keep it from sticking together.

Sauté the corn. Husk the corn and slice the kernels from the cobs. Heat the canola oil in a medium sauté pan over medium heat. Add the kernels and sauté for 3 to 4 minutes. Sprinkle with a little salt and pepper if you wish; then transfer to a paper towel–lined plate to drain.

(recipe continues)

VEGETABLES ARE BETTER FROM YOUR FARMERS' MARKET

It should be no surprise to anyone that fresh is always better. Whenever you can buy local, freshly harvested vegetables, the flavor is always going to be better. We support our local growers whenever we can and urge you to do the same: They are very valuable to the preservation of small farms and creation of artisanal foods, and their hard work should be commended. While it may not always be possible to get to your local market, try your best to buy local goods—your food will take on a whole new taste and feeling.

Blanch the vegetables. Bring a large pot of water to boiling. Add the
Swiss chard and cook for 2 minutes. Keep the pot of water boiling
while you transfer the chard to a colander (use tongs) and rinse
under cold water to stop the cooking. Add the asparagus and carrots
to the boiling water and cook for 3 minutes. Drain the asparagus and
carrots and submerge in a bowl of ice water to stop the cooking.
Drain when cool and blot dry with kitchen towels.

Cook the sauce. Heat the butter and olive oil a large sauté pan over
medium heat. Stir in the garlic and gently sauté until aromatic—
about 1 minute. Stir in the shallots and cook 1 minute. Stir in the
corn, asparagus, Swiss chard, and carrots and cook for 2 minutes. Stir
in the cream; heat through. Taste the sauce and season with salt and
pepper as you wish.

Complete the sauce. Meanwhile, bring a large pot of water to
simmering over high heat. When the sauce is ready, add the
orecchiette to the simmering water and reheat for 15 seconds;
drain in a colander and immediately stir into the sauce. Spoon the
orecchiette, vegetables, and sauce into 4 individual pasta bowls,
dividing equally and ladling any excess sauce over each serving. Top
with some Parmesan; serve immediately, passing more Parmesan at
the table.

BBQ'D WILD KING SALMON WITH SWEET CORN

SERVES 6

TODD: Wild king salmon runs in the Pacific Northwest in the summer and has such a bold, distinctive flavor that it can stand up to this combination of BBQ sauce, corn salad, and corn coulis. This is an especially good choice for a festive summer lunch. Make the corn salad, coulis, and BBQ sauces the day before; it will make your life a lot easier when you go to put this dish together.

3 medium ears fresh sweet corn

½ cup thinly sliced shallots

1 tablespoon canola oil, plus more for brushing

1 cup roasted red bell peppers (see Chef's Appendix), cut into thin strips

¼ cup fresh basil leaves, thinly sliced

1 tablespoon Lemon Vinaigrette (recipe page 240)

Salt

Freshly ground black pepper

6 pieces skinless salmon fillet (about 6 ounces each)

1½ cups Sweet Corn Coulis (recipe follows)

1 cup T. Gray's BBQ Sauce (recipe follows)

Potato chips for serving (optional)

Make the corn salad. Husk the corn. Slice the kernels from the cobs. Heat 1 tablespoon oil in a medium sauté pan over medium-low heat. Stir in the kernels and shallots and sauté until soft—4 to 5 minutes. Transfer to a medium bowl. Add the peppers, basil, Lemon Vinaigrette, 1 teaspoon salt, and ¼ teaspoon black pepper; stir to mix and set aside. If you make the salad ahead of time, remove it from the refrigerator in time to reach room temperature.

Barbecue the fish. Preheat a gas or charcoal grill to high. Brush the salmon fillets on both sides with a little oil and sprinkle with salt and pepper. Place the fillets on the grill, top side down, and cook for 3 minutes. Turn the fillets over, brush with BBQ sauce and cook for 3 minutes more—until medium rare (the flesh will begin to tighten but the centers should be still be soft). Brush the salmon with a little more BBQ sauce and cook just until the sauce becomes shiny—about 3 more minutes.

Compose the plates. Warm 6 dinner plates in a warming oven or microwave. Heat the Sweet Corn Coulis in a small saucepan over medium-low heat just until it begins to simmer. Pour ¼ cup of the Coulis onto each plate, mound some of the sautéed corn mixture on the Coulis, dividing equally, and top with a salmon fillet. Drizzle additional BBQ sauce around the plate. Serve immediately, with potato chips on the side if you like. Reserve any leftover Coulis or BBQ Sauce for another use.

(recipe continues)

SWEET CORN COULIS
MAKES ABOUT 3 CUPS

Sauté onions and corn. Coarsely chop 1 small yellow onion. Husk
3 ears of corn and slice the kernels from them; discard only 2 of
the cobs. Heat 1 tablespoon grapeseed or canola oil in a medium
saucepan over medium heat. Add the onions and sauté for 3 minutes.
Add the corn kernels and sauté for 5 minutes. Add the 2 remaining
corncobs.

Make the Coulis. Stir in ½ cup vegetable stock (see Chef's
Appendix), then add 1 cup heavy cream and ¼ teaspoon turmeric.
Bring the mixture to simmering; then simmer gently over medium-
low heat for 30 minutes. Remove and discard the corncobs. Puree
the Coulis in a blender and then pour through a mesh strainer into a
small saucepan (or food storage container if not using immediately).
Season with salt and pepper to taste.

T. GRAY'S BBQ SAUCE
MAKES ABOUT 3 CUPS

Season and sauté onions. Coarsely chop 1 small Vidalia onion. Heat
1 tablespoon canola oil in a medium saucepan over medium heat
until slightly hot. Stir in the onions, 1 tablespoon ground sumac,
1 tablespoon ground dried chipotle pepper, and ¼ teaspoon red
pepper flakes, sauté until the onions are golden—for 5 to 8 minutes.

Make the sauce. Pour in 3 cups of apple cider vinegar, scraping the
pan to deglaze. Bring to boiling over medium-high heat; lower the
heat to medium-low and simmer until the liquid is reduced by two-
thirds. Pour in 2 cups of Coca Cola and reduce by half, adjusting the
heat in the same way. Stir in 2 cups of ketchup and simmer for 10
minutes. Purée the sauce in a blender and then pour through a mesh
strainer into a small bowl (or food storage container if not using
immediately). Season with salt and pepper to taste.

GRILLED WILD ROCKFISH FILLETS WITH AVOCADO AND SALSA

SERVES 6

TODD: Rockfish, which is actually striped bass, is an amazing fish: It has a tight but silky texture and a bright, mild flavor. You can substitute with any delicate fin fish, such as sea bass, snapper, mahi-mahi, or grouper if rockfish isn't available at your fish market. I've paired it with Avocado, Mango, and Red Onion Salsa, which just speaks to summer and complements the subtle flavor of the rockfish. Do not prepare the salsa more than an hour in advance as its acidity will cause the avocadoes to disintegrate.

FISH:

6 pieces skinless rockfish fillet (about 5 ounces each)

2 tablespoons olive oil

2 sprigs fresh thyme

1 garlic clove, sliced

Salt

Freshly ground black pepper

¼ cup fresh cilantro leaves for garnish

SALSA:

1 ripe tomato

2 avocados, diced

1 mango, peeled, pitted, and diced

1 small red onion, finely diced

1 jalapeño pepper, minced

1 garlic clove, minced

4 scallions, thinly sliced crosswise, including part of the green

1 lime

½ cup olive oil

1 tablespoon sherry vinegar

1½ teaspoons salt

⅛ teaspoon freshly ground black pepper

Marinate the fish. Mix the oil, thyme, and garlic in a shallow dish. Lay the fish fillets in the dish, turning to coat. Cover the dish and refrigerate for 2 hours.

Prep the tomato for the salsa. Bring a medium pot of water to boiling over high heat. Drop the tomato into the water and cook for 1 minute. With a slotted spoon, transfer the tomato to a bowl of ice water to stop the cooking. Use a paring knife to peel the tomato, then core it and squeeze out the seeds. Chop the tomato.

Make the salsa. Combine the tomato, avocados, mangos, onions, jalapeños, garlic, and scallions in a large bowl. Grate the zest from the lime and add it to the bowl. Squeeze the juice from the lime into a small bowl; add the oil, vinegar, salt, and pepper, and whisk together. Pour the oil mixture into the tomato mixture and stir together. Taste the salsa and add more salt or pepper as you wish. Cover and refrigerate until ready to serve (no more than 1 hour).

Grill the fish. Preheat a gas or charcoal grill to high. Transfer the fish fillets from the marinade to the grill, sprinkle with salt and pepper. Cook 4 minutes, then turn and sprinkle salt and pepper over the second side; cook until the fish is firm to the touch and opaque—4 minutes more. Arrange the fillets on a platter; spoon some salsa over them and sprinkle the cilantro on top. Serve immediately, passing additional salsa at the table.

Avocados and a Kibbutz Summer

ELLEN: Whenever anyone asks me about my time on the kibbutz in Israel I automatically think Hass Avocados, as they were the main crop of Kibbutz Kfar Hanasi. At the time, Israel was just getting started with its avocado production, which is flourishing today. The oddly shaped, green, bumpy-skinned fruit with the big pit was new to me, but on the kibbutz it was everywhere (as were glasses full of water, with the iconic pit half-submerged, skewered by toothpicks and resting on the rim). All of us "volunteer farm workers" hoped for the white roots to sprout from our avocado pits so we could leave a tree in Israel upon departure.

My summer on the kibbutz coincided with the advent of the boom box, and we worked the harvest to nonstop Bob Dylan. After long days picking, high in the trees, you'd think we'd have gotten tired of both Dylan and avocados, but it was quite the opposite—I still adore both!

I tried those avocados 100 different ways but the simplest turned out to be the best, and still is. Here's how we ate them: Make toast from challah or another white bread, and butter it liberally while it's still warm. Then immediately spread lots of mashed, perfectly ripened avocado on it and sprinkle coarse salt over the avocado. That's all there is to it.

I have always attributed this tradition to English origins, for no other reason than the fact that the residents of the kibbutz had English and German roots. To this day, summer avocados recall my time on the kibbutz. I still prefer to eat them the way I so often did there—it's my guacamole. Enjoy!

ROCKFISH, BACK FROM THE BRINK

One of the greatest recent accomplishments in the food world has been the replenishment of rockfish stocks in the Chesapeake Bay via strict fishery management. After an extended moratorium, rockfish has now returned to markets and restaurant menus, but only during limited stretches of time throughout the year. The season for the fish is basically spring and summer; the females head back to their freshwater spawning grounds in April and May.

HARRI'S SARDINE SANDWICH WITH MUSTARD BUTTER

MAKES 4 SANDWICHES

TODD: When sardines are canned, the heads of the fish (herring, brisling, sprats, pilchards) are removed, then they are eviscerated, cooked (usually steamed), dried, and packed in liquid, usually water, oil, or tomato sauce. They can come with the skin and bones intact or skinless and boneless. I happen to like the skin; if you don't care for it, discard it. The bones, however, must be removed—their texture is too unpleasant in my opinion. Thankfully, Ellen is a pro at it.

ELLEN: And it doesn't matter to me what they're packed in—I love them any which way (see Sardines, Fresh and Canned, below).

2 tablespoons unsalted butter, softened

1 tablespoon mayonnaise

1 teaspoon whole grain mustard

1 teaspoon Dijon mustard

Salt and freshly ground pepper to taste

8 slices rye bread

Two 3.75-ounce cans sardines (oil-packed), pin bones and spine removed (see Chef's Appendix)

½ cup very thinly sliced red onions

8 soft, sweet lettuce leaves (such as butter or Boston)

MAKE IT PARVE. *Substitute margarine for the butter.*

Make the mustard butter. With a fork, cream the butter in a small bowl or glass measuring cup. Mix in the mayonnaise and mustards. Taste, and add salt and pepper if you wish—the amount will depend on your preference and the seasoning of the mustards you start with.

Assemble the sandwiches. Toast the bread. Arrange all 8 slices on a work surface; spread some of the mustard on each. Top each of 4 slices with a lettuce leaf and add the sardines and then the onions, dividing both equally. Top with another lettuce leaf and slice of bread. Cut each sandwich in half and serve.

Sardines, Fresh and Canned

ELLEN: I was only eight or nine years old when my grandfather, Harry Henkin, taught me how to debone sardines, using a technique I use to this day. He and my grandma Rose were the resident managers of an apartment building in the Glover Park section of Washington, D.C. On weekend visits, I would go on long walks with Grandpa and when we'd get back to their apartment, Grandma Rose would set out a big platter of fish delicacies: pickled and creamed herring, gefilte fish, canned smoked fish and oysters, and sardines packed in tomato sauce.

That's when Grandpa and I would get to work, using the side of a fork to gently pry open the sardines at their belly flaps and

lay their fillets on a plate, skin-sides down. Then we'd pry the spines up, peel them away and put them in a little bowl, anxious to pile up the sardines on crackers, top them with sour cream and sliced onions, and devour them.

TODD: Harry loved those sardines and so did Ellen, but to be honest, I didn't get what all the fuss was about.

ELLEN: That's an understatement. It was a real revelation to Todd that Jewish people ate canned fish, especially sardines. They were not on the top of his list of things to try, but he did anyway, just to appease me.

Soon after we were married, we had a sardine epiphany. We went on a rare evening out to a nice restaurant (we were pretty poor in those days) and wound up at Obelisk in Dupont Circle. The chef there, Peter Pasten, was known for his simple, elegant, Mediterranean-influenced cooking. The menu was very limited and one of the dishes he served was grilled fresh sardines, dressed with a little olive oil and fresh lemon. I had never tasted a fresh sardine before—I didn't even know they came that way—and that night Todd and I both had a "wow" moment. They were so delicate and bright.

TODD: After that night at Obelisk, fresh sardines became a regular part of my cooking repertoire. I really love them now. When we were in Paris last summer, we stopped at a little bistro near Saint-Germain and noticed there were sardines on the menu. I ordered them thinking we'd be experiencing some kind of fancy Parisian interpretation. Not only were they just canned sardines, but they were served right in the can with the lid still attached, plunked on a paper doily like a serious dish. It cost 24 euros for that can of fish, and Ellen hasn't let me live it down since then.

RYE BREAD SALAD WITH CUCUMBER AND ASPARAGUS

SERVES 4 TO 6

ELLEN: This is a version of the Italian bread salad known as panzanella, a dish that offers a tasty way to use up stale pieces of country bread: You toss them in dressing with vegetables (especially tomatoes) and let the bread soak up all the juices and soften. Since I love rye bread so much, it made sense to substitute it in this recipe.

TODD: This is definitely one of Ellen's favorite dishes. It's generally served as a starter (and you can do that) but we often add extra vegetables and eat it for lunch. It's a great way to show off the delights of asparagus in the spring and early summer (see Thoughts on Asparagus, page 165). The vibrant green blanched asparagus look great with yellow tomatoes or cherry or heirloom tomatoes if yellow are hard to find (see Say Yes to Heirloom tomatoes, page 224).

ELLEN: We do love this salad in summer, but really, it's great in any season. In the fall we use roasted squash and in the winter, I make it with eggplant and peppers.

1 large loaf artisan-made rye bread (not sliced)

½ cup olive oil

1 teaspoon salt

⅛ teaspoon freshly ground black pepper

24 asparagus spears

1 large cucumber, peeled, halved lengthwise, and cut into ¼-inch thick slices

2 medium yellow tomatoes, cut into 1-inch chunks

1 medium red onion, quartered and thinly sliced

1 cup pitted and chopped green or black olives

1 garlic clove, minced

1½ cups Sherry Mustard Vinaigrette (see recipe page 165)

18 to 24 fresh basil leaves

Toast the bread. Preheat oven to 350°F. Cut the bread into 1-inch cubes; you should have about 4 cups. Toss the bread with the olive oil, salt, and pepper in a large bowl. Spread on a baking sheet and toast in the oven, stirring occasionally, until the bread is golden brown on all sides—15 to 20 minutes. Cool on the baking sheet on a wire rack.

Blanch the asparagus. Bring a medium saucepan of lightly salted water to boiling over high heat. Add the asparagus and boil until just tender—2 to 3 minutes. Using tongs, transfer the asparagus to a bowl of ice water and allow to chill completely (add more ice if you need to). Transfer the asparagus to paper towels or kitchen towels to drain; cut into 1-inch lengths.

Mix the salad. Place the bread and asparagus in a large bowl. Add the cucumber, tomatoes, onions, olives, and garlic. Cut 8 of the basil leaves into thin strips; add to the bowl. Pour in the Sherry Mustard Vinaigrette and toss to mix. Cover and refrigerate the salad for 20 minutes. Serve garnished with more basil leaves.

DINNER

OLIVE-OIL POACHED COD 261

GRILLED YELLOWFIN TUNA SKEWERS
WITH RUSTIC TOMATO SAUCE 263

ANNIE'S SOUTHERN FRIED CHICKEN 265

ASPARAGUS RISOTTO WITH PARMESAN
TUILES 269

GRILLED LONDON BROIL WITH
CHANTERELLE MUSHROOMS 271

OLIVE-OIL POACHED COD

SERVES 6

ELLEN: Cod came like most grocery store fish in the 60's and 70's, sitting water-logged on a styrofoam square wrapped in plastic. So it wasn't until Todd came along that I got a chance to enjoy that fish.

TODD: Olive-oil poaching was a cool technique in the late '90s that I became fascinated with when I saw famed chef Charlie Trotter and others utilizing it. I still use it, especially for thick, meaty cuts of fish because it keeps them moist all the way through. The touch of oil imparts a velvety finish to the fish, so you don't need to top it with a sauce or relish. That makes it a fuss-free summertime cooking method. Summer Corn Succotash with Black-Eyed Peas (page 276) would be a perfect accompaniment.

1 liter olive oil

4 sprigs fresh thyme

4 garlic cloves, crushed

2 bay leaves

6 pieces cod fillet (5 ounces each)

Salt

Freshly ground black pepper

Summer Corn Succotash with Black-Eyed Peas for serving (optional, recipe page 276)

Pour the oil into a medium sauté pan or saucepan; heat to 250°F over medium-low heat (measure on a candy thermometer). Add the thyme, garlic, and bay leaves. Sprinkle salt and pepper over fillets. Working in batches if necessary, gently submerge the fillets in the oil and cook until the flesh is opaque and begins to tighten—6 to 8 minutes. Use a slotted spatula to lift the fillets from the oil and transfer to a serving platter. The fish should retain enough oil to act as its own sauce.

LIME-MINT MARINADE

MAKES ABOUT ¾ CUP

Whisk together ½ cup olive oil and 2 tablespoons freshly
squeezed lime juice in a small bowl or glass measuring cup;
whisk in 4 finely minced garlic cloves, 2 tablespoons chopped
fresh mint leaves, 1 tablespoon chili powder, 1 teaspoon salt,
and ¼ teaspoon freshly ground black pepper.

GRILLED YELLOWFIN TUNA SKEWERS WITH RUSTIC TOMATO SAUCE

SERVES 6

TODD: In the summer, Ellen, Harrison, and I and a couple of other families would go down to the Outer Banks and there was always one day that was set aside for tuna fishing. We would bring back the fresh-caught tuna and feast on it for three or four days. You can't beat grilled tuna with a basic tomato sauce for an easy dinner on a summer night. Calling a simple dish rustic makes it sound a little special—basically it means chunky here (we add diced tomatoes to a pureed sauce for texture).

ELLEN: By the way, you can grill tuna steaks instead of making skewers. If you're doing the skewers, make sure to soak the bamboo sticks for several hours first to prevent them from catching fire—or use metal skewers. The recipe doesn't call for them, but feel free to add bell pepper chunks to the skewers.

SKEWERS:

1 pound yellowfin tuna, cut into large cubes

Lime-Mint Marinade (recipe follows)

1 zucchini, cut into ¼-inch thick rounds

1 yellow squash, ¼-inch thick rounds

1 Vidalia onion, cut into large chunks

TOMATO SAUCE:

One 28-ounce can peeled plum tomatoes

1 tablespoon olive oil

1 medium yellow onion, finely diced

2 garlic cloves, minced

One 14-ounce can diced tomatoes

Sugar to taste (optional)

¼ cup chopped fresh basil leaves

Marinate the skewers. Thread the tuna, zucchini, yellow squash, and onions onto the skewers, dividing equally and alternating a couple of vegetables between the fish pieces. Lay the skewers on a platter; pour the Lime-Mint Marinade over them, turning them to coat evenly. Cover and refrigerate for 2 hours.

Make the tomato sauce. About an hour before you're ready to grill the skewers, put the plum tomatoes through a food mill (you can puree them in food processor if you don't have a food mill). Heat the oil in a medium saucepan over medium heat. Stir in the onions and garlic and cook until shiny and aromatic—2 minutes. Stir in the plum tomatoes and diced tomatoes; cover the pan and lower the heat to low. Cook the sauce (barely simmering) until thickened and slightly sweet to the taste—about 40 minutes. Add a small amount of sugar if you prefer your sauce on the sweet side. Remove from the heat and stir in the basil.

Grill the skewers. Preheat a gas or charcoal grill to high. Lift the skewers from the marinade (let excess marinade drip off but leave

(recipe continues)

a coating on the food so it doesn't stick to the grill) and arrange them on the grill rack. Cook until the vegetables are lightly charred and fish is just cooked through, turning to char each side—5 to 6 minutes total. Transfer the skewers to a platter and sprinkle with salt and pepper. To serve, ladle some warm tomato sauce onto each diner's plate and top with a skewer.

Steve Turnage and Virginia Produce

ELLEN: Steve Turnage's Rappahannock Fruits and Vegetables was the first farm we visited and really got to know. It was also featured in the *Chef's A'Field* television series that highlighted how chefs incorporate farm-fresh ingredients into their cooking. Todd was one of the initial chefs to appear on the show.

TODD: At Galileo, I was buying log-grown shiitakes from Steve. They were the best shiitakes I've ever seen, before or since. From there, Steve expanded his business into tomatoes, melons, and greens. One summer weekend back in the mid-'90s, we stopped at Steve's farm in Warsaw along the way to Rappahannock. We rode a tractor around, picking up various melons and tomatoes, and using his sheath knfe, the kind hunters use, to cut wedges out of them, took a bite to check for sweetness and ripeness and throw the half-eaten fruits back into the field. We went around the farm tasting the differences between all the various varieties.

That is where the friendship with Steve began. We took our staff down there one summer for our company picnic in August.

I don't hear much from him through the winter, but then the calls start in mid March, telling me what's about to be available, usually in the first week of April: wild field spinach, kale, and mustard greens. Soon to follow, in late April or early May, would be sugar snap peas, the log-grown shiitakes, and the beginnings of the asparagus season, with some of the most beautiful purple asparagus you'll ever lay your eyes on. Steve's crops progress through the late spring and into early summer with: English peas, spring onions, bi-colored sweet corn, peppers, zucchini, and a stunning variety of tomatoes. In the fall come the most brilliant butternut and Kabocha squash and heirloom tomatoes.

I've been buying from Steve since the day we opened Equinox, and the cooks, sous-chefs, and chefs who passed through my kitchen and went on to other places then became customers of Steve's. Not only do I feel a connection to the product, but I have helped a small farmer grow his family business, earn a fair wage, and maintain the integrity of his product. It's a paradigm in which everybody wins: the cook, the farmer, and the guest.

ANNIE'S SOUTHERN FRIED CHICKEN

SERVES 6

ELLEN: Growing up in Washington, my family had a housekeeper named Annie Barley, who made the best fried chicken (see Annie Barley, page 266). She would batter and dip it in crushed up cornflake crumbs—you know, the ones that came in the box with the big red rooster on it? She used an iron skillet with four inches of oil in it. Whenever I came home from school and that chicken was frying, I knew it was going to be a great dinner.

TODD: We still make fried chicken this way from time to time, especially for a summer picnic with friends and family, and serve it with big bowls of Red Cabbage Coleslaw (page 57) and Fingerling Potato Salad (page 279).

Canola oil for frying

3 cups all-purpose flour

1 teaspoon salt

¼ teaspoon freshly ground black pepper

3 cups egg wash (see Chef's Appendix)

4 cups cornflake cereal, crushed

9 chicken thighs

9 chicken drum sticks

Fry the chicken. Preheat the oven to 350°F. Pour 3 inches of oil into a deep skillet or heavy saucepan (fill a skillet no more than halfway) and heat over medium heat to 300°F (measure on a candy thermometer). Mix the flour, salt, and pepper in a shallow dish. Place the egg wash and cereal each in shallow dishes. Working in batches, dip each chicken piece in the flour, shaking off the excess, then in the egg wash, and finally in the cereal, pressing the crumbs with your hands to adhere to all sides; add the chicken to the skillet and fry until the crust is nice and crispy on all sides. Transfer the chicken to a paper towel–lined plate to drain.

Complete the cooking. The chicken will be done when the juices run clear where the meat is pierced with a skewer; if the frying hasn't completely cooked it, transfer the pieces to a baking dish and complete the cooking in the oven. (If the chicken is done after the frying step, lower the oven temperature to 225°F and keep the first batch of chicken warm while you cook the remainder.)

(recipe continues)

Annie Barley

ELLEN: Todd and I are convinced that while we were growing up we were often doing the same exact thing at the same exact time—watching the same television show, going to the same concert or movies, and we know we were in the same room at the same time on several occasions before we ever actually met. Parallel lives, but with lots of intersections.

Annie Barley is a good example of that phenomenon. Annie was the housekeeper who worked for my family for eighteen years, pretty much my entire childhood, starting in 1968 when I was four years old and leaving us when I graduated from college at twenty-one and my youngest brother, Elliot, finished high school.

To say she had a profound effect on me is an understatement. My mother and father both worked, so Annie essentially raised my brothers and me. She was there when we came home from school and into the evening, tending to our needs, putting up with our mishegoss, and trying to maintain order in a chaotic household.

Most of the cooking fell to Annie, which was all right by us because she was a great cook. I'd hang out with her in the kitchen while she put dinner together. She smoked Salems, often leaving one hanging off the countertop and then forgetting about it, thereby adding another burn mark to the lineup along the counter's edge—that was definitely the 70's!

Our favorite dish of hers was her fried chicken (Annie's Southern Fried Chicken, page 265), coated in cornflake crumbs and fried to golden crispiness in a big cast-iron skillet bubbling with oil. We always called it Annie's Jewish fried chicken even though it wasn't particularly Jewish at all. I guess it was just because we were Jewish and that's where she was making it.

She was a Southerner who lost her husband and her son in Vietnam. The civil rights movement was in full swing in Washington, but growing up in our Upper Northwest world on Morrison Street, it was something I didn't really understand, until Annie took us into her world on trips to her house on North Capitol Street. She opened my eyes to what was really going on in D.C.

Fast forward to 1995. Annie was at our wedding and walked right up to Todd, whom she had not officially met before, and said, "I know you. I used to meet my sister in a restaurant in Fredericksburg, Virginia, called The Happy Clam and you were working there." She actually remembered him!

So on weekends off, Annie was eating at the same restaurant where Todd worked. How crazy is that? If that's not enough, after Annie left us, she went to work for a doctor's family. Dr. Bob Kane, it turned out, was a regular of ours at Equinox and was the doctor who performed cataract surgery on Todd's grandmother in Fredericksburg years before. You see, parallel lives and intersections!

ASPARAGUS RISOTTO WITH PARMESAN TUILES

SERVES 4 TO 6

TODD: Although risotto is considered a peasant dish and can indeed fall in line with a thrifty approach to cooking, to me risotto always has an elegant air about it. That's why we like to garnish this one with crispy, cracker-like wafers of baked Parmesan cheese called *tuiles*, which means "tiles" in French. This risotto really presents summer asparagus in their best light (see *Thoughts on Asparagus*, page 165). Using vegetable stock keeps the dish vegetarian, but your risotto would get an extra boost of asparagus flavor if you use the pieces you trim from the spears in that stock. For pointers on *making risotto, see Making Risotto*, page 32.

1½ cups grated Parmesan cheese (6 ounces)

3 tablespoons canola oil

1 medium yellow onion, minced

2 cups carnaroli or arborio rice

2 cups dry white wine (such as Chablis or Sauvignon Blanc)

6 cups hot vegetable stock or chicken stock, preferably homemade (recipes in Chef's Appendix)

36 large asparagus spears, peeled and any tough ends removed

2 tablespoons mascarpone cheese

1 tablespoon unsalted butter

1 teaspoon freshly grated lemon zest

1 teaspoon salt

⅛ teaspoon freshly ground black pepper

Make the tuiles. Preheat the oven to 325°F. Line a baking sheet with parchment paper. Measure ¾ cup of the Parmesan and spoon it into thin 3-inch diameter rounds on the baking sheet. Bake until the cheese melts, turns golden brown, and begins to firm—5 to 6 minutes. Transfer the baking sheet to a wire rack and let the tuiles cool; remove from the baking sheet and set aside.

Prep the asparagus. Starting at the base, slice the asparagus stalks diagonally into small pieces, leaving the tips in 1-inch lengths. Bring a medium saucepan of lightly salted water to simmering over high heat. Add the asparagus tips (set the cut stalks aside) and boil until just tender—2 to 3 minutes. Drain the tips in a colander and rinse under cold water to stop the cooking. Blot dry on a kitchen towel and place in a small baking dish; set aside.

Cook the risotto. Heat the oil in a medium saucepan over medium heat. Add the onions and cook, stirring occasionally, for 2 minutes. Stir in the rice, cook for 2 minutes, stirring occasionally (this technique is called toasting). To deglaze the pan, stir in the wine and continue cooking, stirring once or twice, until the wine has been completely absorbed by the rice or has evaporated—about 3 minutes. Add the stock in three 2-cup additions, adding the sliced asparagus stalks with the second addition; after each addition allow the rice to absorb the liquid (do not stir) and then free the rice from the sides of the pan with a wooden spoon before adding more stock. Preheat the oven to 275°F when you add the third addition of stock.

Complete the risotto. When the third addition of stock has been absorbed by the rice (about 15 minutes after adding) stir in the mascarpone, butter, and remaining ¾ cup Parmesan, stirring until the risotto appears smooth and creamy. Place the baking dish with the asparagus tips in the oven to warm briefly. Stir the lemon zest, salt, and pepper into the risotto and then immediately spoon it into individual dishes. Top each serving with a few asparagus tips and add some Parmesan tuiles to the side of each.

GRILLED LONDON BROIL WITH CHANTERELLE MUSHROOMS

SERVES 6 TO 8

TODD: My mom often marinated London broil in bottled Italian dressing and grilled it for a quick, midweek dinner. It was a less expensive red meat alternative to strip steaks or fillets, so it made regular appearances on our dinner table. I jazzed this version up by using a balsamic-soy marinade and adding chanterelle mushrooms. These can be costlier than other kinds, so feel free to use whichever type you prefer: oyster, shiitake, crimini, or even button mushrooms.

One 3-pound London broil

2 tablespoons salt

½ teaspoon freshly ground black pepper

2 sprigs fresh rosemary

2 cups Balsamic-Soy Marinade (see page 306 Chef's Appendix)

3 cups chanterelle mushrooms (or shiitake or oyster mushrooms), cut in half

1 cup sliced shallots

2 garlic cloves, minced

¼ cup canola oil

Marinate the steak. Season the steak with 1 teaspoon salt and ¼ teaspoon pepper, dividing over both sides. Place the steak and rosemary in a resealable plastic food storage bag (or similar container). Pour in the Balsamic-Soy Marinade; seal the bag and turn to coat the steak with marinade. Refrigerate for 2 hours.

Grill the steak. Heat a gas or charcoal grill to high. Remove the steak from the marinade, letting the liquid drip off. Sprinkle 2 tablespoons salt evenly over both sides of the steak and then grill it to medium-rare—6 to 8 minutes per side. Transfer the steak to a platter, cover, and keep warm. If you'd like to serve the marinade as a sauce, transfer it to a small saucepan, bring to simmering, and simmer for at least 3 minutes; keep warm.

Sautée the mushrooms. Heat the oil in a medium sauté pan over medium-high heat. Stir in the mushrooms, remaining ½ teaspoon salt, and remaining ¼ teaspoon pepper; cook until the mushrooms begin to soften—3 to 5 minutes. Stir in the shallots, garlic and cook until the mushrooms are lightly caramelized—3 to 5 minutes more. Taste the mushrooms and add more salt or pepper if you wish. Use a slotted spatula to transfer the mushrooms to a paper towel–lined plate to drain. To serve, slice the beef against the grain, making ⅛ to ¼-inch thick slices. Divide the slices among six (or up to eight) dinner plates and spoon the mushrooms on top, dividing equally. Drizzle with a little hot marinade if you wish.

SIDES

FIVE-BEAN SALAD 273

HOMEMADE DILL PICKLES 275

SUMMER CORN SUCCOTASH
WITH BLACK-EYED PEAS 276

FINGERLING POTATO SALAD 279

CUMIN-SCENTED PAN-FRIED
EGGPLANT 281

FIVE-BEAN SALAD

SERVES 10 TO 12

ELLEN: As a vegetarian, I tend to make bean salads a lot and when I do, I make a huge batch; that way we have a good, healthful, protein-rich dish to snack on or have with meals for a few days—and it tends to taste better after a couple of days as the flavors all meld together. It's a perfect party dish because it goes with everything. Feel free to cut the recipe in half or add whatever other ingredients strike your fancy, and use fresh corn in the summer if you can.

2 cups fresh or frozen corn kernels

1 cup oven-dried tomatoes (recipe in Chef's Appendix)

One 15.5-ounce can cannellini beans, rinsed and drained

One 15.5-ounce can great northern beans, rinsed and drained

One 15.5-ounce can dark-red kidney beans, rinsed and drained

One 15.5-ounce can black beans, rinsed and drained

One 15.5-ounce can chickpeas (garbanzo beans), rinsed and drained

1 bunch scallions, thinly sliced crosswise, including part of the green

1 red (or orange or yellow) bell pepper, cored, seeded, and finely diced

1 medium red onion, finely diced

2 tablespoons chopped fresh mint leaves

1 tablespoon chopped fresh parsley

1 cup Lemon-Lime Vinaigrette (recipe follows)

Salt

Freshly ground black pepper

Fresh parsley for garnish

Cook the corn. Bring a medium pot of water to boiling over high heat. Add the corn and simmer for 3 minutes. Drain in a colander, rinse under cold water, and set aside to cool to room temperature.

Mix the salad. Place the tomatoes, all five types of beans, the scallions, peppers, and onions in a large bowl; add the corn and stir to mix well. Add the mint and parsley and pour in the Lemon-Lime Vinaigrette; mix well. Taste the salad and add salt or pepper as you wish. Cover and refrigerate until ready to serve—at least 1 hour—so the flavors can meld. Serve the salad garnished with fresh parsley.

LEMON-LIME VINAIGRETTE

MAKES ABOUT 1½ CUPS

Add to the container of a blender ½ cup extra-virgin olive oil, ½ cup canola oil, ¼ cup Champagne vinegar, 1 tablespoon Dijon mustard, 1 tablespoon honey, 1½ teaspoons freshly squeezed lemon juice, 1½ teaspoons freshly squeezed lime juice, 1 finely chopped garlic clove, ½ teaspoon salt, and a sprinkling of freshly ground black pepper. Purée until well mixed. Transfer to a small jar and refrigerate until ready to use.

HOMEMADE DILL PICKLES

MAKES 48 PICKLES

ELLEN: I remember as a kid seeing all the pickle carts on the Lower East Side in New York. I could only guess at the years of technique that go into all the different pickling brines for those full sour and half sour pickles loaded with garlic and dill.

TODD: This is a basic pickling brine that doesn't call for garlic cloves, but add them if you wish (see Pickled Foods Belong in Your Repertoire, page 164). To develop the flavor of these pickles, let them sit for two weeks in the refrigerator before eating. Because the jars are not sterilized and sealed, these pickles must be kept refrigerated and eaten within 45 days. If you wish the pickles to have a longer shelf life, purchase the proper canning equipment and follow the manufacturer's instructions for preserving and canning.

4 tablespoons kosher salt

1 teaspoon whole black peppercorns

1 tablespoon pickling spice

1 teaspoon dill seeds

½ teaspoon mustard seeds

6 cups water

½ cup white wine vinegar

1 tablespoon red wine vinegar

12 small cucumbers, quartered lengthwise

1 bunch fresh dill

Make the pickling brine. Place the salt, peppercorns, pickling spice, dill seeds, and mustard seeds in a small saucepan. Stir in the water, white wine vinegar, and red wine vinegar. Bring to simmering over high heat, stirring to dissolve the salt. Remove from the heat.

Make the pickles. Stand the cucumbers on end in glass jars that have airtight lids. Pour the hot brine into each jar, covering the cucumbers. Add several sprigs of dill to each jar. Cover and refrigerate for 14 days before using to allow the pickling to take effect. Store the pickles for up to 3 months in the refrigerator.

SUMMER CORN SUCCOTASH WITH BLACK-EYED PEAS

SERVES 4 TO 6

TODD: Succotash gets a bad rap because people usually think about the sad, overcooked dish our mothers made from canned corn, lima beans, and mushy red peppers, but when done the right way, it can really be a winner. It's a great way to take advantage of all the great corn the summer offers (see Summer Gold: Corn, page 276). We use fresh black-eyed peas when we can get them, but canned ones work just fine. You could also use cooked, freshly shelled beans, like butter beans, fava beans, or lima beans, or frozen shelled edamame. Leftover succotash makes a nice salad the next day if you add a little bit of vinaigrette to it, such as Lemon Vinaigrette (page 240) or Sherry Mustard Vinaigrette (page 165).

5 baby carrots, cut into ¼ inch thick rounds

3 medium ears fresh sweet corn

1 tablespoon canola oil

1 tablespoon unsalted butter

1 medium red onion, minced

1 garlic clove, minced

One 15.5-ounce can black-eyed peas, rinsed and drained (or 1½ cups fresh)

1 red bell pepper, cored, seeded, and finely diced

5 scallions, thinly sliced crosswise, including part of the green

1 teaspoon salt

⅛ teaspoon freshly ground black pepper

MAKE IT PARVE. *Use margarine or olive oil instead of butter.*

Blanch the carrots. Bring a large pot of water to boiling over high heat, add the carrots and cook until crisp-tender—3 to 4 minutes. Drain in a colander and rinse under cold water to stop the cooking.

Prep the corn. Husk the corn. Slice the kernels from the cobs (you should have about 2 cups).

Cook the succotash. Heat the oil and butter in a large sauté pan over medium heat until the butter begins to sizzle. Stir in the onions and garlic, cook until aromatic—2 minutes. Stir in the corn and beans and cook 3 minutes. Stir in the carrots, red peppers, scallions, salt, and black pepper. Cook, stirring occasionally, until heated through—3 to 5 minutes. Taste the succotash and add more salt or black pepper if you wish. Serve immediately, family style.

Summer Gold: Corn

ELLEN: For us, the height of corn season always marked the time for relaxation, because that's when we usually wound up taking our summer trips to the Jersey Shore, the Eastern Shore, or the Northern Neck of Virginia.

TODD: Corn is a key ingredient on my summer menus because it is so versatile. It's sweet and savory at the same time, so it's no wonder that it shows up at brunch, lunch, and dinner at our home and in nearly every course at Equinox. Our former pastry chef, Tom Wellings, even loves to make corn ice cream for dessert.

"Is that Silver Queen corn?" people like to ask every summer, as if they are measuring all other corns against some kind of sense memory benchmark. I remember the late, great John Apple (a *New York Times* travel writer) calling me and asking about Silver Queen corn and what I knew. After multiple phone calls to my farmers, I came to discover that Maryland's beloved Silver Queen strain had been replaced by the Argent strain of corn because it was more durable and could withstand temperature fluctuations better than Silver Queen.

Still, our local corn (such as Argent, White Magic, 81W) is succulent, sweet, and tender. It's amazing cooked or raw in salads, grilled in the husk, in succotash, as part of a relish . . . you name it. Be it white, yellow, or bi-colored, it would not be unusual to have corn turn up six or seven times on any given Equinox menu in the summertime.

FINGERLING POTATO SALAD

SERVES 6

ELLEN: We love fingerling potatoes in our house—roasted with sea salt in the winter and in potato salad in the summer. They're perfect for potato salad because they're small, are less starchy than Russets and Idahos, and seem meatier to me. Make the salad at least several hours in advance (overnight is better) so the flavors have a chance to meld.

1 pound fingerling potatoes, cut in half lengthwise

2 celery ribs, finely diced

1 small Vidalia onion, minced

⅔ cup mayonnaise

¼ cup crème fraîche or sour cream

¼ cup minced fresh chives

1 tablespoon chopped fresh tarragon

1 teaspoon salt

½ teaspoon freshly grated lemon zest

⅛ teaspoon freshly ground black pepper

Cook the potatoes. Bring a large pot of salted water to simmering over high heat. Add the potatoes and cook until tender—4 to 6 minutes. Drain the potatoes in a colander and set aside until they reach room temperature.

Mix the salad. Place the potatoes in a large bowl. Add the celery and the Vidalia onions and stir to combine. Mix together the mayonnaise, crème fraîche, chives, tarragon, salt, lemon zest, and pepper in a small bowl. Add the mayonnaise mixture to the potato mixture and stir until well mixed. Taste the salad and add more salt or pepper if you wish. Cover and refrigerate until ready to serve—at least 1 hour—so the flavors can meld.

CUMIN-SCENTED PAN-FRIED EGGPLANT

SERVES 4 TO 6

TODD: Japanese eggplants are elongated and much thinner than the large, fat variety we're used to seeing. They lend themselves nicely to pan-frying because they yield nice, little medallions. I also find their flesh a little meatier and less seedy than large eggplants.

4 Japanese eggplants

2 cups all-purpose flour

Salt

Freshly ground black pepper

1 cup egg wash (see Chef's Appendix)

2 cups panko bread crumbs

⅓ cup canola oil

½ teaspoon cumin powder

½ teaspoon garlic powder

Saffron Mayonnaise for serving (optional, recipe in Chef's Appendix)

Prep the eggplant. Cut the eggplants lengthwise into ¼ inch thick slices. Sprinkle salt over both sides of each slice and place them in a colander to drain for 30 minutes. Mix the flour, ½ teaspoon salt, and a sprinkling of pepper in a shallow dish. Place the egg wash and bread crumbs each in shallow dishes.

Crust the eggplant. Remove the eggplant from the colander and blot dry with paper towels. Dip each slice into the flour mixture, shaking off the excess, then into the egg wash, and finally into the bread crumbs, being sure to coat both sides.

Fry the eggplant. Heat the oil in a large sauté pan over medium heat. Mix the cumin, garlic powder, ¼ teaspoon salt, and a sprinkling of pepper in a cup. Working in batches if necessary, add the eggplant slices and sprinkle with some of the cumin mixture. Fry until golden brown, turning once and sprinkling the other side with more of the cumin—about 2 minutes per side. Transfer the slices to a paper towel–lined plate to drain. Serve with Saffron Mayonnaise on the side if you wish.

DESSERTS

APRICOT SALAD WITH POPPY SEEDS
AND BALSAMIC SYRUP 283

STRAWBERRY RHUBARB COBBLER 284

CHILLED MANGO SOUP WITH
BLACKBERRIES 287

FIG AND PORT WINE BLINTZES 288

VANILLA AND PEACH MELBA 291

APRICOT SALAD WITH POPPY SEEDS AND BALSAMIC SYRUP

SERVES 6

TODD: Apricots at the height of their season are so sweet that they need only gentle prodding to turn them into a winning summer dessert. Bay leaf and thyme add a savory touch to the poaching syrup, poppy seeds provide texture, and balsamic syrup imbues a touch of tartness and drama.

6 ripe apricots

1 cup dry white wine (such as Sauvignon Blanc)

1 cup water

1 cup sugar

1 bay leaf (optional)

1 sprig fresh thyme (optional)

2 teaspoons poppy seeds

Thinly sliced fresh basil or fresh thyme leaves for garnish

BALSAMIC SYRUP:

½ cup good quality balsamic vinegar

2 tablespoons sugar

Blanch the apricots. Bring a large pot of water to boiling. While it is heating, use a paring knife to cut an X in the bottom of each apricot, with the slits running at least halfway down the side of the apricot (this prepares the apricots to be peeled and cut into quarters). Gently add the apricots to the boiling water and let boil until the skin is visibly loosened—for 30 seconds to 1 minute. Immediately remove them from the water using a slotted spoon and place in a bowl of ice water to stop the cooking. Once they have cooled completely (after only 2 to 3 minutes), remove the apricots from the ice bath and gently peel off and discard the skins; set the ice bath aside. Following the X pattern made earlier, quarter the apricots and remove the pits.

Poach the apricots. Pour the wine and water into a medium saucepan, stir in the sugar, and bring to simmering over medium heat. Add the bay leaf and thyme sprig, if using, and the apricots. Lower the heat to low and simmer until the apricots are tender and easily pierced with a paring knife—5 to 10 minutes. Immediately remove the pan from the heat and cool it over the ice bath to stop the cooking. Stir the apricots gently to avoid smashing them but to help facilitate the cooling process. Set aside in the pan of poaching liquid.

Make the balsamic syrup. Stir together the vinegar and sugar in a small saucepan; bring to barely simmering over low heat and cook until the syrup just coats the back of a spoon. Remove from the heat and let cool.

Assemble the salad. Using a slotted spoon, gently transfer the apricots from the poaching liquid to a medium serving bowl. Add the poppy seeds and toss gently to mix. Drizzle the balsamic syrup over the top and garnish with the fresh thyme leaves or thinly sliced fresh basil. If you wish, refrigerate the poaching liquid to use again.

STRAWBERRY RHUBARB COBBLER

MAKES ONE 10-INCH DIAMETER COBBLER

ELLEN: This dish is one of the first dishes I perfected as a "married lady," so it has a special place in my heart. Todd loved it, or at least he said he did, so it helped me get over the intimidation I felt about cooking for a chef. Rhubarb was an exotic ingredient to me then; now it's part of my repertoire, because its tartness complements the sweetness of strawberries so nicely. They're a classic combination. With each bite, your taste buds try to figure out, "Is it tart or is it sweet?" I like a dish that has edge like that.

TODD: A good way to address the tartness issue is to serve the cobbler with a big scoop of vanilla ice cream on it. Problem solved.

1 pound fresh strawberries

1 pound fresh rhubarb

1⅓ cups all-purpose flour

¾ cup sugar

1½ teaspoons baking powder

½ teaspoon salt

5 tablespoons cold unsalted butter, cut into pieces

½ cup heavy cream, plus more for brushing

Prepare the fruit. Hull the strawberries and cut into quarters. Remove and discard any leaves from the rhubarb and cut the stalks into ½-inch lengths. Place the strawberries and rhubarb in a medium bowl; add ½ cup of the sugar and stir to coat the fruit.

Make the dough. Preheat the oven to 375°F. Whisk together the flour, the remaining ¼ cup sugar, the baking powder, and salt. Add the butter and then rub the flour mixture and butter between your fingers to combine and crumble into pea-size pieces. Add the ½ cup cream and stir until just combined using a fork.

Bake the cobbler. Butter a 10-inch ovenproof skillet or 8×10-inch baking dish or casserole and spoon in the fruit. Pat the dough into a disc; pinch off small pieces and flatten each, then arrange in a random pattern over the top of the fruit—like dumplings. (If you prefer, you can roll out the dough on a lightly floured surface into a piece sized to cover your dish and then gently lay it over the fruit.) Brush the dough with a little cream. Bake until the crust is golden and the fruit is bubbly. Transfer to a wire rack to cool before serving.

MANGO TIPS

Mangoes have a large, flat seed in the middle that just about runs the length of the fruit. Use a sharp slicing knife to slice all the way through along both sides of the seed, leaving you with two oval-shaped pieces of fruit. (If you start slicing and hit the seed, just move your knife over a little bit and go again.)

Cut a 1-inch cross-hatch pattern in the flesh of each oval without slicing through the skin. Grasping an oval by its sides, flex it open. Use your slicing knife to cut the squares of mango flesh away from the skin. Repeat with the other oval.

There won't be very much fruit left around the seed, but there will be some. Slice the flesh from around the circumference of the seed, adjusting your knife away from the seed as you come into contact with it. Pare the flesh away from the skin and cut it into cubes. Discard the seed and the skin.

CHILLED MANGO SOUP WITH BLACKBERRIES

SERVES 4

ELLEN: Cold soups are rooted in Ashkenazi cuisine, all beginning with the ubiquitous borscht, since beets were so abundant in Eastern Europe. That dish is a blending of sweet and sour. We consider this soup to be a modern–day extrapolation, made with fruits we are lucky to have available to us: mangoes, limes, and blackberries.

TODD: This dish is a great example of a less-is-more concept. Cook fresh mangoes lightly with some sugar, lime juice, water, and vanilla bean, purée, strain, and chill, and *basta!* The blackberries add a nice contrast of color against the vivid yellow soup and bursts of tartness. A perfect summer refresher.

3 cups diced peeled mangoes (see Mango Tips, opposite)

½ cup sugar

¼ cup water

1 vanilla bean (see page 211)

Juice of 1 lime

½ pint fresh blackberries

Fresh mint sprigs for garnish

Make the soup. Place 2 cups of the mangoes, the sugar, and water in a small saucepan. Split the vanilla bean in half and scrape the seeds into the pan; also add both halves of the pod to the pan. Bring to simmering over medium heat and cook until the mangoes soften—about 20 minutes. Remove the vanilla pods and transfer the soup to the container of a food processor or blender and process until smooth. Pour the soup through a mesh strainer into a medium bowl; stir in the remaining 1 cup diced mangoes and the lime juice. Cover and refrigerate for several hours to chill.

To serve, divide the blackberries among four dessert bowls. Spoon the soup into the bowls, dividing equally. Dot each serving with a sprig of mint.

FIG AND PORT WINE BLINTZES

MAKES 10 TO 12 BLINTZES (6 SERVINGS)

ELLEN: I urged Todd to include a blintz recipe in the summer section because I'm crazy about them (see Falling for Blintzes, page 7). He matched it with another of my food crushes: figs. I went wild for them in Israel years ago and now ask any of my family members and friends going on trips there bring back dried figs for me. When they do, Todd knows it's time to make this recipe for dessert.

TODD: We use dried figs (black mission, but Turkish browns are fine, too) because of their concentrated flavor. Moreover, fresh figs might make the filling too wet, causing a soggy blintz. Another advantage of using dried figs is that they make the recipe suitable for any time of the year. When fresh figs are available, though, I garnish lavishly with them as you can see in the photo—they certainly add an extra dimension.

CREPES:

4 tablespoons unsalted butter, softened

1 cup whole milk

2 large eggs

½ cup all-purpose flour

Cold unsalted butter for greasing sauté pan

FILLING:

2 cups dried black mission figs

1½ cups water

1 cup port wine

1½ cups cream cheese (12 ounces), softened

½ cup ricotta cheese

1 tablespoon honey

¼ teaspoon salt

Pinch freshly ground black pepper

Confectioners' sugar and 4 finely diced fresh figs for serving

Prepare the batter. Melt 2 tablespoons of the butter; let cool slightly. Whisk together the milk and eggs in a small bowl; then whisk in the flour until well combined. Pour the batter through a mesh strainer into another small bowl. Stir in the melted butter. Cover the bowl and refrigerate for at least 1 hour.

Prepare the figs for the filling. Place the dried figs, water, and port in a small saucepan and bring to simmering over medium heat; lower the heat to low and cook until the figs absorb the liquid—about 10 minutes. Remove the pan from the heat and set aside until the mixture is lukewarm. Transfer the mixture to a chopping board and finely chop—it should turn into a pulp.

Mix the filling. Using a wooden spoon, blend the cream cheese and ricotta cheese in a medium bowl. Stir in the fig pulp, honey, salt, and pepper until well combined.

Cook the crepes. Line a 10-inch plate with paper towels. Heat an 8-inch nonstick crepe pan or skillet over medium heat. Rub the pan with cold butter and immediately add ¼ cup crepe batter. Cook until the crepe is slightly caramelized on the bottom—about 2 minutes. Using a pancake turner, turn the crepe over and cook the second side until slightly caramelized—about 2 minutes more. Transfer the

crepe to the paper towel–lined plate. Repeat this process until all the batter has been used; place additional paper towels between the cooked crepes.

Fill the crepes. Spoon a dollop of filling onto each crepe, covering about a third of the area nearest to you but leaving an empty margin at the sides. Fold the margin at each side up and over the filling, then roll up the crepe—like a cylindrical envelope. Turn "flap down" until ready to cook.

Cook the blintzes. In a skillet large enough to hold all the blintzes, melt the remaining 2 tablespoons of butter over medium heat and then pan-fry the blintzes until they are golden-brown on both sides—about 4 minutes per side. To serve, arrange the blintzes on individual plates, dust with confectioners' sugar, and top with a spoonful of the diced fresh figs

VANILLA AND PEACH MELBA

SERVES 5 TO 10

TODD: A pairing of two great summer fruits—peaches and raspberries—and a riff on the classic dessert named after opera singer Nellie Melba. To me the Tidewater peaches we get in the summer from Steve Turnage of Rappahannock Fruits and Vegetables (see Steve Turnage and Virginia Produce, page 264) are some of the best peaches I've ever eaten, so they shouldn't be messed with too much. I poach them in vanilla syrup, peel them, and serve them with raspberry sauce and vanilla whipped cream (substitute vanilla ice cream, if you prefer).

2¾ cups water

½ cup dry white wine (such as Chablis)

1½ cups sugar

1 vanilla bean (see page 211)

4 ripe peaches

1 pint fresh raspberries

Vanilla ice cream

Poach the peaches. Use a paring knife to cut a 1-inch-long X in the bottom of each peach (this prepares them for peeling and cutting in half). Pour the water and wine into a medium saucepan and stir in 1 cup of the sugar. Split the vanilla bean pod lengthwise, scrape the seeds into the wine mixture, and then add the pod to the pan. Bring to barely simmering over medium heat. Gently add the peaches; lower the heat to low and simmer until tender and easily pierced with a paring knife—7 to 12 minutes, depending on their ripeness. Remove the vanilla bean pod and, using a slotted spoon, transfer the peaches to a bowl of ice water to stop the cooking. Pour the poaching liquid into a medium bowl and set aside. When the peaches are cool enough to handle (after only a few minutes), remove them from the ice bath and gently peel off and discard the skins. Cut each peach in half; remove and discard the pit. Submerge the peaches in the poaching liquid; cover the bowl and refrigerate until ready to serve.

Make the raspberry sauce. Mix the raspberries and the remaining ½ cup sugar in a small saucepan. Heat over medium heat and cook, stirring frequently, until the raspberries release all their juices and the sugar is dissolved. Transfer the mixture to a blender and purée. Pour through a fine mesh strainer into a small bowl; cover and refrigerate at least 1 hour.

To serve, divide the raspberry sauce among four shallow dessert bowls. Place 2 peach halves on each (hollow side up or down—it's up to you). Top with a dollop of vanilla ice cream. If you wish, refrigerate the poaching liquid to use again.

HOLIDAY MENUS

ROSH HASHANAH

A dairy menu to welcome the Jewish New Year.

CURRIED BUTTERNUT SQUASH SOUP
WITH GRILLED SOURDOUGH BREAD 19

SALT-BAKED RED SNAPPER 43

CARAMELIZED CAULIFLOWER WITH
ALMONDS AND RAISINS 202

BRUSSELS SPROUT PETALS SAUTÉ 63

ROASTED POTATOES WITH ROSEMARY 58

ALMOND BISCOTTI 67

APPLE STRUDEL 68

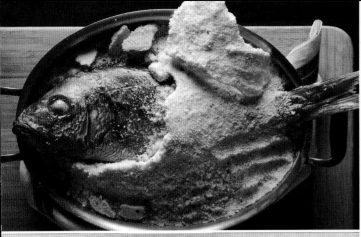

YOM KIPPUR

To break the fast at the end of the Day of Atonement, the holiest day of the year for Jews; this menu is parve.

EGGPLANT CAVIAR WITH PITA CHIPS 172

SALAD OF YOUR FAVORITE GREENS, WITH A VINAIGRETTE DRESSING OF YOUR CHOICE (SEE CHEF'S APPENDIX)

BAKED SALMON WITH POTATOES AND GREEN OLIVES 41

PICKLED HEIRLOOM BEETS WITH HARD-BOILED EGGS 129

BAKED SPAGHETTI SQUASH WITH TOMATO FONDUE 60

PENNSYLVANIA DUTCH APPLE DUMPLINGS 142

HANUKKAH

Hanukkah, or the Festival of Lights, is an eight-day holiday that commemorates the rededication of the Holy Temple in Jerusalem in the second century BCE. We like to celebrate it with this meat menu.

SWEET RED PEPPER HUMMUS 168

CHOPPED LIVER WITH SWEET
MARSALA ONIONS 8

MATZO-STUFFED CORNISH
GAME HENS 126

BRAISED CABBAGE 134

YUKON GOLD AND SWEET
POTATO LATKES 3

TRI-COLOR LENTIL SALAD WITH BALSAMIC
VINEGAR AND PINE NUTS 247

DAIRY-FREE BROWNIES 139

PASSOVER

A meat menu to commemorate the story of Exodus, when the Israelites were freed from slavery in ancient Egypt.

SALAD OF ROASTED HEIRLOOM BEETS WITH CAPERS AND PISTACHIOS 240

NOT EXACTLY AUNT LIL'S MATZO BALL SOUP (OMIT THE NOODLES) 95

BAKED GEFILTE FISH 85

TODD'S MODERN DAY BRISKET 122

QUINOA SALAD WITH FIGS AND MINT 171

WILTED SPINACH WITH SESAME SEEDS 195

MANGO, PINEAPPLE, AND POMEGRANATE SALAD 205

APRICOT HAMANTASCHEN (PASSOVER VERSION) 214

CHEF'S APPENDIX

SPICE BLENDS

I like to use different spice blends in my cooking. They are versatile and fun to mix and match with different types of dishes. If there are particular spices that you like to cook with, try mixing or blending them for a rub or to add to a marinade.

BBQ SPICE MIX

MAKES ABOUT ½ CUP

¼ cup chili powder

1 tablespoon finely ground coffee

1 tablespoon salt

1 teaspoon smoked paprika

1 teaspoon light brown sugar

½ teaspoon garlic powder

¼ teaspoon freshly ground black pepper

Whisk together all the ingredients in a small bowl. The mix can be stored in an airtight container for up to 3 months.

AROMATIC SPICE BLEND

MAKES ½ CUP

This mix of ground toasted spices is great to rub on meat or poultry before cooking. To toast the spices, read Toasting Seeds and Nuts, page 317. Use a mortar and pestle to grind the seeds after they cool.

2 tablespoons ground toasted cumin seeds

2 tablespoons ground toasted coriander seeds

1 tablespoon ground toasted fennel seeds

1 tablespoon onion powder

1 tablespoon salt

1 teaspoon garlic powder

½ teaspoon freshly ground black pepper

Whisk together all the ingredients in a small bowl. Store airtight for up to 3 months.

PICKLING SPICE BLEND

Use this mixture of aromatic spices and herbs to flavor a pickling brine. And feel free to be creative; you can add garlic and other spices or herbs to complement the food you are pickling (see Pickled Foods Belong in Your Repertoire, page 164). If you create a sachet of your blend, the small seasonings will be easy to remove from the brine when you are finished pickling.

2 bay leaves

1 star anise

2 sprigs fresh thyme, broken into short pieces

12 black peppercorns

1 teaspoon coriander seeds

1 teaspoon fennel seeds

To make a spice sachet: Place the spice blend in the middle of a square of cheesecloth; fold up the cloth over the spices and tie closed or bind with kitchen twine.

VINAIGRETTES

These slightly acidic dressings have so many uses, from finishing a salad to punching up lentils to working as marinades. In fact, I even like using vinaigrettes in meat and fish dishes, where they make a nice alternative to butter sauces.

LEMON VINAIGRETTE

MAKES 1 CUP

⅓ cup freshly squeezed lemon juice (about 2 medium lemons)

⅓ cup olive oil

⅓ cup canola oil

1 teaspoon salt

⅛ teaspoon freshly ground black pepper

Strain the lemon juice into a small bowl. Add the olive oil, canola oil, salt, and pepper. Whisk together until combined.

LEMON-LIME VINAIGRETTE

MAKES ABOUT 1½ CUPS

½ cup extra-virgin olive oil

½ cup canola oil

¼ cup Champagne vinegar

1 tablespoon Dijon mustard

1 tablespoon honey

2 tablespoons freshly squeezed lemon juice

2 tablespoons freshly squeezed lime juice

1 garlic clove, finely chopped

½ teaspoon salt

Sprinkling of freshly ground black pepper

Add all the ingredients to the container of a blender and puree until well mixed. Transfer to a small jar and refrigerate until ready to use.

BALSAMIC VINAIGRETTE

MAKES ABOUT 1 CUP

¼ cup balsamic vinegar

2 tablespoons sherry vinegar

1 teaspoon honey

1 teaspoon whole grain mustard

¼ cup olive oil

¼ cup canola oil

Salt

Freshly ground black pepper

Whisk together the balsamic and sherry vinegars, honey, and mustard in a small bowl. Add the olive and canola oils and whisk until well combined. Season with salt and pepper to taste.

RED WINE VINAIGRETTE

MAKES ABOUT 3 CUPS

¾ cup reduced red wine (see page 316)

¼ cup red wine vinegar

1 large egg yolk

1 tablespoon whole grain mustard

1½ teaspoons honey

1 cup canola oil

1 cup olive oil

Salt

Freshly ground black pepper

Place the reduced wine, vinegar, egg yolk, mustard, and honey in a blender. Pulse to combine and then slowly drizzle in the canola and olive oils, pulsing every so often to combine; run the blender for 30 seconds to fully emulsify. Transfer to a storage jar; season with salt and pepper to taste. Store in the refrigerator for up to 2 weeks.

SHERRY MUSTARD VINAIGRETTE

MAKES ABOUT 1 CUP

¼ cup good quality sherry vinegar

2 tablespoons red wine vinegar

1½ teaspoons whole grain mustard

1 teaspoon Dijon mustard

1 teaspoon honey

¼ cup canola oil

¼ cup olive oil

Salt

Freshly ground black pepper

Whisk together the vinegars, mustards, and honey in a small bowl. Add oils and whisk until well combined. Season with salt and pepper to taste.

MARINADES

LIME-MINT MARINADE

MAKES ABOUT ¾ CUP

½ cup olive oil

2 tablespoons freshly squeezed lime juice

4 garlic cloves, finely minced

2 tablespoons chopped fresh mint

1 tablespoon chili powder

1 teaspoon salt

¼ teaspoon freshly ground black pepper

Whisk together the oil and lime juice in a small bowl or glass measuring cup; whisk in the garlic, mint, chili powder, salt, and pepper. The marinade can be stored, covered, for 3 days in the refrigerator.

BALSAMIC-SOY MARINADE

MAKES ABOUT ¾ CUP

½ cup balsamic vinegar

2 tablespoons soy sauce

2 tablespoons maple syrup

Salt

Freshly ground black pepper

Whisk together the vinegar, soy sauce, and maple syrup in a small bowl or glass measuring cup. Season with salt and pepper to taste. The marinade can be stored, covered, up to 1 month in the refrigerator.

CREAMY DRESSINGS AND SAUCES

LIME SOUR CREAM

MAKES ABOUT 1 CUP

1 cup sour cream

1 tablespoon mayonnaise

1½ teaspoons freshly squeezed lime juice

¼ teaspoon freshly grated lime zest

1 tablespoon finely chopped fresh chives

Whisk together the sour cream, mayonnaise, and lime juice in a small bowl. Add the lime zest and chives; stir to combine. Cover and refrigerate until ready to serve.

MINTED LEMON YOGURT

MAKES 1 CUP

1 cup plain or vanilla low-fat yogurt (Ellen favors vanilla)

3 finely chopped fresh mint leaves

½ teaspoon freshly grated lemon zest

½ teaspoon freshly squeezed lemon juice

¼ teaspoon honey (if you're using plain yogurt)

Pinch of salt

Pinch of freshly ground black pepper

Whisk together all the ingredients in a small bowl until combined; cover and refrigerate until ready to serve.

RÉMOULADE SAUCE

MAKES ABOUT 1½ CUPS

1 cup mayonnaise

¼ cup ketchup

1 tablespoon sour cream

¼ teaspoon Tabasco Sauce

⅓ teaspoon freshly grated lemon zest

¼ teaspoon salt

⅛ teaspoon freshly ground black pepper

4 cornichon pickles, finely chopped

1 tablespoon capers, rinsed, drained, and finely chopped

1 tablespoon finely chopped chives or scallions

With a fork, blend the mayonnaise, ketchup, sour cream, Tabasco Sauce, lemon zest, salt, and pepper in a small bowl; stir in the pickles, capers, and chives. Cover and refrigerate until ready to use.

RUSSIAN DRESSING

MAKES ABOUT 1½ CUPS

1 cup mayonnaise

¼ cup ketchup

1 tablespoon sour cream

¼ teaspoon Tabasco Sauce

¼ teaspoon salt

⅛ teaspoon freshly ground black pepper

4 cornichon pickles, finely chopped

1 tablespoon finely chopped scallions, including a little of the green part

With a fork, blend the mayonnaise, ketchup, sour cream, Tabasco Sauce, salt, and pepper in a small bowl; stir in the pickles and scallions. Cover and refrigerate until ready to use.

SAFFRON MAYONNAISE

MAKES ABOUT 1⅓ CUPS

1 cup white wine (such as Chablis)

1 large shallot, finely minced

½ teaspoon saffron threads

1¼ cups mayonnaise

1 teaspoon freshly squeezed lemon juice

Pinch of salt

Pinch of freshly ground black pepper

Stir together the wine and shallots in a small saucepan. Bring to boiling over medium heat; gently boil until the liquid is reduced to 1 ½ tablespoons (that's 4 ½ teaspoons). Stir in the saffron threads and cook just until they are soft; pour the mixture into a small bowl and set aside until cool. Stir in the mayonnaise, lemon juice, salt, and pepper, mixing well. Cover the bowl and refrigerate until ready to use (or up to 1 month).

TARRAGON MAYONNAISE

MAKES ABOUT 1¼ CUPS

1 cup mayonnaise

1 tablespoon chopped fresh tarragon

1 tablespoon minced fresh chives

½ teaspoon freshly grated lemon zest

Salt

Freshly ground black pepper

Whisk together the mayonnaise, tarragon, chives, and lemon zest in a small bowl. Taste the mayonnaise and season with salt and pepper if you wish. Cover and refrigerate until ready to use.

ZESTY MAYONNAISE

MAKES ABOUT ⅔ CUP

½ cup mayonnaise

¼ teaspoon freshly squeezed lemon juice

¼ teaspoon freshly grated lemon zest

Dash of Tabasco Sauce

¼ teaspoon salt

Pinch of freshly ground black pepper

2 tablespoons minced fresh chives

With a fork, blend the mayonnaise with the lemon juice, lemon zest, Tabasco Sauce, salt, and pepper in a small bowl; stir in 2 tablespoons minced fresh chives. Cover and refrigerate until ready to use.

CONDIMENTS AND FOUNDATIONS

BREAD CRUMBS

To make bread crumbs, begin with brioche or white sandwich bread. The method is easy: slice the bread then, remove the crust for a lighter color crumb mix, or leave the crust on for a darker mix. Heat the oven to 300°F. Arrange the slices on a baking sheet and bake until it is lightly toasted and slightly cooked and dried out—10 to 15 minutes, turning several times. Let the slices cool on a wire rack. Then crumble them into the container of a food processor fitted with a metal blade and process until fine crumbs form—fine crumbs make a more delicate filler or coating. Store at room temperature in an airtight container for up to 1 month.

We like to crush purchased coarse dry bread crumbs (such as Panko crumbs) before using, too, so their texture is finer. You needn't toast them; all you have to do is put them in the container of a food processor and process for 30 seconds.

HERB BOUQUET

I like to infuse the flavor of fresh herbs into my cooking. This is one of the best ways to boost flavor and add complexity to a dish. If you tie your herbs into a bouquet before adding to the pan, the cooking liquid will absorb their flavor and you can then easily remove them so that there are no stray leaves in the finished dish. Which herbs you choose to use is a personal preference. I like a mix of 3 sprigs thyme, 2 sprigs sage, and 1 sprig rosemary as a rule, or sometimes parsley is nice, too; you might like oregano, marjoram, and mint. To make a bouquet, simply wrap butcher's twine securely around the bunched herbs, tying a good knot that won't come loose.

ROASTED GARLIC

You may roast whatever quantity of garlic you wish. This recipe yields approximately 2 cups roasted garlic cloves—adjust the amount of oil up or down if you choose to roast more or less.

4 whole garlic bulbs
Salt
Freshly ground black pepper
4½ teaspoons olive oil

Preheat the oven to 350°F. Separate the cloves from a garlic bulb but do not peel them. Scatter them in a pie pan or small roasting pan. Sprinkle with salt and pepper, drizzle with olive oil, and toss to mix. Roast until the skins begin to pop and the flesh is soft—about 20 minutes. The roasted cloves can be refrigerated in a food storage container for up to 1 week. To use, squeeze the flesh out of the skins.

To roast a whole garlic bulb, simply slice off and discard the top; then sprinkle the cut surface with salt and pepper and drizzle with olive oil. Wrap bulbs in foil and roast for 30 to 40 minutes; when bulbs are ready the tops should be golden brown and lightly caramelized and the cloves should be tender.

ROASTED GARLIC JUS
MAKES 1 CUP

This is a sophisticated sauce for lamb.

1 cup demi-glace, homemade (see page 314)
12 roasted garlic cloves (see above)

Combine the demi-glace and garlic cloves in a small saucepan and bring to simmering over high heat; lower the heat to medium-low and simmer for 3 minutes. Keep warm until ready to serve. Or pour into a food storage container and refrigerate up to 1 week. When ready to serve, heat in a small pot over medium-low heat until hot.

ROASTED GARLIC PASTE
MAKES ABOUT ½ CUP

24 roasted garlic cloves (see above)
Salt
Freshly ground black pepper

If not yet peeled, squeeze the garlic cloves out of their skins. Place them on a cutting board. Using the back of a knife or metal spatula, press down on the cloves until they form a paste—work the knife back and forth to do this. Transfer the paste to a small dish, sprinkle with salt and pepper, and stir to mix. The paste can be stored, covered, in the refrigerator for up to 3 weeks.

ROASTED BELL PEPPERS

You can roast a pepper on the top of a gas stove or in your oven. Here are both methods; for either, you need metal tongs:

Stove top roasting. Turn a gas burner to medium-high. Place the pepper directly on the burner grate; allow the pepper skin to char, turning frequently so it doesn't catch on fire. The skin should be black and blistered and begin to peel away.

Oven roasting. Heat the oven to 350°F. Rub the pepper all over with olive oil. Place on a baking sheet in the oven and bake until the skin is black and blistered, turning when each side blisters.

Complete the pepper prep. Place the roasted pepper(s) in a stainless steel bowl and wrap with clear plastic food wrap; set aside until cool enough to handle—about 30 minutes (the pepper will steam in the bowl as it cools). With a small paring knife (professionals wear heavy rubber gloves and use their fingers), peel the charred skin off the pepper. Cut the pepper lengthwise into segments and remove and discard the seeds; cut the pepper segments into medium dice (pieces a little bigger than ½-inch square)—or whatever size your recipe directs—on a cutting board. If not using immediately, place in an airtight container and store in the refrigerator for up to 1 week (roasted peppers do not freeze well).

CARAMELIZED ONIONS
MAKES ABOUT 2 CUPS

¼ cup canola oil

2 cups thinly sliced yellow onions (2 medium onions)

¼ teaspoon salt

Heat the oil in a medium sauté pan over medium heat. Stir in the onions and salt and cook for 4 minutes. Lower the heat to low and continue to cook the onions, stirring often, until they turn amber in color—20 to 30 minutes. Drain in a colander and store in the refrigerator until ready to use, for up to 4 days.

PICKLED RED ONIONS
MAKES ABOUT 2½ CUPS

2 cups water

1 cup red wine vinegar

1 cup sugar

1 teaspoon salt

½ teaspoon freshly ground black pepper

¼ teaspoon mustard seeds

¼ teaspoon coriander seeds

1 bay leaf

4 cups thinly sliced red onions (about 2 red onions)

Combine the water, vinegar, sugar, salt, and pepper in a medium saucepan; bring to simmering over medium-high heat, stirring to dissolve the sugar. Wrap the mustard seeds, coriander seeds, and bay leaf in a small piece of cheesecloth, tying closed with kitchen twine. Add this spice sachet and the onions to the sugar mixture and bring to boiling over high heat; immediately remove the pan from the heat and set aside to let the onions reach room temperature in the pickling liquid. Discard the spice sachet and if not ready to use the onions, transfer them with the pickling liquid to a food storage container and refrigerate for up to 3 weeks.

OVEN-DRIED TOMATOES
MAKES 24 PIECES

I like this technique because it produces tomatoes that have a concentrated sweetness and lend a slightly roasted flavor to any dish in which they're included.

12 ripe Roma tomatoes

¼ cup olive oil

4 springs fresh thyme

2 garlic cloves, minced

½ teaspoon salt

¼ teaspoon dried oregano

Freshly ground black pepper

Preheat the oven to 225°F. Bring a medium pot of water to boiling over high heat. Drop the tomatoes into the water and cook for 1 minute. With a slotted spoon, transfer the tomatoes to a bowl of ice water to stop the cooking. Use a paring knife to peel the tomatoes; cut each lengthwise in half and scoop out and discard the seeds.

Place the tomatoes in a shallow baking dish or on a baking sheet. Drizzle the oil over them. Pluck the leaves from the thyme sprigs and sprinkle over the tomatoes along with the garlic, salt, oregano, and a little pepper; toss to mix well. Bake until the tomatoes are slightly blistered and appear soft and roasted—4 to 6 hours—stirring gently every 60 minutes to ensure even cooking. Transfer the tomatoes to a wire rack to cool, leaving them in the baking pan. They will keep in an airtight container in the refrigerator for up to 2 weeks.

SALT AND PEPPER

Seasoning a recipe with salt and pepper is one of the most basic techniques for enhancing the flavor of our food. I prefer to use kosher salt or fine sea salt when I cook and try to stay away from iodized or processed salts. Using freshly ground pepper from a mill also makes a big difference: Your pepper flavor will be brighter, cleaner, and more visible when you grind peppercorns when ready to use, as opposed to reaching for packaged ground pepper. For a more robust accent or when a recipe calls for coarsely ground pepper, you may wish to crack the peppercorns in a mortar and pestle instead of grinding them.

Using the right amount of salt and pepper can make a huge difference to the taste of your finished dish. This is obviously a personal thing as well—some people prefer the taste of more or less salt or pepper. The amount of these seasonings specified in my recipes is a suggestion, and you should feel free to adjust it to suit your preferences. Also, some people have health issues that require moderate salt intake, and if someone in your home has to limit his or her salt, then you must cut back.

STOCKS, JUS, AND DEMI-GLACE

Because it is the base of so many recipes, I'm a big advocate for making stock (and its cousins jus and demi-glace) from scratch. The superior flavor "homemade" adds to your cooking is definitely worth the effort (really, it's just time, these are not difficult to make). See The Story on Broth, Stock, and Quick Stock on pages 20–22 for more about these. One tip: As you read the following recipes you'll see directions to "skim off impurities"; by this chefs mean you should remove and discard any foam, scum, and grease that rise to the surface. However, if you prefer, you can use readymade chicken, vegetable, or fish stock that is available in any grocery store, and for veal stock, begin with purchased demi-glace (also readily available), diluting it with 2 to 3 parts water as explained on page 313.

CHICKEN STOCK

MAKES 8 TO 10 CUPS

One 3-pound chicken, quartered, or 3 pounds uncooked chicken bones

1 medium yellow onion, quartered

2 celery ribs, chopped

1 carrot, chopped

2 garlic cloves, crushed

2 sprigs fresh thyme

2 bay leaves

12 black peppercorns

1 tablespoon salt

If using a quartered chicken, trim and discard any excess fat, and then wash the pieces under cool water. Place the chicken quarters or bones

in a stockpot just large enough to hold them comfortably. Add all the remaining ingredients to the pot and pour in water to cover. Bring to simmering over medium heat; skim off any impurities. Lower the heat to low and simmer, uncovered, gently for 4 hours; check every so often and add more water as necessary to keep the chicken and vegetables covered.

Pour the broth through a mesh strainer into a bowl or food storage container; it will keep in the refrigerator for 4 days or in the freezer for up to 1 month. Pick any meat from the bones and save for another use. Discard the vegetables and bones.

ROASTED CHICKEN JUS

MAKES 2½ CUPS

This is a brown chicken stock cooked in the oven and then reduced to a glaze consistency.

2 pounds uncooked chicken bones

1 tablespoon canola oil

2 celery ribs, chopped

1 medium yellow onion, chopped

1 carrot, chopped

2 garlic cloves

2 sprigs fresh thyme

12 black peppercorns

1 cup dry red wine (such as Cabernet Sauvignon—an inexpensive one is fine)

1 tablespoon tomato paste

1 teaspoon salt

Preheat the oven to 325°F. Place the bones in a roasting pan and drizzle with the oil. Roast, stirring several times so they cook evenly, until the bones turn light golden-brown—30 to 40 minutes total. Leaving the oven on, transfer the bones to a paper towel-lined plate to drain and wipe the pan dry. Return the roasted bones to the pan; add the celery, onions, carrots, garlic, thyme, and peppercorns. Pour in the wine and stir in the tomato paste and salt. If appropriate, add water to cover. Return the pan to the oven and cook for 4 hours, adding water as necessary to keep the bones covered.

Pour the liquid from the pan through a mesh strainer into a small saucepan; discard the bones. Bring the liquid to boiling over medium heat and boil gently until it is reduced to 2 ½ cups, skimming off any impurities. Transfer the jus to a food storage container; it will keep in the refrigerator for 1 week or in the freezer for up to 1 month.

FISH STOCK

MAKES 4 TO 5 CUPS

1 pound fish bones, preferably from flat fish such as flounder or sole

1 medium yellow onion, chopped

2 celery ribs, chopped

1 small carrot, chopped

2 garlic cloves, crushed

2 sprigs fresh thyme

1 teaspoon freshly grated lemon zest

2 bay leaves

12 peppercorns

1 teaspoon salt

¾ cup dry white wine (such as Chablis or Sauvignon Blanc)

6 cups water, more as needed

Combine all ingredients in a small stockpot, adding more water if necessary to cover the bones and vegetables. Bring to simmering over medium heat, skimming off any impurities. Lower the heat to low and gently simmer, uncovered,

for 45 minutes. Pour the stock through a mesh strainer into a bowl or food storage container; it will keep in the refrigerator for 3 days or in the freezer for up to 1 month. Discard the bones and vegetables.

VEAL STOCK AND DEMI-GLACE DEFINED

See About Veal Stock, page 47

VEAL STOCK

MAKES ABOUT 4 QUARTS (16 CUPS)

This recipe makes quite a bit of stock, but that's a blessing since it must cook for 24 hours. Freeze it in 1-quart containers (or smaller) so it's handy for later use. If you are pressed for time, by all means begin with a prepared version of demi-glace (available in most grocery stores or online, such as Demi-Glace Gold brand), and dilute it with 2 to 3 parts water—this is a fine and practical option to making your own veal stock.

10 pounds veal bones, cut from the leg

6 celery ribs, chopped

3 carrots, chopped

3 medium yellow onions, chopped

6 garlic cloves, crushed

Handful of mushroom stems (optional)

1 bunch of parsley (leaves and stems)

4 bay leaves

2 cups dry red wine (such as Cabernet or Burgundy)

¼ cup tomato paste

Place the bones in a large stockpot and pour in water to cover. Bring slowly to boiling over medium heat, skimming off any grease that rises to the surface. Simmer 20 minutes, then drain in a colander, discarding the liquid, and rinse the bones under cool water.

Wash the stockpot and return the bones to it. Add the carrots, celery, onions, garlic, mushrooms if using, parsley, and bay leaves. Whisk together the red wine and tomato paste in a small bowl and then add to the stockpot. Pour in water to cover the bones and vegetables; bring to simmering over medium heat. Lower the heat to low and simmer gently, uncovered, for 24 hours, skimming off any impurities. Check every so often and add more water as necessary to keep the bones and vegetables covered. Pour the stock through a mesh strainer into a large bowl or food storage container; it will keep in the refrigerator for 1 week or in the freezer for up to 3 months. Discard the bones and vegetables.

DEMI-GLACE
MAKES ABOUT 3 QUARTS (12 CUPS)

To make demi-glace, return the strained veal stock to a clean stockpot; bring to simmering over medium heat. Add salt to taste; simmer, uncovered, over medium-low heat until it is reduced to the desired thickness. Typically chefs reduce veal stock by three-quarters so it becomes glazelike, for instance, reducing 1 gallon down to 1 quart—or even further.

VEGETABLE STOCK

1 large yellow onion, chopped
2 carrots, chopped
3 celery ribs, chopped
2 garlic cloves, crushed
1 large tomato, quartered
2 sprigs fresh thyme
2 bay leaves
1 gallon water (16 cups)
1 teaspoon salt

Place the onions, carrots, celery, garlic, tomatoes, thyme, and bay leaves in a 4-quart stockpot. Pour in the water, stir in the salt, and bring to simmering over medium-high heat. Lower the heat to medium-low and gently simmer, uncovered, for 3 hours. Check every so often and add more water as necessary to keep the vegetables covered. Pour the stock through a mesh strainer into a bowl or food storage container; it will keep in the refrigerator for 1 week or in the freezer for up to 3 months. Discard the vegetables.

TECHNIQUES IT'S GOOD TO KNOW

WARMING BREAD

Preheat the oven to 300°F. Arrange bread slices, pitas, or rolls on a baking sheet and place in the oven for 4 to 5 minutes, or a little longer if you'd like them to have a bit of a crunch.

BLANCHING

A pre-cooking process by which fruits and vegetables are briefly boiled and then drained and placed under or in cold water to stop the cooking. Blanching gives ingredients a head start on doneness, which allows them to be added to a recipe shortly before serving, prevents them from becoming overcooked or discolored, or compensates for different cooking times among various ingredients. Blanching also loosens the skins of tomatoes and stone fruits for easy peeling. The blanching time varies with the size of the ingredient or the result desired, so it's specified with the recipes in this book.

MELTING CHOCOLATE

Chocolate melts faster if you chop it first.

Microwave method: Place the chocolate in a small microwave-safe bowl and microwave on High for 30 seconds; remove and stir. If not completely melted, repeat the microwaving. Stir until smooth.

Stove top method: Place the chocolate in the top of a double boiler, over (but not in) boiling water. Stir occasionally until the chocolate is melted. Melted chocolate will "seize" (separate and become grainy) if even a drop of moisture mixes with it and there's no fix for this, so be careful that no steam or water falls into the pan with the chocolate.

CLEANING CHICKEN LIVERS

See Chicken Liver Prep, page 9.

DRAINING CHEESE OR YOGURT

To remove all excess liquid from a curd cheese such as ricotta or from yogurt, line a fine-mesh strainer with a double thickness of cheesecloth large enough to be able to pick up the ends, bring them together above the strainer, and twist them so as to wring excess moisture from the cheese. Suspend the strainer over a bowl and add the cheese to the cheesecloth. Allow the cheese to drain for 30 minutes, then bring the cloth ends together and twist gently to wring.

EGG WASH

This "eggy" liquid is a mix of whole eggs and water that is used to adhere crumb coatings to food that is to be fried or to glaze baked goods. For 1 cup, mix 2 large eggs with 6 tablespoons cool water, whisking until combined. If using for a savory dish, you can add a sprinkling of salt and pepper.

JULIENNE

This is a technique for cutting vegetables into very thin, matchstick-like pieces. They're ideally about $1/16$-inch thick; their length can vary, but is usually no more than a couple of inches. Start by cutting thin lengthwise slices of vegetables such as leeks, carrots, or zucchini. Lay the slices flat and then cut them crosswise into sections of the length you want. Finally cut each of these sections lengthwise to complete the julienne.

COOKING PASTA

I advocate adding lots of salt to the water when boiling pasta—it should taste like sea water. When the pasta is done (still a bit firm to the bite), drain it in a colander and rinse under cold water to stop the cooking. If not immediately incorporating sauce, transfer the pasta to a bowl and toss with a little olive oil to keep it from sticking together.

FRYING FOOD

It's important to get the temperature right when you're frying food such as falafel or latkes—or chicken. When making falafel at Muse Café, we use a little tabletop fryer that regulates the heat of the oil, but at home we just heat the oil in a pot. It's a good idea to have a candy thermometer on hand to take the guesswork out of heating the oil to the proper temperature.

REDUCING RED WINE

By reducing red wine you cook out the alcohol and concentrate the fruit flavor; the result makes a good foundation for a red wine sauce or a vinaigrette. I love using Cabernet Sauvignon or Burgundy for reducing. You want to always use a decent wine but don't go over the top. A good

rule of thumb: If you wouldn't drink it, then don't cook with it.

Pour 1 liter of wine into a medium saucepan. Bring to boiling over medium-high heat. Boil, uncovered, until reduced by three-quarters (until about 1 cup remains)—this should take about 30 minutes. Let cool. Transfer to a storage jar and refrigerate for up to 1 month.

DEBONING SARDINES

We think the bones in sardines have an unpleasant texture so we remove them. To do this, gently slice the sardine in half lengthwise with a paring knife, pry up the tail end of the spine with the knife tip, and then lift the spine between your fingertips.

SAUTÉING

Learning the technique of sautéing—cooking small pieces of food in a little fat, usually without liquid—is very important. Chefs sauté everything from fish, meat, and vegetables to pasta. Typically you sauté in a sauté pan (a shallow pan with a flat bottom and curved sides) or skillet, cooking over medium heat and using a fat such as oil or butter. The pan is heated, the fat is then put into the pan, and the food you are cooking follows. Allow the food to cook over medium heat (or as indicated in your recipe), with minimal stirring, until caramelized on all sides, or for vegetables, until softened or wilted. When meat and fish are properly sautéed they are caramelized and golden brown.

TOASTING SEEDS AND NUTS

You can toast seeds and nuts in a toaster oven or your regular oven. Ellen likes to spray them with olive oil and sprinkle them with salt before toasting—this gives them a flavor boost and helps them to brown. Preheat the oven to 325°F. Spread the seeds or nuts on a baking sheet and bake until nicely toasted, stirring or shaking as necessary so they evenly brown—for about 5 minutes. Let the seeds or nuts cool before you crush them or add them to room temperature or cold ingredients. That's all there is to it.

USING VANILLA BEANS

To use a vanilla bean, split the pod lengthwise and scrape the tiny seeds into whatever you are making. For syrups and sauces, sometimes you add the pod, too, in order to maximize the flavor, and remove it when finished simmering the syrup or sauce. Your recipe will indicate which method to use. For more information, see Vanilla Beans Are Something to Love, page 211.

VEGETABLE PREP

It is important to always wash fresh vegetables before using them, even if they are to be peeled. Wash under cool water and be sure to scrub if necessary with a soft scrub pad (or even a kitchen towel) to remove any hidden dirt. Blot dry or drain in a colander. Peel them with a vegetable peeler. Vegetables that are not to be peeled should be dried before using unless you are immediately adding them to a pot of water. If you are using vegetables as a garnish and want to retain their tops, be sure to scrape around the tops with a small paring knife.

In this book it is assumed that vegetables are washed and peeled, with tops and roots trimmed away, before using unless a recipe specifies otherwise or when peeling is not usual, as for radishes or mushrooms. It is also assumed that leafy greens are washed and spun or blotted dry.

INDEX